AN ANTIETAM VETERAN'S MONTANA JOURNEY

AN ANTIETAM VETERAN'S MONTANA JOURNEY

The Lost Memoir of James Howard Lowell

EDITED BY KATHARINE SEATON SQUIRES

Forewords by Ken Robison and Castle McLaughlin, PhD

THE History PRESS

Published by The History Press
Charleston, SC
www.historypress.com

First published 2018

Manufactured in the United States

ISBN 9781467139670

Library of Congress Control Number: 2018936088

Notice: The information in this book is true and complete to the best of our knowledge. It is offered without guarantee on the part of the author or The History Press. The author and The History Press disclaim all liability in connection with the use of this book.

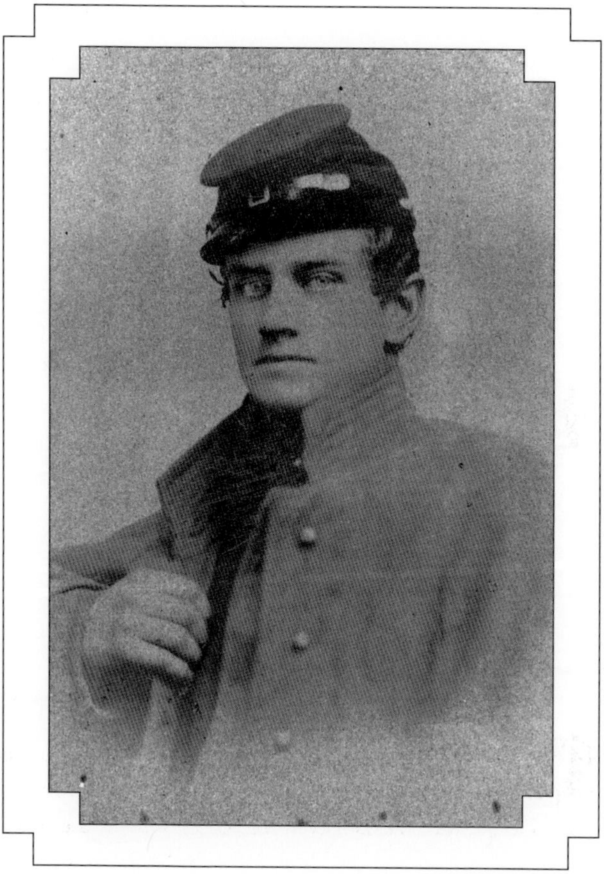

James Howard Lowell, Manassas, 1862. *Courtesy of Allen Sewell.*

For Meredith and Cole

There are but few important events in the affairs of men brought about by their own choice.

—Ulysses S. Grant

CONTENTS

Contents

Foreword

THE WEST OBSERVED

The westward expansion of the United States during the nineteenth century was arguably the most defining event in American history. Between the 1849 California gold rush and the advent of the railroad in the late 1860s, some 500,000 Euro-Americans walked or rode to California, Oregon, and other points west. Merrill J. Mattes, historian of the trails those travelers forged, has estimated that only one in every 250–500 people left a written record of the experience. That so few people wrote about traveling as many as two thousand miles across a foreign and demanding landscape filled with perils in pursuit of an unknown future seems astonishing today, when self-documentation has become a lifestyle. But it is a revealing statistic, one that testifies to the cultural and psychological impact of literacy and mass media. In the mid-nineteenth century, most Americans had little formal education, and few developed the kind of self-consciousness about their place in the world that we now take for granted.

James Lowell's reminiscent account of his participation in the post–Civil War migration west is a welcome addition to the slim corpus of surviving diaries and journals, many of which have been published in recent decades. Like Lowell, most immigrants were young men bound for mining camps in the intermountain west. But Lowell differed in ways that shaped both his experience and his narrative. Relatively well educated, Lowell read widely, wrote well, and carried with him letters of introduction. His friends and associates were professionals; Lowell himself would become an attorney. Once across the Missouri River, he joined a tacit class of gentlemen, placing him among social and civic leaders in frontier settlements and broadening his prospects beyond mining and hunting. Ultimately a teacher, county official, and attorney in Fort Benton, Montana, Lowell wrote that he felt "an exultation" at contributing to "the up building of a community or State."

Yet Lowell was an adventurer, not a settler, and his experiences were remarkable. He was a veteran of the Civil War. Like Jack Crabb in the film *Little Big Man*, the "westering" Lowell moved from one circumstance to another, changing personas and meeting an unfolding series of historical actors. His recounting of these experiences is sometimes cinematic and begins *en medias res*: "One day in April 1865, I was pacing the platform of a railway station in Pittsburg, Pennsylvania, and counting the number of planks thereof, for I had nothing else to do while waiting for a westbound train." Moments later, he happened to meet the future territorial governor of Utah, the first of many influential people he encountered during his six-year sojourn in the West. Among them were politicians, entrepreneur David A. Butterfield, General Grenville M. Dodge, Mormon leader Brigham Young, the Gros Ventre leader Horse Capture, and fur trade giant Alexander Culbertson, who asked Lowell to transcribe his life story. All of these people played significant roles in the colonization of the West.

In the fall of 1865, Lowell accepted his first job: driving a freight wagon in the inaugural trip of the Butterfield Despatch, then launching a new route from Atchison, Kansas, to Denver. Like most citizens, Lowell was apparently unaware that Butterfield's trail through the Smoky Hill Valley bisected the territory of the Cheyenne and Lakota Dog Soldiers, formidable defenders of native lands and cultures. The stage running ahead of Lowell's wagon train was attacked at Monument Station by a party of warriors that probably included Charles Bent, the son of famous trader William Bent. Dog Soldiers also took all the livestock, mostly mules, from Lowell's party of freight wagons but did not press a direct attack. As a result, the freight crew was marooned and on their own for thirty-one days, until the company drove in oxen to replace the mules. Lowell was fortunate to be in the vanguard of traffic crossing the Smoky Hill country, because the conflicts that ensued ignited a ten-year war for the Plains that culminated in the Battle of Little Big Horn during the summer of 1876.

Lowell's passage across Kansas was just the first of his close calls, all of which he relates in a matter-of-fact fashion. Lowell was a careful observer and an unadorned but expressive writer. His manuscript reads like a highlights reel, carrying readers from Mormon settlements to mining camps, into crowded saloons where men fight over women, and through quiet mountain passes occupied only by eagles, antelope, and the sound of the wind. His cast of characters includes riverboat pilots, wolf hunters, and vigilantes, a heroic Indian chief, a scarred Spanish mustang, and a mystical mountain man. Sensing the epic nature of the era, Lowell sometimes quotes Shakespeare, Kipling, and Homer in order to more fully convey the dramas of frontier life.

Unlike many of his contemporaries, Lowell was aware that his experiences were part of a profound change, and many of his descriptions vividly bring people and events to life. He probably did not realize that his first-person account also expressed a perspective on those changes particular to white men of his status and generation. Indeed, some passages suggest that Lowell was driven by a belief in the tenets of Manifest Destiny, although he does not use that term. Thus, his lively narrative is at once history, literature, memoir, and cultural document. The publication of Lowell's manuscript will be welcomed by all who seek to understand a pivotal moment in nineteenth-century America, not from the present, but as lived experience.

—Castle McLaughlin, PhD
Curator, Peabody Museum of Archaeology and Ethnology,
Harvard University

FOREWORD

The epic struggle of the Civil War had just ended when young James H. Lowell made his way west. During, and because of that great conflict, several factors made the Upper Missouri region a great magnet for Lowell and thousands of other adventurers. The remote region, long dominated by native Blackfoot Indians, had opened to the fur trade in the 1830s. By 1846–47, the Fort Benton trading post had begun operations as the Upper Missouri Outfit of the American Fur Company, an extension of St. Louis on a wild, scenic, and resource-rich frontier.

The arrival of the first steamboats at the Fort Benton levee in the summer of 1860 coincided with the completion of the Mullan Military Wagon Road and brought a regiment of army dragoons. This strategic road linked Fort Benton, the head of navigation on the Missouri River, to Fort Walla Walla, the head of navigation on the Columbia River.

The beginning of the great Civil War in 1861, followed by the discovery of gold southwest of Fort Benton one year later, brought a sudden influx of thousands to the mining camps and riches to a few but failure to many more. A struggle ensued between the North and the South for control of the gold flowing out of the new placer mines. To solidify Union control and bring law and order to the region, the Territory of Montana was created in 1864.

As Union forces prevailed in Missouri and the western theater of the war, the new territory became a relief valve for the great pressure cooker of the Civil War. Montana Territory became the exile home of choice for many Southern families whose plantations were devastated and their slaves freed, as well as a haven for Confederate soldiers, some prisoners on parole, others wounded in battle, and disillusioned deserters.

With the end of the Civil War and in response to increasing incidents with Indians along the river and on the old Mullan Road, the U.S. Army constructed Camp Cooke, its first military post in Montana Territory, at the mouth of the Judith River, ninety miles below Fort Benton. This marked the beginning of major new military business for the steamboat lines and Fort Benton, with boats carrying recruits and supplies upriver. Camp Cooke was soon replaced by Fort Shaw in the Sun River Valley, while an infantry company remained at Fort Benton.

This expansion was the environment into which James Lowell arrived in August 1869. Equal in excitement to the river traffic arriving at Fort Benton was the overland transportation industry required to carry the massive flow of cargo and passengers. Stage lines, bull trains, and mule trains crowded the roads and trails. "All trails lead out of Fort Benton" was a familiar phrase, and the trails and roads radiated from the town like spokes on a wagon wheel. The combination of steamboats and freighting kept Fort Benton prosperous for two decades, until the railroads arrived.

As citizens struggled to maintain law and order in this wild frontier environment, Lowell provides exciting, new commentary on Fort Benton society and events, including the little-known shadowy activities of local vigilantes. This was a time of made and lost fortunes and colorful characters—and James Lowell was there.

—Ken Robison
Historian, Fort Benton, Montana

EDITOR'S NOTE

Commencing in 1872, Civil War veteran and Boston native James Howard Lowell handwrote this recollection of his travels out West in a bound journal without the benefits of revision. He left contemporary references that suggest he completed the work in the late 1890s. With the aim of clarity, I have taken the liberty of modernizing some of the punctuation and spelling to preserve flow and consistency. I've also added some paragraphing and subheadings to ease navigation through the material. My goal was to retain the period flavor and some of the nineteenth-century capitalizations while increasing readability.

Similarly, I have corrected the spelling of proper names. Lowell spelled his mining partner's name William H. Claggett, when, in fact, the surname is spelled with one G. Clagett's name was also misspelled when traders named a post adjacent to Camp Cooke Fort Claggett. The cursive of the original journal is remarkably legible—the letters to his future wife, Kate Mary Roberts, less so. Illegible passages are so noted.

In some instances, Lowell's language represents the ethnocentrism of his day. I have retained some nineteenth-century terms that modern readers will find offensive, such as references to squaws, savages, "virgin territory," and the "nigger engine," a capstan engine used by river men to release steamboats from sandbars on the Missouri River. At the time, the use of these terms was commonplace.

Editor's Note

I have abbreviated our author's name, JHL; his sweetheart and later wife, Kate Mary Roberts, as KM; and AVMJ for *An Antietam Veteran's Montana Journey*. For researchers who might require examination of the original spelling and punctuation, the manuscript will be scanned and deposited in archives. For more information, see www.lowellmemoir.com.

PREFACE

In my family, we refer to my great-great-grandfather's handwritten manuscript as "the journal." I grew up knowing this slim, leather-bound volume rested in a plastic box in my mother's dresser drawer, quietly degrading amid her turtlenecks. It was rather a mystery to my sister Liz and me why our mother wouldn't consider sharing this wonderful account of James Howard Lowell's travels out West after his Civil War service. Over the years, Liz and I showed copies of the manuscript to a handful of history teachers and professors. Inevitably, upon returning the photocopies of the handwritten manuscript, they would look me in the eye and say, "You *must* get this published," with a look of entreaty that I never forgot. We knew it was something special, but our mother was old school, and her response to our queries was that the journal was private family business. My sister and I understood the manuscript's value to historians as primary source material and to general readers as pure enjoyment. Unless it were typed and published, the narrative would be lost.

Lowell began recording his story a year after he returned to the East with the words "Dull Day Jottings 1872," but he neglected to date the closing page of the manuscript. Clues in the text suggest that Lowell completed the work in the 1890s. Those chronological hints are noted.

The journal itself has degraded to the point where it is a rather poignant experience to handle it. One feels as if one were fingering the papery skin of the man who wrote it. The leather of the cover is crumbling, the spine is broken, and the pages are brown and covered with fading script, but Lowell's cursive hand remains easy to read. Few cross-outs appear. His style reveals a wry, self-deprecating humor as he narrates his travails out West as a miner and neophyte lawyer. The content leaves no doubt the author had grit.

As a former journalist, in 2012, I undertook to rescue the journal from my mother's dresser drawer and commenced typing its 129 handwritten pages. I read volumes of period history and plied historical records to put into context the events and places Lowell describes and to learn more about his life. The nineteen-year-old Lowell enlisted at the outbreak of the Civil War in July 1861 and was wounded at Antietam a little more than a year later. At the start, I had no idea what wounds he had suffered or why he failed to return home to Boston after the war.

For context, in Section II, I've included selected correspondence written contemporaneously to his wartime nurse and later wife, Kate Mary Roberts. In her hometown of Harrisburg, Pennsylvania, Roberts waited six years for Lowell's return. This section also features excerpts of Lowell's letters regarding his Civil War service with the Massachusetts Thirteenth Regiment, Company A. In addition to his private correspondence, Lowell contributed anecdotes to the Thirteenth's circulars, pamphlets that served as invitations to the regiment's annual reunions in Boston. The circulars provided a means for old friends to stay in touch and preserve memories. For biographical context and to spread fodder for Civil War buffs, I have included some of these writings in Section II. They give a fuller picture of Lowell's life preceding the events described in the journal and a taste of the values and esprit de corps of the men. The familiar camaraderie of the mining camps out West gave the young veterans time to heal both physically and spiritually in the wilderness. While many kept diaries of their daily activities and expenses, few wrote literary accounts of this era of western migration.

Snippets of Lowell's correspondence, including a late-life exchange with the explorer Charles W. Cook, give us perspective on the character of the later Judge Lowell.

Full transcripts of Lowell's correspondence with Kate Mary Roberts and his contributions to the Massachusetts Thirteenth circulars can be found at www.lowellmemoir.com.

ACKNOWLEDGEMENTS

I can't thank enough my newly discovered cousins Tim Sewell and Allen Sewell for sharing their collections of James Howard Lowell papers and photos. They are the grandchildren of Lowell's youngest daughter, Kate Roberta (Lowell) Sewell, and I am the great-grandchild of his second son, James Henry Lowell, the fellow who inherited the manuscript. Without the support of Tim and Allen, this volume would have been bereft of good likenesses of our hero and much biographical information.

Another descendant of a Massachusetts Thirteenth soldier, Bradley Forbush, has been a willing collaborator and a font of regimental trivia. Along with Art Rideout and Greg Dowden, Brad compiled a comprehensive history of the Massachusetts Thirteenth, available online at 13thMass.org. Brad built a career as an artist and animator, but he is, at heart, a historian.

To the Fort Benton, Montana historian Ken Robison, I owe a debt of gratitude. Ken steered me toward good sources, introduced me to The History Press and wrote a foreword for the book when he was exceedingly busy with his own work. I couldn't have done it without him. Thank you.

Likewise, Castle McLaughlin did a close reading of the manuscript, then suffered several interruptions to her day as I extracted a trace of her expertise as curator of North American ethnography at the Peabody Museum of Archaeology and Ethnology at Harvard University. She gave me valuable notes and wrote a foreword. Her positive feedback in 2012 gave me the confidence to move forward. Thank you.

To my editor, Artie Crisp: How do you manage to convey a smile in every email message? Every problem is a molehill. It was a dream for me to have Lowell's work appear in print, and you got it done. Thank you.

And thank you to copy editor Abigail Fleming, for making it accurate; Anna Burrous, for making it beautiful; and the whole family at The History Press.

To Ezra Zeitler, cartographer extraordinaire, my hat's off. I approached Ezra early on and vowed that I *really was* writing this book and that someday I would hire him to make the maps. Thank you.

Kudos to photographer Harold Ross, who provided the main cover photo and several other Montana beauty shots, and to photographers Camron Flanders, Kelly Morris, Ken Archer, and the dashing John Squires.

And thanks to the staff of the Montana Historical Society in Helena, including Jeff Malcolm, who guided this intruding easterner through its collections. Shouts out to my archival allies: Coi at the Denver Public Library, Melissa at History Colorado, Hannah at the Mansfield Library at the University of Montana–Missoula, Eileen at MSU-Billings, Jason and Heather at MSU-Bozeman, Jenny at the Minnesota Historical Society, Paul at the University of Wisconsin–La Crosse, McKayla at the Utah Historical Society, Madeleine and Mae at BYU, and Robin and Jonathan at the National Parks Service, Yellowstone.

To genealogist David Curtis Dearborn, now retired, and David Allen Lambert, chief genealogist at the New England Historic Genealogical Society, I owe many thanks for help in researching Lowell's early life and untangling the tendrils of the family tree. We learned that all three of us are related. Isn't everyone?

To the inimitable Careen Shannon, immigration attorney, activist, writer, and editor of legal textbooks used the world over—my dear and respected friend dating back to our high school years—thank you for your close reading of an early draft and for catching many of my *errata*. More importantly, thank you for boosting my confidence with your positive feedback.

To my sister, Elizabeth Lowell Seaton-Frankfort, thank you for your support. My children, Meredith and Cole Simonds, now grown, put up with my distraction and late dinners—thank you.

Last of all, I thank my extraordinarily patient and supportive husband, John Spencer Squires, who encourages my intensity and enthusiasm. You get me, and that gives me rein to forge ahead. I promise to return to the twenty-first century.

INTRODUCTION

An *Antietam Veteran's Montana Journey* describes James Howard Lowell's experiences as a wagon train driver, hunter, placer miner, Indian trader, attorney, and civil servant from 1865 to 1871. Finding a means to success, a *place* in life, was indeed a challenge for this Civil War veteran and son of Boston. Initially, the twenty-two-year-old was not seeking to get rich from a lucky find in the gold fields. Instead, he was prospecting for a position. Having taken several years off from his Boston apprenticeship in lithography to serve in the war, what to do after the war became a puzzle he had to piece together through trial and error. Lowell had experienced the close bond of fighting men, witnessed the horrors of battle, and lain wounded in the Miller cornfield at Antietam. A reporter from the *New York Sun* saved him from bleeding to death from a gunshot wound to his left leg by dragging him to relative safety behind haystacks on the Poffenberger Farm. In a regimental circular for his Massachusetts Thirteenth fellows in 1920, Lowell wrote, "Antietam has always been a theme of deep interest—a sort of starting point in my life."[1] He and at least eight other boys from the regiment recovered from their wounds in a makeshift hospital in the Sunday school room of a German Reformed church in Harrisburg, Pennsylvania. There, Lowell met his future wife, Kate Mary Roberts, a volunteer nurse who sang in the women's quartet. "A rule was early laid down that all emotions except those of cheerfulness should be stifled; and I recall no infraction of this law," Lowell recalled.[2] He recovered in Harrisburg and served off the field of battle in Gettysburg for the remainder of the war.

Years later, writing to Kate Mary from a mining camp in Montana, Lowell admitted he failed to understand what power had lured him out West after the war. One could ask why a Boston kid would end up in Benton, Montana, doing odd jobs and practicing a crude form of frontier law with no training aside from self-study. Why did he stray so far while his sweetheart languished in Harrisburg? One could imagine that pride and stubbornness had a bit to do with it. Lowell's letters, featured in Section II, offer a sense of the private frustration he experienced, unable to earn enough cash to return home and marry. After surviving the most deadly and violent struggle in our history—with nearly twenty-three thousand missing, killed, and wounded at the Battle of Antietam alone—Lowell confessed to Kate Mary the idea of returning to the drawing rooms of Boston and to his lithography career held little appeal: "You are not the only one who has been 'mystified' by my choosing 'such wild places' to live in."[3] Lowell was not alone. Veterans drifted out West by the thousands after the war, lured by the promise of placer gold and adventure. After experiencing the camaraderie of their service years, the exploration of the West provided a romantic alternative to the drill of home life. They craved intensity and required time and healing before settling down.

A passage from Ulysses S. Grant's memoir characterizes the breed of young men who stampeded west in the gold rush before the war, but his observations could pertain to Lowell's generation as well:

> *Many were young men of good family, good education and gentlemanly instincts. Their parents had been able to support them during their minority, and to give them good educations, but not to maintain them afterwards.... Some realized more than their most sanguine expectations; but for one such there were hundreds disappointed, many of whom now fill unknown graves; others died wrecks of their former selves, and many, without a vicious instinct, became criminals and outcasts.... Those early days in California brought out character.... The immigrant, on arriving, found himself a stranger, in a stranger land, far from friends.... Many became discouraged. Others would take off their coats and look for a job, no matter what it might be. These succeeded as a rule.*[4]

Likewise, Lowell bounced back from his failures as a miner and was not above digging ditches if manual labor would pay for a daily serving of pork chop and beans. Despite his being a Boston Yankee and a Union veteran operating in a territory populated by southern Democrats, he stayed out of trouble and procured offers of employment wherever he landed. No doubt, his wounded leg gave him trouble, but he never once mentioned in his writings the injury that must have pained him as he tramped through waist-high drifts of snow in one of his near-death escapes from exposure.

Back in Harrisburg, Kate Mary Roberts waited and corresponded for six years. Her letters are lost, but a relation deposited copies of Lowell's hopeful communications postmarked Atchison, Denver, Salt Lake City, Helena, Diamond City, and Benton in the Montana Historical Society Research Center archives after his death. They appear in Section II.

Also in Section II is the wistful late-life exchange Lowell launched with an early explorer of the Yellowstone region, Charles W. Cook.[5] Lowell and Cook were contemporaries who worked the Montana mining camps clustered around Diamond City in the late 1860s. In his later years, Lowell read Cook's account of his 1869 Yellowstone expedition with envy:[6] "You may justly be proud. I would love to have been along."[7] In a letter Lowell wrote to Cook a year before his death, Lowell ruminates briefly on his motives for going out West and offers a rare mention of his own memoir: "I obeyed the call to go out where things awaited opening up.…When I located here [Kansas] I wrote with some detail the seven years spent west, five in Montana."[8] In response, the aged Cook described the responsibility of fending for the bushels of gold taken out of Diamond City: "I handled gold as a farmer does wheat. This all came into my hands unweighed and uncounted. At the time I did not see anything unusual or peculiar in my position."[9] Cook settled in White Sulphur Springs, Montana, near the area where Lowell had worked a promising claim in Thompson's Gulch. Their letters offer a poignant reminiscence of two old "mineys" reflecting on life in the camps.

To more fully understand the pioneers who were hardened to outdoor life by their Civil War service, letters recounting Lowell's war experiences round out Section II.

THE JOURNEY

Armed with a letter of introduction and his Spencer repeating rifle, Jim Lowell's path westward commenced in August 1865, four months after Lincoln was assassinated. It traced from eastern Kansas along the northern Smoky Hill route with the first and disastrous D.A. Butterfield wagon train to Denver. This richly outfitted train suffered a wagonload of calamities, including an Indian attack. On the plains of Kansas, Lowell learned to hunt buffalo to feed the party and mastered the long lash and crude lingo of the bull whacker. In November 1865, the Butterfield Overland wagon train limped into Denver, where Lowell gratefully parted company. He talked his way into a job clerking at the Planter's House hotel in Denver.

Restless to push on further and capitalize on an offer of employment, he set out the following spring and survived some late blizzards on the trail from Denver to Salt Lake City. In the Mormon city, the territorial governor of Utah permitted Lowell to sit quietly on the sidelines while he conducted business with the Mormon leader, Brigham Young, and the apostles Heber C. Kimball and George A. Smith, whom Lowell described. Impressed by Mormon enterprise but still failing to find employment in Salt Lake, Lowell joined yet another wagon train headed north to Helena, Montana, where he learned placer mining from an old forty-niner and found fellowship in the surrounding gold camps.

When Lowell's hard-won mining claim east of Helena revealed little color, he did what ambitious young men still do when things don't pan out—he commenced reading law. To keep body and soul together while he studied, Lowell boarded a stagecoach and headed farther north to set out his shingle as an attorney in Benton, Montana. Historians have called Benton the "World's Innermost Port."[10] The settlement was the final stop on the trip up the Missouri River from St. Louis. Steamboats conveyed passengers, trade goods, and Indian annuities upriver and hauled furs, buffalo robes, and gold south from the territories to the States. In Benton, Lowell practiced what he characterized as "tomahawk jurisprudence," and on a couple of occasions, he attempted to prevent the casual execution of *ex parte* vigilante justice. His eyewitness anecdotes fill out the details of the many published accounts of vigilantism in Montana with one of the few firsthand accounts of Benton's vigilance committee from the period.[11] He leaves a mystery, however, as to the identity of the swaggering "Master of Ceremonies," the chief executioner of the period, whose maxim was, "If you see a man looking for trouble, accommodate him."

Along with stewarding legal cases for both prosecution and defense, Lowell taught a bit at the settlement's first school and patronized the nascent reading room at the Chouteau County courthouse.[12] Despite the rocky launch of his legal career, Lowell would go on to become a respected attorney and judge in his adopted home of Holton, Kansas, where he served as mayor, police judge, and county attorney of Jackson County.

The memoir serves up many courses of frontier hardship, but dessert arrives near the end of the story with a taste of Lowell's feast and trading adventures with a band of River Crow and Gros Ventres near the mouth of the Judith River. With goods obtained from the Benton merchant, Thomas C. Power (later, one of Montana's two first senators), Lowell's trading endeavor was a last-ditch effort to inflate his pockets and return to the States. He enlisted an interpreter, Bob Gordon, to locate the barterers, and together they journeyed downriver in a thirty-foot mackinaw piled with blankets and other goods. After a harrowing turn through Deadman Rapids, they awaited the trade at Gordon's cabin, near the abandoned army post at Camp Cooke.[13] Lowell described the small fortress ingeniously designed to protect Gordon and his native wife, Ca-but, from Sioux attack. Ca-but's story—how she became his devoted wife after he nursed her to health—is a gem of storytelling, as is Lowell's account of the trading feast and barter. The story reaches a dramatic climax as Lowell makes another near-death escape. Ultimately, his partner Gordon's fate wasn't so lucky.

Lowell also weighs in with his perspective on an important historical event that took place northwest of Benton, the Baker Massacre, also known as the Marias Massacre. In January 1870, the Second U.S. Cavalry under Major Eugene M. Baker shot, slashed, and burned at least 173 Piegan Blackfeet who were wintering on the Marias River, including 53 women and children.[14] One contemporary account claims the death toll was much higher, at 217: mainly women, children, the sick, and elderly.[15] What made the carnage more infamous was the revelation that Baker's troops had slaughtered the wrong Indians—not the Blackfeet band led by Mountain Chief, who had been marauding and killing settlers, but a peaceful Piegan band rife with smallpox that the army brass had specifically instructed Baker to *avoid*. Their leader, Heavy Runner, had even obtained a pass of safety signed by Lieutenant Colonel Alfred Sully to prove that his people were at peace. Witnesses said Heavy Runner died waving his safety pass.[16]

When the facts leaked out that the army had mowed down another innocent camp of natives, the outcry in the eastern press marked a turning point in the history of American Indian affairs.[17] The federal government had been planning to shift civilian control of Indian affairs back to the military. News of the massacre scuttled those plans. Yet the Baker Massacre remains relatively obscure when compared to the notoriety of Sand Creek (1864) and Wounded Knee (1890), despite the fact that a comparable number of Native Americans were killed.[18] Lowell also offered his take on Indian medicine and the Piegan method of treating smallpox.

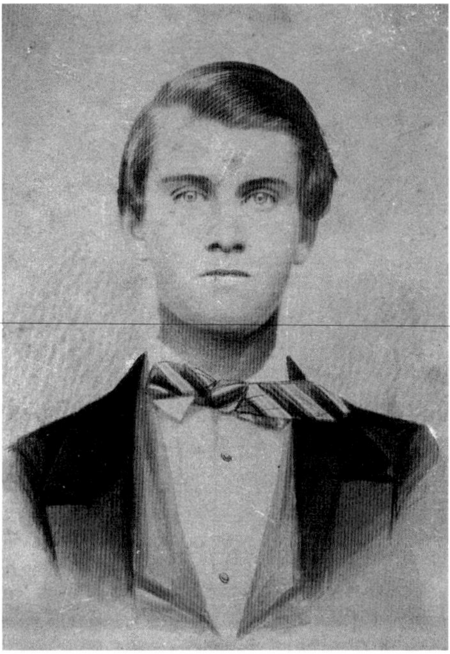

James Howard Lowell, late 1850s–early 1860s. Lowell's elder brother, John Zanidorus Lowell, was an artist, designer and engraver before he enlisted and served three stints in the Union army. In 1861, the elder Lowell suffered a wound at the Battle of Ball's Bluff. He died in 1865. John Zanidorus likely created this image of his younger brother when the younger Lowell was serving as a lithography apprentice before the war. *Courtesy of Tim Sewell.*

In the town of Benton and Fort Benton, north of town, the white settlers supplied a wholly different set of characters to the narrative. A survey of the western literature from the period would lead one to believe that gambling, bar fights, hurdy-gurdy girls, and prostitutes were the early Montana man's exclusive recreations. That impression would fall just slightly off the mark. Whether or not Lowell's account was cleaned up for posterity—which it likely was—he clearly acted as an early force for civilization in Benton as a prosecutor, defense attorney, schoolteacher, and Choteau County assessor. In 1871, Montana governor Benjamin F. Potts appointed Lowell to organize the bylaws of Dawson County, Montana. At the time, Dawson was America's largest territorial county by geographical size. Tellingly, Lowell failed to mention teaching classes at the newly formed school, although Fort Benton historian Joel Overholser mentions the young man as one of the town's first teachers, along with Misses Power, Culbertson, and Clevenger.[19] One is left with the impression that manliness was a highly regarded virtue by Lowell, and teaching schoolchildren did not fit into the image he sought to cultivate back east.

While Lowell admired the manly in mankind, he was not above relishing the comforts of civilization. In one episode, he recalled the joy of sleeping between sheets for the first time in years. In the dreary winters of the mining camps and in Benton, Lowell missed the civilizing influence of women. He expressed admiration for pioneer women and their capacity to maintain their persons and keep clean, orderly homes in the wilderness. Lowell was not the only young man who missed the society of women. A California diarist recorded a similar complaint in 1850: "To one who was born and brought up where there were more women than men, it is hard to realize what a hardship it is to be deprived of their company."[20]

Despite the apparent loneliness for civilized conversation and the evidence of his ardent letters to Kate Mary, Lowell never mentioned his former nurse in the manuscript. The young suitor delayed returning stateside until he had achieved a measure of financial success.

The story is replete with escapes, chance encounters, and stirring descriptions of the landscape of the Old West. Lowell had a literary bent that revealed an artistic nature and almost spiritual reverence for the territory that surrounded him. Despite proffered modesty regarding his literary powers, the memoir offers a rich account of the natural beauty of the plains, the Montana wilderness, the Missouri River, and, particularly, the vast herds of buffalo, elk, and antelope that populated the land at that time. His nostalgia for the era of great herds, steamboat traffic, and the American Indians, whom he described as high priests of nature, reveals sympathy for a slower and more primitive time.

Part I

THE MEMOIR

DULL DAY JOTTINGS *1872*

A First Few Words

The old-fashioned Pioneer is about extinct in this generation. You might find a specimen or relic bearing the trademark in fugitive retirement in the Rockies or the Sierras. Time and the railroads have done what wild beasts, Indians, and the privations of an inhospitable wilderness could not do—retire the Pioneer. Time was, he was the vanguard to push the borderline westward, but in the later '60s, the railroads usurped the role, and the pilot of the locomotive elbowed aside the stage driver, the bull whacker, and the mule skinner—the adventurous Argonauts of the plains—and marked as well the speedy disappearance of Nature's reign of man and beast. The old pioneer was a tremendous force, and we live today largely on those sterling qualities that gave a fiber to his manhood—iron, to edge resolve with.[21] The boundaries of the region known as the West have been constantly shifting, so that probably within the lifetime of a few old folks, it lay along the foothills of the Alleghenies, then later to the banks of the Mississippi, and still later—at the time we will speak of, in the '60s—along the bluffs of the Missouri. Beyond this line, there lay the region of Tradition, Prophecy, Adventure, Discovery, Enterprise, and Heroism—the West! How captivating to the senses of virile youth, the young manhood of that period, to him who had tasted the severities of Militarism, the twin sister of Adventurism, to find in this vast arena an escape from the commonplaces of existence;

the temptation of abolishing the frontier, of ranging the little known and mysterious solitudes beyond the border, of possessing it and its hidden store; the exultation of being a factor in subjugating its virgin ruggedness, and in the up-building of a community or State!

A Change of Base

One day in April 1865, I was pacing the platform of a railway station in Pittsburg, Pennsylvania, and counting the number of planks thereof, for I had nothing else to do while waiting for a westbound train. A carriage drove up, and from it there alighted an elderly gentleman who soon settled down to counter-striding the platform and apparently working out the same problem in arithmetic. He had a large head and bore a distinguished appearance. His age must have been past sixty. He spoke to me, and finding we were in the same plight and waiting for the same train, there was no reason except the disparity of our ages (mine being twenty-two) to prevent an acquaintanceship. He would stop off at St. Louis, but only for a short time, as he was going to Utah. We had a section together in the sleeper and the sociability of the man to St. Louis leaves a pleasant recollection, and as the circumstance of meeting him changed somewhat the trend, or course, of my western life, I have occasion to remember it. It was plain to see that he was a personage of some account—was traveled—and I felt flattered by the warmth of his fatherly treatment and greatly entertained with his converse. As we moved into St. Louis and were about to part, cards were exchanged and he said that I might find it of advantage to go on to Salt Lake City, where he was to take a position, and if I did, to hunt him up. My ticket terminus was St. Joe. And for a few days I looked around there for a train, either mule or bull train, for Denver. St. Joseph was then a raw specimen of settlement seated back on the rising slope from the river—a sort of fringe of civilization, straggling and unsightly—treeless and barren surfaced. I found there was no outfitting of overland trains at St. Joe and therefore went to Atchison, another topsy-turvy, embryonic western city, illogically built along some broken bluffs on the west bank of the Missouri river. It was the starting point of the Overland Mail for the mining regions and California, the headquarters of the stage companies, and one of the chief points on the border for the transshipment from cars and steamboats to the wagon trains bound for Colorado, Idaho, Montana, and Utah. Huge warehouses and yards stored massive machinery for working mines and goods for feeding and clothing miners. A new venture in transportation had just been started by one D.A. Butterfield with Eastern capital, named "Butterfield Overland Despatch."[22] Up until this time, this freight and passenger traffic had been along the Platte River to Nebraska, to its forks, and thence along the south fork to Denver. Now it was designed to carry the same along the Smoky Hill River. The new company with unstinted means was outfitting its first line of coaches and its first wagon trains, the latter to have fifty wagons and the finest mules and equipment; the idea being to make a swift and thorough initial trip to Salt Lake. The season was very wet, and preparations went along slowly. I had letters to the Butterfield people and soon was on good terms with a younger brother of D.A. It happened that one day the clerk who spelled off the freight that was discharged on the levee from the steamboats was ill, and I had his job that day. While checking off the goods, my attention was arrested by a consignment marked "Charles Durkee Salt Lake City," the name of my quondam traveling mate whose half-forgotten card I brought forth from a pocket. On inquiry, I was told that the gentleman had recently been appointed by President Johnson as Governor of Utah, and that he had that day arrived in Atchison and stopped at the Massasoit, at which hotel I was also lodged. I met him there at noon with a "How do you do Governor," whereat he smiled and made me known to his staff.[23] I was a good deal tongue-tied at this turn of affairs, but he was affable and proposed me to join his party, who had decided to drive across over the Platte route, then patrolled by soldiers: I, to furnish one horse. This I could not do, for my arrangements had been made to go with the crack train of Butterfield. The Governor then gave me charge of the goods of his on that train to keep an eye on. They left the next day.

THE PLAINS ACROSS

Kansas to Colorado, 1865

Some frontier poet, in order to give rhythm as well as rhyme to his border verse, invented the expression, "The Plains Across," one that became expressive of a pilgrimage across the plains at the time this writing treats of and a gem of border vernacular. The Butterfield project of a shipping route via the Smoky Hill River was opulent in promise but disastrous of outcome—not so much because of any inherent or natural difficulties, but rather because of the meteoric conception in the brain of an impractical man. A superficial exploration had been made of the route to Denver about 1863, and a report favorable for a line of six hundred miles between Atchison and Denver had been made. Butterfield was the alleged proprietor of the scheme that took form in the spring of the year I was there, 1865. It was mapped out that a route out of Atchison southwesterly, via Grasshopper Falls (now Valley Falls), thence intersecting the Old Fort Riley military road a little northeast of Topeka, following this route and crossing Soldier Creek a few miles northwest of Topeka, thence on the north bank of Kansas River, westward up the river to Fort Riley to Junction City, thence along the Smoky Hill fork. No definite route was specifically mapped. It was defined only in general terms. Changes were subsequently made, but not till after this first train I went with had made its passage. Certain stations were located, but none established after Fort Riley. [Near Junction City, Kansas.]

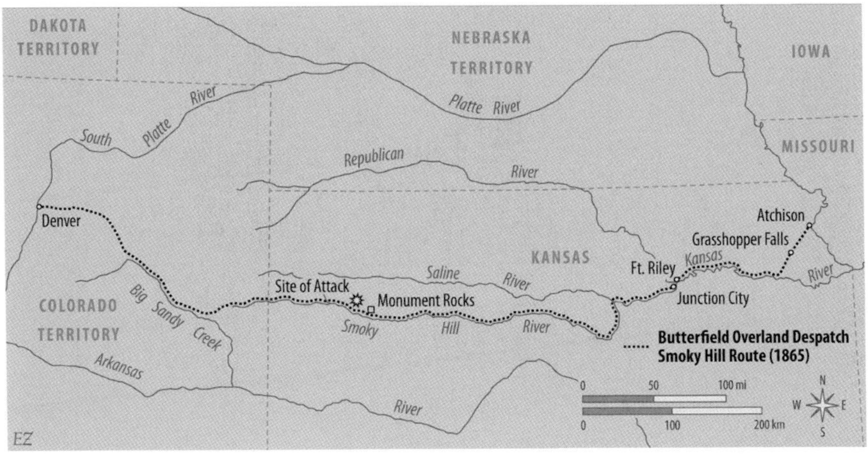

Map by Ezra Zeitler.

THE CAREER AND FATE of this wagon train has had publicity only in the most general terms. Its wreck has been attributed to hostile Indians that harassed it, but this is only a part of the truth. It has been recorded that the train reached Denver September 23, 1865. This is erroneous, for I have abundant proof that it reached there in November of that year in letters that I wrote on the ground and other sources of fact, aside from the personal memory I have of the event.[24] We pulled out of Atchison about August 20, 1865; the wagon Master was one Devine, a blacksmith of that town, an oldish man of the Missourian type. He had a husky screaming kind of voice and no end of energy. The roads were terribly muddy and the rains persistent. It was several days before we crossed at Grasshopper and as many weeks before reaching Fort Riley, a distance of about 120 miles. From Riley we were in terra-incognito—the mythical Kingdom of Quivira—a stretch of land—undulating plain, having an altitude from 600 to 3,000 feet sloping upward to the west; wholly devoid of swamps with a rare occasion of a tree line growing dispiritedly before us, and across this territory, this train of fifty wagons now began its journey along the Smoky Hill without so much as a trail to guide its course—a region as virgin as when Francisco Vasquez de Coronado with his army of Explorers came there from New Mexico to the bison plains of Kansas in 1540.[25] There lay illimitable stretches of a brownish green surface, rolling like long waves of the seas and broken by a small stream at intervals but more often seamed with coulees. These enlarged into huge ravines, waterless and arid—blocking passage that made it necessary to divert our course to head them off. There were sand dunes belting north and south, to traverse which required doubling and trebling the teams. The train was provided with two guides chosen to facilitate the passage. Instead, they brought us broadside to these natural obstacles, and days were spent in tacking, meandering, returning, and tacking again, either through the indecision or misdirection of the guides. This vast area west of Riley was peopled by innumerable buffalo and antelope, giving animation to the otherwise dreary expanses. A sentimental person might say that the existence of these creatures relieved the landscape of its monotony, which was true, but in another view, they were a nuisance. They made a wallow of the stinted water, so polluting it that its use for drinking and cooking was well nigh prevented, and this was a daily experience for as far as the eye could reach. The surface of the earth was a heaving mass of animal life: it seemed covered with a mantle of brown fur. At times, as we advanced, the huge drove would quietly separate to our right and left leaving a lane along which we traveled. We were 100 miles south of the Platte route. Grazing was plentiful for our beasts; our fuel was buffalo chips, and we carried a limited amount of food staples, relying upon the company's coaches to follow with these supplies. Trouble came to our animals as we traversed the Saline River country. There, the soil is sandy and saturated with alkali, and from contact, the mules contracted sores on their fetlocks and legs of a character so malignant, our Veterinary was unable to cope with it. The hospital, or "calvey yard," as plainsmen called it, was kept heavily reinforced.[26] This feature also contributed to delay the train, but more serious jolts than any mentioned awaited us.

Before the start from Atchison, I got to know two brothers named Chamberlain, who, like myself, were initiates into Western life. We three prepared for this "Plains Across." Each was provided with a horse and equipment and a mongrel rig of wearing, partly citified and partly border ruffian or cowboy. Our arsenal was a revolver each. My Spencer rifle (a repeating breach-loading Spencer, firing seven shots) and the Chamberlains' were provided by the train with the Ballard gun. We were the self appointed Nimrods [hunters] of the expedition and took part in the cooking and other odd jobs that came up. The train was amply manned; everything new and shiny—a medicine chest, extra beasts in the "calvey yard," a Ballard [gun] for each person, and a finer array of mule flesh never pulled a train the plains across. I remember having a prejudice against a few that made up the personnel of the outfit; they seemed dark-visaged and evil-eyed, but I reasoned to myself that it was only the difference between the mannered

East and the ill-conditioned West and that the sooner I adapted myself, the better. We had hardly gotten out of Atchison before an "odd job" turned up and lasted for days. Washouts and mud crossings stalled the teams, and our shoulders were at the wheels constantly. This labor continued until we were halfway to Riley.

With Riley ended the habitable portion of Kansas, and up to this point, fairly good order had been preserved in the trains, but it was plain to see that a rebellious spirit pervaded the trainmen, or at least a portion of them, and that there was contempt for the authority of the boss. This ripened into open insubordination and mutiny very shortly, when the train was precipitated beyond the restraints of civil and martial authority. Abe Devine lacked the quality of command; his mastership of the train ceased at the border of habited Kansas. The drivers, the vicious portion of them, gave free rein to their contempt of him; he became the butt of their gibes and ribaldry. The wagons straggled along at the will of their drivers; the better element kept together. The liquors in the freight were ravaged, and wild, drunken, and debauched men flourished their whips and revolvers from the box seats by day and brutish orgies vocalized the night. It frequently occurred that the corralling of the wagons at nightfall was short of its complement. Some belated and sometimes one or more not appearing caused delay in rallying the fugitives. The Chamberlains and self hovered on the flanks in pursuit of the buffalo and antelopes. It was great sport, and our providing gave us a good standing with all; grass was abundant, the game in splendid condition, and hoodoo buffalo (sick, crippled run-down animals) that usually hover on the skirts of the herd were scarce, and consequently, the wolves and coyotes, plentiful as the buffalo, were handicapped for a living. They resorted to ham-stringing them, and their hunger made them bold and obtrusive. We three slept under a wagon, and I have had one of these brutes nose the blanket that covered me. On one of our excursions, we had dallied behind the train out of its hearing and had to our credit two antelope, which we had secured about nightfall. Realizing the ease with which one may get lost in the maze of undulating plain, we hastened to sling our game to the saddles and hunt out the track taken by the train. It was a chance to find it and occupied us till long after midnight. Meanwhile, we were constantly beset with surrounding wolves, who yapped almost at our heels in headlong rushes to capture the meat. Their number was legion, and their howlings were like demons. I have never since known of so determined an attack by wild brutes. A fitful glimmer disclosed, at length, the campfire, toward which we rolled as the light streaks of morning painted the East. But this romancing was shortly to have an end.

An emergency occurred, when one night, several of the whackers—having shifted into two wagons a valuable lot of the freight—made off with them on the back track. I cannot recall that any effort was made to follow them. The desertion made it imperative for us to take the reins of the vacant boxes. The ringleaders being gone, order was partially restored, and the worn-out authority of Devine showed some signs of life, but the free lance of the three jolly rovers of the plains was broken, and I and the Chamberlains began the schooling in mule craft. A mule is unknown to him who knoweth not the nature thereof. It is not alone the long lashed whip that spurs a mule to its duty—his eyes, his features, his limbs, and his relations, are reviled in the most free and fearless manner and with the aridest liberty of speech and always emphasized with the use of one of the names of the holy trinity. By some subtle perception of the brutes, a driver unskilled in this acquirement—do what he may—is a failure.

A succession of sand dunes was to be passed and required a doubling up of trains to cross them. A memorable object of national scenery were the chalk or soft limestone structures rising out of the earth, which, seen from afar, had every appearance of a city with its temples, pinnacles, statues,

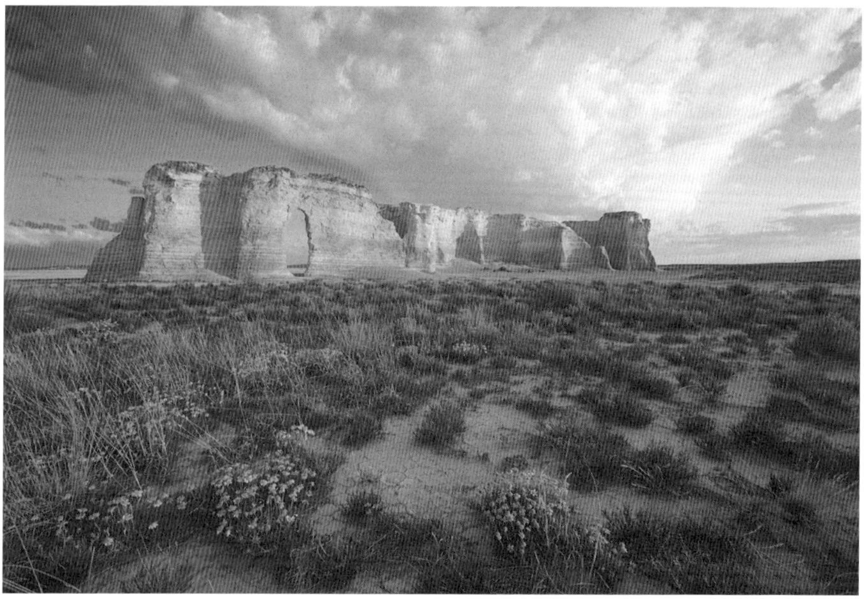

Monument Rocks, the Badlands, Kansas. *Photograph by Camron Flanders.*

colonnades, terraces, chimneys, and towers. The glinting substances upon the natural objects heightened the effect. It was difficult to divest oneself of the conviction that a city was being approached.

While driving down a hill one day, my lead mules turned at something in the grass and overturned the wagon, breaking a wheel. The boss was furious and addressed me with great freedom. He had always mistrusted me. And some Yankee ways of mine he had disapproved of, and he had made a point of showing his dislike for Yankees generally, and myself in particular, in a hundred ways. I dare say he was right, but I cherish a dislike for that man, Abe Devine, to this day. For a while, I was out of a job.

We had proceeded to within fifty miles of what was called Monument Station (but no stations had been equipped yet), and one night, had got things snug—corral formed—and the animals out to feed. Toward midnight, we were routed out. The night herders announced that the herd had been surprised and all the animals except the cripples were run off by Indians. Pursuit was out of the question. The corral was put in shape for defense, weapons examined, and in the morning, we espied the enemy in war costume popping into sight and then disappearing Indian fashion and coming up again as much as to say, "You're a beleaguered Party." In outfitting this train for speedy movement, and to make a record as such, the plan was that it should depend largely for its commissariat upon the coaches that were to be sent out en route for Denver.[27] This had been done, but the next coach came along without stores and found us tied up. After some parley and urging by one of the passengers, an ex-colonel of a Pennsylvania regiment in the war, the coach undertook to go on. The second coach—and last—turned back. The colonel's coach proceeded to Monument Station, and while nooning—the animals out feeding—an attack was made upon the party. They put up as good a defense as they could, when a signal from the Indians came for a parley. One of them in Indian rig with a white man's voice gave the colonel's party an option to go away unhurt and leave the plunder.[28] This was accepted as a prudent measure against such odds, and leaving the coach and animals, they retraced their steps towards our position, a distance of fifty miles, where they arrived, a sorry lot of tourists, the following day. Each had removed his footgear to ease the wear and tear and hasten the journey. I met the colonel in Denver some months after, and he was limping yet.[29]

It became a matter of interest how to feed the party, now certainly cut off, and daily hovered around with redskins whose purpose it seemed to be to force us to abandon the train. Stores had run low, and the party was rationed. We were strong enough to stand off any amount of hostiles. To attack them, even if successful, would be of little relief: our position was in the open, and there was no reason to think they would attack us behind the wagons arranged corral fashion. It was simply the game of freeze out. One morning, in the opposite direction from the beleaguers, appeared a hoodoo buffalo. A hoodoo is one that, either through sickness or injury, seeks the outskirt of the herd and companions by himself til recovered. An Irishman of our party borrowed my Spencer and approached the beast and luckily brought him down in his tracks. A rush with knives and axes was made, while the others in the corral attended to the hostiles, who heard the report of the gun and showed up actively in consequence. The spoil was lugged in and cooked by the "chips." Judged from the point of total abstinence, the meat was good, though it lay closer to the bone than was desirable.

Dilemmas of this kind always have a humorous side, and in this instance, a cheerful feeling ran through the thirty-one days of our quarantine. Not one but would have done creditable work whatever befell, and song and jest enlivened the siege. General G.M. Dodge, on the thirty-first day, came over the rise from Denver with a rescuing body of cavalry.[30] Following were a drove of bulls to haul the trains in to Denver. This was about the last of September or early October. Butterfield and his Lieutenant Colonel [Isaac E.] Eaton of the Butterfield Overland were with the troops that came in. I recall the meeting of Butterfield and my friend Devine the wagon boss. It was easy to see that Butterfield attributed all the calamities to *Devine* Management, and when he found Devine half-screened behind a wagon, as if guilty, he looked at him in silence awhile as if he would like to annihilate him, and then as quietly as if addressing a lady, he delivered a torrent of anathema—much of it wholly undeserved and unmerited and brutal.

The Bulls were speedily in harness and lumbering along Denver-ward, while the troops apparently sought the trail of the disappearing reds. We had passed the antelope realm and were now with the main herd of buffalo that blanketed the earth all around us. Some pretense of equipment of the "stations" appeared—a tent, or rude structure—part stable and part office, where men were to be seen. Better order and method prevailed in the train. It was a novelty to be driving four or six yoke of bulls, but the emergency required it and better luck came out of it, but it was not until November that we pulled into Denver.

Altogether, the journey was a pretty piece of frontiering; the uniform view was of a rolling virgin prairie. Prairie merged into plain inhabited only by nature's dumb creatures and impressing one with the measureless extent of the territory—the nights vocal with the chorusing yelp of wolves and coyotes. The morning would find these creatures squatting around us, impatiently waiting the breaking of camp to seize the crumbs and remains of our breakfast in ferocious rivalry.

The appearance of the train as it lumbered into Denver was in strange contrast with the train that pulled out of Atchison in August. Capital's unsparing hand had equipped the finest outfit that ever journeyed the plains across: mules selected from the choicest, and a surplus of them, new wagons and fittings, every detail of the best. Against all experience and in total disregard of the natural conditions that prevail during the winter months along the route to Salt Lake City, the train was then ordered to proceed on from Denver. [Lowell withdrew his services and remained in Denver.] It struggled through the Black Hills and over the Laramie Plains, encountering pitiless snows and fierce winds and blighting cold. Harassed by famishing wolves and predatory hostiles on the Green River, the climax was reached: the train looted of its freight and practically wiped off the face of the earth. Some of its men perished, and others only escaped through sufferings.

DENVER

Clerking at the Planter's House Hotel

At that time, Denver was a mining town, but aspiring and peopled with mixed elements—the sturdy and ambitious—the moral and the depraved. It was the gateway to the mines of Central and Georgetown. The most pretentious building was the mint. Gambling halls were maintained on its principal street, and while I was there, the winter of '65–'66, these places were assailed by the Vigilantes and closed out. I recall the Skull and X-bones, which these self-constituted promoters of the peace plastered upon their doors. Enterprise and a rude activity entered into all the industries. The chief hotel was the Planters, famous as having housed many Eastern celebrities: Speaker Colfax, Foster, president of the senate, Doolittle, and many others touring the territory put up at this hostelry.[31]

It was a two-story frame, plainly furnished, having on the ground floor a long and wide room. At one end was the office, at the other end a bar. Two billiards tables furnished the center. While looking around for something to do, I stayed there awhile, then to Central [City] and Blackfoot and returned broke. The morning after my return, I went to the clerk of the hotel and, in a few words, stated to him the situation and offered to go in as an assistant. In fact, it was more a demand than an offer. Mr. Bishop, the clerk, was willing to be relieved from so much work and installed me. The hotel was owned by Peacock and Meek, two old miners who were innocent of any education and, as to writing, could only scribble their names. They were suspicious of Bishop, and it was not long before I was put in charge and Bishop discharged. Although I was under no fixed salary, they allowed me

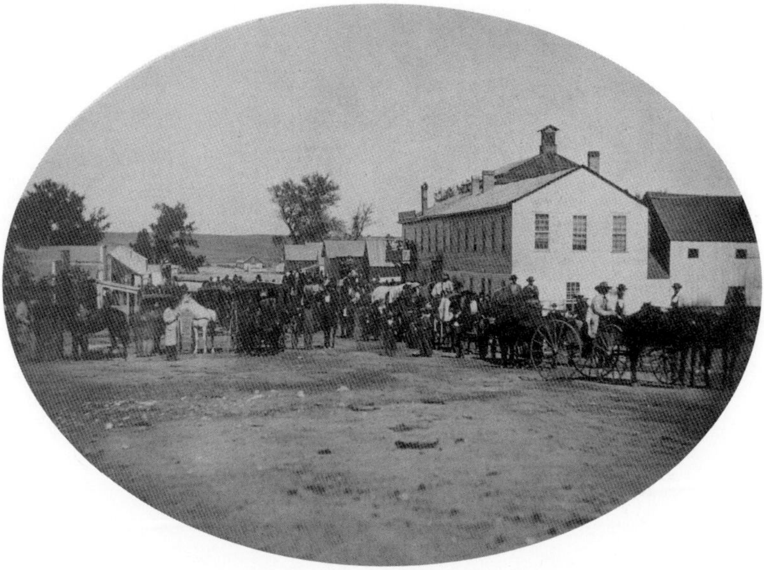

Planters House, 1864. *Reproduced by permission from History Colorado, 20004772.*

$75 per month from the time I entered, which was soon increased to $100. In this way, I was thrown into the society of many prominent men, Eastern tourists, statesmen, artists, and public characters.

Sunday was a great day at the hotel, and an especially good dinner was provided for the miners, who came in that day in crowds from the mines. I had printed bills of fare with absurd and frenchy menu cards. Ex-Governor Gilpin lived there; he was the first territorial governor, a little past the prime and quite dignified.[32] It was probably because of my interest in literature that put me so much in his society. His room was plainly furnished. I recall one morning I went there with him and his burning his hand while poking the fire in the little stove and his antics over it and his loss of dignity. In some way, he had been connected with the earliest exploration of the territory, and the government gave him many leagues of land in the San Luis Valley. His bearing was soldierly, and he said he had been with [Major General John Charles] Fremont. He was, however, a Quaker at this time and was interesting in his reminiscences.

I had some funny experiences as hotel clerk and will mention one. A shabby genteel young man offered to pawn a guitar, which was in a green bag, as barter for supper, lodging, and breakfast. I set the instrument aside, and he went in to his supper; a little later, he brought in another green bag saying that

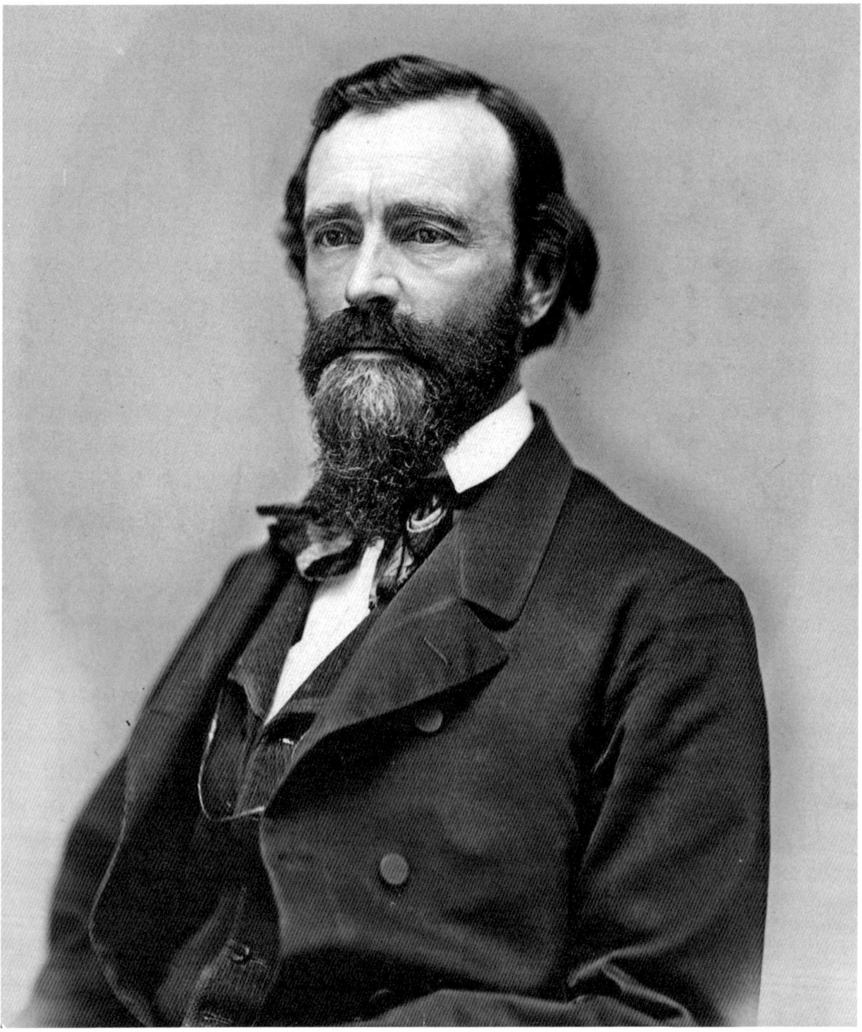

William Gilpin, first governor, Colorado Territory. *Reproduced by permission from History Colorado, 10025405.*

he had an engagement to play the guitar at a dance and wanted to substitute the violin in the second bag. Without examining, I took it, and he went off with the guitar, had his lodging and breakfast, and was seen no more. A day or two after, I happened to think of him and took a look at the violin. It had neither bridge nor catgut. It was split from end to end and had a sad and wrecked appearance. Conscience stricken, I told Peacock and Meek about it, and amid much hilarity, I was compelled to order the drinks for the house.

SALT LAKE CITY BOUND, *1866*

As spring approached, some irresistible lodestone attracted my thoughts upon Salt Lake City. There was a young man at the hotel awaiting some chance of getting there, and between us, arrangements were made to start in the month of March 1866. My good employers used every way to dissuade me, urging, as one reason, the impassable route via the Black Hills and Laramie Plains at so early a season, and persuasively, a flattering offer to stay with them. It is in vain now to try to account for so unwise a step or the folly that persisted in it. Equipped with three nags—one for the pack—and provisioned for the trip, we left Denver via the one stage route to the range's base and skirted along the foothills northerly to a stream named Cache la Poudre, where we arrived in the weather almost like summer. It was about midafternoon when one of our animals received injuries that compelled us to abandon it. This was a serious loss and required a rearranging of our stores. From this stream, we pushed on to Virginia Dale that same evening, where we arrived late and in snow, ankle deep. The sudden transition to cold induced us to sleep inside the station, for that was all there was of Virginia Dale except a shoeing shop and barn. It was the last habitation we were to see for many a day.

We were now one hundred miles from Denver and on the northern border of Colorado. The morning found us crossing into the Domain of Dakota (now Wyoming), a region devoid of any pretense of frontier life. Before us rose the stretches of Laramie Plains blanketed with snow a foot deep—a treeless plateau. The distance across to Fort Halleck, some one hundred miles, was slow journey and through huge drifts. This we traveled on foot; mostly, an unceasing headwind of great violence kept us company. We spied a log hut at Coopers Creek in which we took refuge and took an inventory of ourselves and belongings. It was a relief from the customary method of kicking away the snow to lay our blankets for the night. Here, as usual, we picketed out our nags, whose living was upon the bunch grass from which they pawed the snow—a nutritious and sustaining growth, even though dried and seasoned, carrying a food quality unknown to tame grasses. Animals readily adapt themselves to uncovering and subsisting upon it without aid of grain. Its tufts grow to a foot and more in height, and when found unpastured, a short time only is required to satisfy a brute. This hut had been made by the soldiers of the fort and probably by the herders of the fort stock. Our faces were swollen through exposure to the wind, and our eyes were so snow blind that it made this place a Welcome Harbor. "A passage perilous maketh a port pleasant." And for the several days that the storm raged, we kept house there. With the stalks of sagebrush for fire, a very comfortable household was maintained. The storm abating, we talked over the situation. My companion had had enough, and nothing could dissuade him from taking the back track by one of the coaches when the road became open to conduit of travel. The snow was now two feet on the level. Several days had elapsed since a coach had ventured to go through, and some time must elapse before travel was resumed. We therefore divided up our stuff,

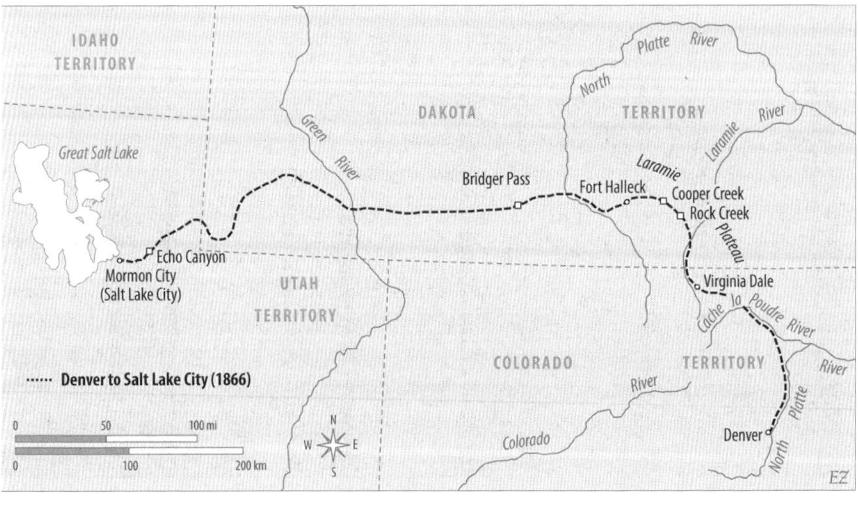

Map by Ezra Zeitler.

and with one of the nags, I started afoot for Fort Halleck, a distance of some forty miles—making Rock Creek the first night. My sight had gone out—snow blind. Started early next morning relying on the instinct of the animal to keep the course. After nightfall, my nag whinnied, and shortly, I heard voices of men and we were escorted into the fort by a party of soldiers.

Nature's chief product within a radius of fifty miles of Halleck was wind, wind, wind: violent and constant. The effect of these winds and blowing sands upon the soft rocks in the open seasons is very curious. There you see the tall, isolated rocks like huge chimneys, sometime round, always smooth as the work of a chisel. The serried walls have fantastic fashionings, apparently from the sands and sediment hurled against them by the forces of the wind, leaving curious specimens of nature's handiwork. Mock fortresses, cathedrals, castles, towers, porches, naves, transepts, and steeples appear with little effort of the imagination. All formed from this laboratory of wind sky-hooting down the stretches of Laramie plateaus.

Tied up at Halleck was a bull train freighted with flour belonging to a man named Ezekiel Newman, who was destined for Salt Lake, or Helena,

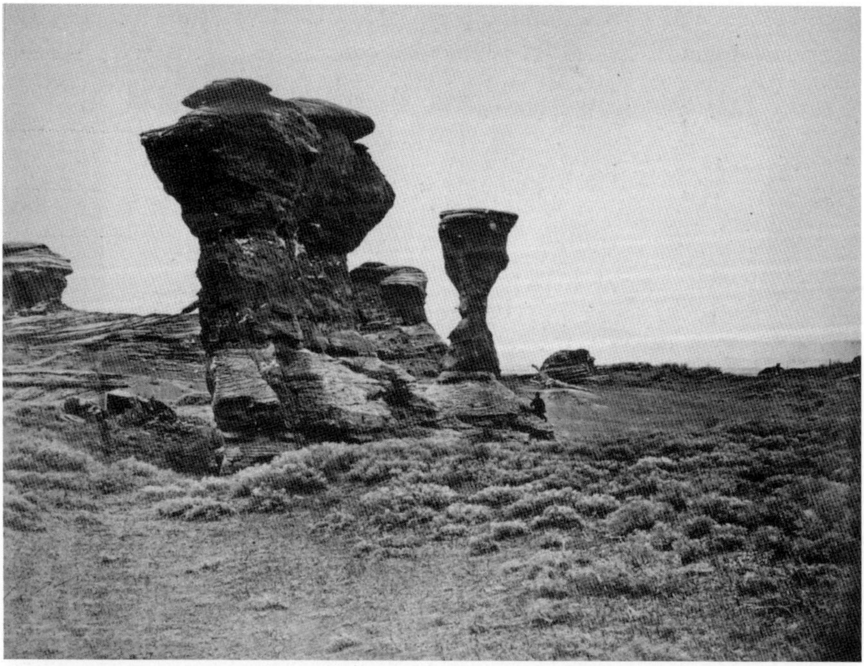

Dial Rock, Red Buttes, Laramie Plains, 1898. *Andrew J. Russell photograph, Library of Congress.*

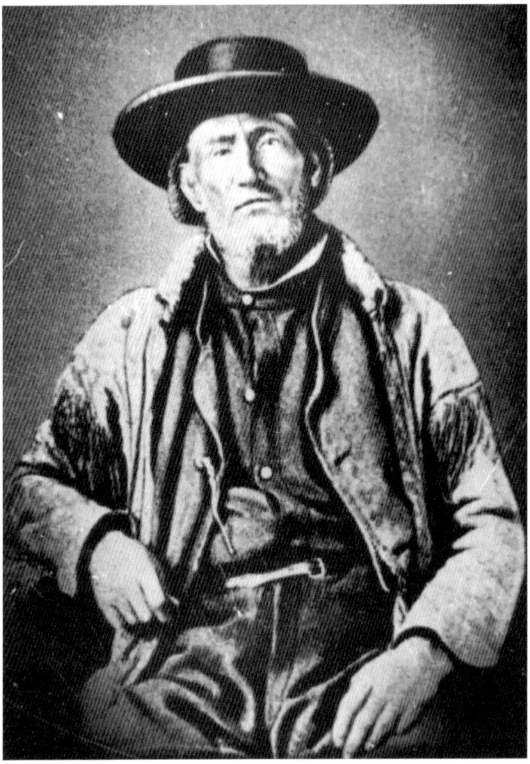

Left: Jim Bridger. *Public domain.*

Below: Bannock Indians, photographer unknown. *Reproduced by permission from the National Park Service, Yellowstone Collection, 02735.*

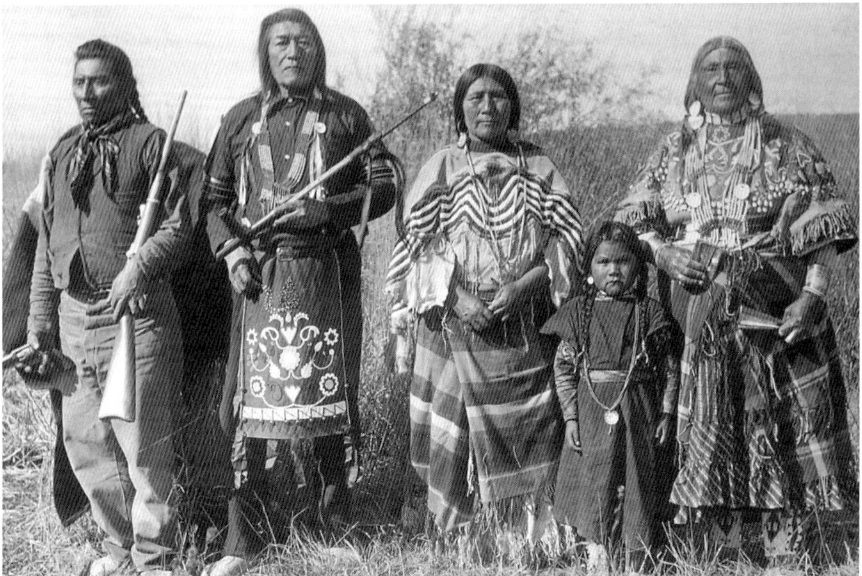

Montana. It was some weeks before favorable transit permitted this train to move, and I engaged to go with it as far as the Mormon City, as correspondent of the owner, who went in advance via coach. My letters were sent daily by the day coach. The wagon boss was a "bad man," laconic in speech, but that speech was the law of the train. "I want to see how quickly you can do it," lacked none of the quality of the most imperative command and was understood as such by the burliest whacker. The stage route was via Bridger's Pass, and there was established a military post by a typical frontiersman, trapper, hunter, and guide, and also a scout. He was discoverer of this pass as early as 1825 and was still living at this fort.[33] As I remember, it was made up of a series of log structures, enclosed with a stockade. The site is admirably situated in a basin of the mountains and supplied with abundance of water from a tributary of Green River. It was by this pass that the traffic was taken across the range.

In due course, Mormon outskirt settlements were passed, and on June 27, 1866, the train emerged through the outlet of Echo Canyon and debouched into the open. It was early forenoon. A clear sky and the sun shone down and illuminated the Great Salt Lake and the Mormon City—a spectacle not easily forgotten.

I forgot to mention that an hour's stop was made on Green River to prospect the famous Moss agate territory there, a fine specimen of which I was lucky enough to kick up, but which I was relieved of through another's cupidity later on. The only Indians seen on this trip were the Bannocks and a band of Shoshones, who were camped peaceably on, and contiguous to, the Green River.

THE MORMON CITY

Lowell Meets Brigham Young

At his time, Brigham Young was at the zenith of his power and fame. The dream of immunity from Federal authority had not yet been fully broken, and the "Destroying Angels" were, in a sense, disorganized. There yet existed a system of espionages. No stranger who entered the gates of Mormonism but was spotted and, if he did not presently depart, was treated to a call of inquiry. A self-invited Mormon came to my room and, in the politest manner, engaged me in a talk concerning my intentions in visiting the city and very frankly told me at parting the purpose of his call. I remained there for about one month at the Salt Lake House, which was kept by a Gentile. One day, having a severe toothache, I asked the clerk to direct me to a good dentist. "If you want the best, he said, go to Brigham's Block where all the professions are located." And so it was that the Block was a large one, having the Prophet's residence, and all about him were skilled representatives of the various professions. The dentist—a young man—courteously answered all questions the surroundings suggested.

I called early at the Executive Mansion, a one-story, but spacious structure outfitted with extreme simplicity. The governor himself let me in, and we talked awhile about the ill-fated trains and the loss of his part of its freight. I got an invitation to call the next forenoon, and I intended there to have it out with him regarding an occupation, as he had promised to place me.

The next day, he was door keeper as before, and after a few words, there came to the door three visitors: Brigham Young and the Apostles

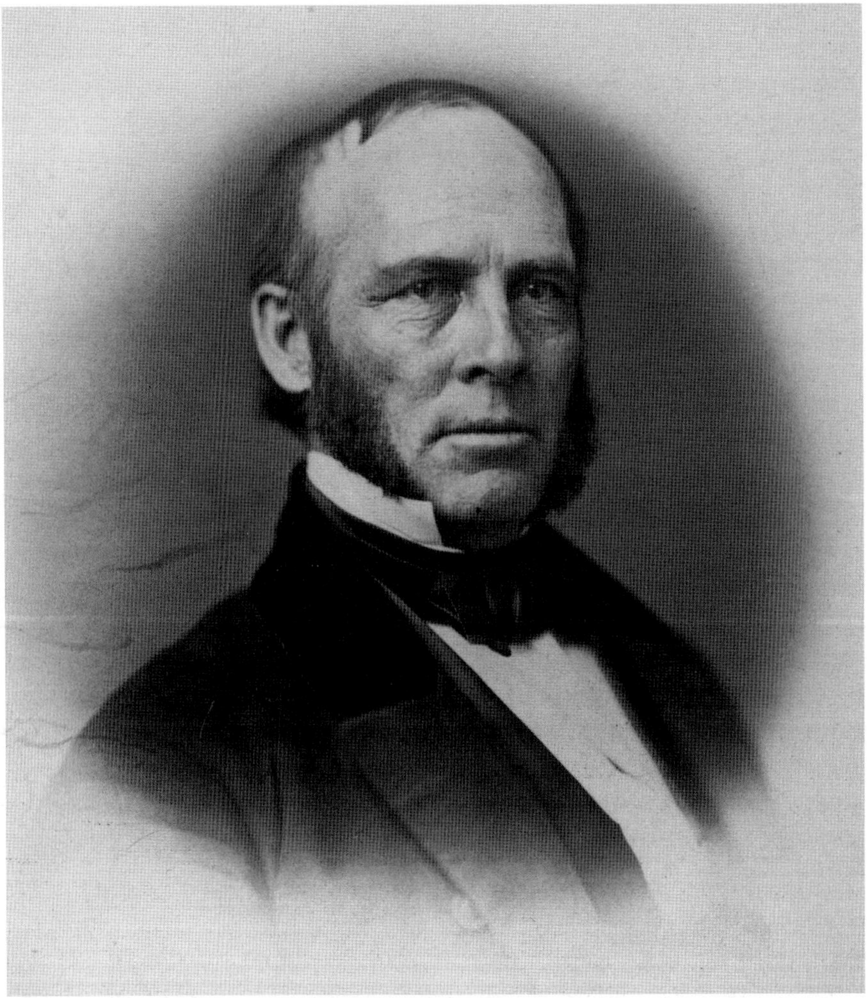

U.S. senator from Wisconsin Charles Durkee, sixth territorial governor of Utah. *Photograph by Julian Vannerson, 1859, Library of Congress, JK1012.M35.*

George Smith and Heber C. Kimball.[34] I was up against it and made as if to retire, but the Governor motioned me to stay, whereupon I lapsed into an interested listener. The whole affair was easy and most informal, the discourse open and frank. The prophet was a tall, well-built man with a strong face who spoke in vigorous and original language—a very self-willed and determined personage. I could imagine how his peoples, made up largely of a subservient class, would regard him, much as Kent did King Lear:

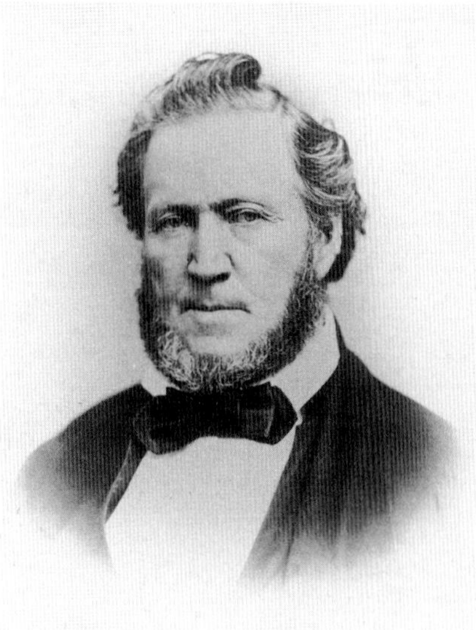

Right: The Mormon prophet Brigham Young. *Reproduced by permission from the Utah State Historical Society.*

Opposite: George A. Smith and Heber C. Kimball (*right*), counselors to Brigham Young. *Reproduced by permission from the Utah State Historical Society.*

> *But you have that in your countenance which I would fain call Master.*
> *What's that?*
> *Authority!*
> [King Lear, 1.4.27–30]

George Smith must have weighed near three hundred pounds and had a trick of turning the discourse into broad good humor, while Heber C. Kimball was a cold, practical man with a hard head, bald and knobby, over which he had the trick of throwing a red bandanna handkerchief and snipping it away again, whether to keep in the Apostolic afflatus or to keep off the flies was uncertain.[35] And this is the story gleaned from the conversation. The theme concerned the Mormon system of proselytizing and colonizing the valley and contiguous territory and naturally discussed the operation of the district divisions of their Government, the temporal and the spiritual of the Latter Day Saints. Brigham was chief spokesman and told how they transplanted people from European countries by sending missionaries, who were authorized to offer the alluring gift of 160 acres of land to the heads of families, passage to America and to Utah, to bestow a team and farming equipment and seed, lumber for buildings and provisions to bridge over until a crop was raised. Their initiatory necessaries—and perhaps others—were paid for out of the church funds, which were obtained by a system of tithing upon the

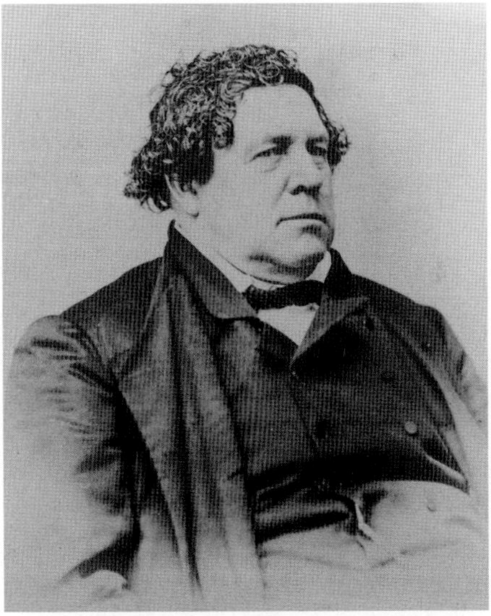

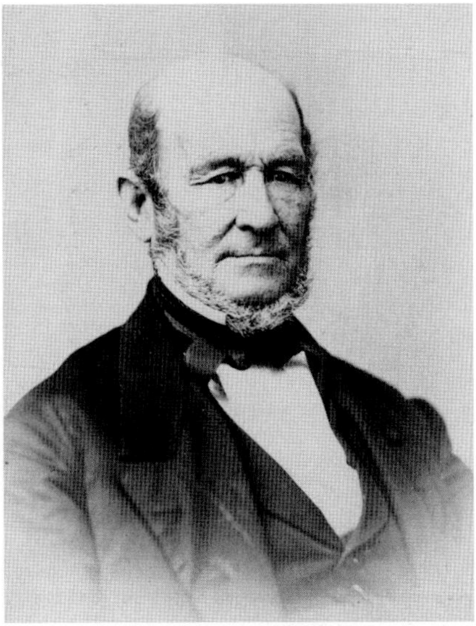

residents in all the several industries. These were by no means gifts, for on the Great Ledgers were charged against the beneficiaries whatever the outlay might be, to be paid for out of the products of their labor. The same system prevailed as to the Mechanics Skillet or otherwise, and probably compassed all kinds of industrial pursuits. In a word, they were set up in business to be tithed later on when sufficiently prosperous. It is easy to see how alluring these offers were to the poorer classes of foreign lands. It is also easy to see why the Mormon Church would ultimately grow rich. There were the elders whose functions concerned the temporal matters, superintending the financial affairs, including the collection of tithes, the placing of converts, and accounting with them. The bishops were the spiritual heads and kept the individuals in touch with church tenets and rules. Residents were thus obtained in exchange for loyalty to church. It was stated that fifty nationalities were represented in the community. And a unique commonwealth of a quiet, frugal, industrious, and self-sustaining population was the result. The conversation covered two or three hours.

The Mormon women and girls were unhandsome; the men were more generally strong-headed and intelligent. All the rural portion and most of the citizens were grotesquely or ill-clad. You can imagine how people of fifty different nationalities, retaining more or less their native garb, would appear. On two occasions, I attended church services, held in an improvised tabernacle called "The Bowery."

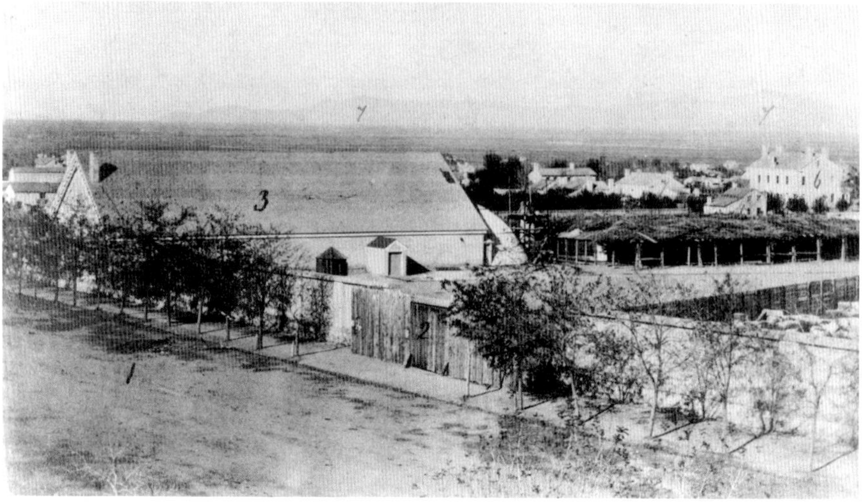

The Old Mormon Tabernacle and Bowery, Salt Lake City, 1847–1854. *Reproduced by permission from the L. Tom Perry Special Collection, Harold B. Lee Library, Brigham Young University, Provo, Utah.*

It was made up of upright posts set in the ground of a superficial height of some ten or twelve feet thatched with boughs and brush and open on all sides, and through which the air cooled to a pleasing temperature. The famous temple had progressed to the laying of its foundations, and no further work was being done that summer. (1866) The temporary meeting place would accommodate several thousand, and it was a good time to note a collective body of Mormons and their varied characteristics and makeup. Brigham preached on one of these occasions and Heber C. Kimball the other. The mastership of the former was too apparent to escape notice. Speaking of the agitation in the Congress and the East regarding their "system," he made a climax in his defiance by saying, "I can count dollar with dollar with any European Prince." I was told that he made it a practice to call by name the woman against whom gossip had laid accusation of some foible or looseness. In all things, he freely applied the Jesuitical doctrine that the end justified the means, in all its rigor.

A party of young people made up for a trip to the Great Lake. The visit extended late into the night and on our return, we reached the halfway house about midnight when it occurred to us that a lunch would be in order. The sign swinging outside informed the public that meals were to be had "at all hours." The house was closed and the lights out, but our loud summons aroused the innkeeper, who, after much banter and insistence, yielded and

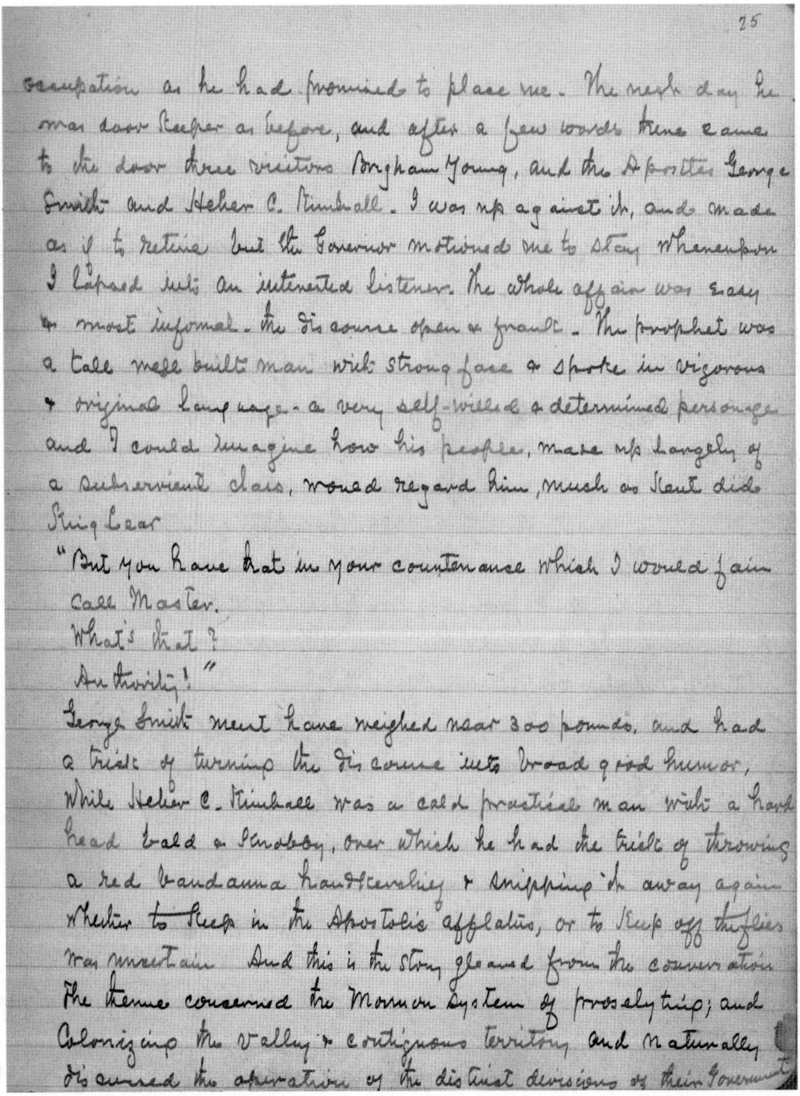

25

occupation as he had promised to place me. The next day he was door keeper as before, and after a few words there came to the door three visitors Brigham Young, and the Apostles George Smith and Heber C. Kimball. I was up against it, and made as if to retire but the Governor motioned me to stay whereupon I lapsed into an interested listener. The whole affair was easy & most informal. the discourse open & frank. The prophet was a tall well built man with strong face & spoke in vigorous & original language - a very self-willed & determined personage and I could imagine how his people, made up largely of a subservient class, would regard him, much as Kent did King Lear

"But you have that in your countenance which I would fain call Master.
What's that?
Authority!"

George Smith must have weighed near 300 pounds, and had a trick of turning the discourse into broad good humor, while Heber C. Kimball was a cold practical man with a hard head bald as [illegible], over which he had the trick of throwing a red bandanna handkerchief & snipping it away again whether ~~to keep~~ in the Apostolic afflatus, or to keep off the flies was uncertain. And this is the story gleaned from the conversation The theme concerned the Mormon system of proselyting; and colonizing the valley & contiguous territory and naturally discussed the operation of the distinct divisions of their Government

Lowell manuscript, page 25.

coldly furnished forth a merry table. A few days later, passing by this tavern, I read a corrected legend, "meals at all reasonable hours." The water supply for drinking, as well as for other purposes, was from a mountain stream so controlled that the gutters along the streets were filled with a rapid current of clear cool water—admirably policed, and under drastic rules, kept free of impurities.

NORTH TO MONTANA

Wintering in Deer Lodge, W.A.C. Ryan

My wagon boss, Mr. Newman, was about to leave the city for Montana—his train of flour had not found a good market there and had been sent forward toward Helena, Montana territory. He proposed that I go and overtake the train and act as before as his correspondent. There seem to be an inability in Governor Durkee to place me, although an offer was made of a place at mines in the southern Utah in which he had an interest. Instead, I took up with Newman's offer, and we took the stage and overtook the train a short way beyond Ogden, where we parted for Helena. I, with the train, passed Virginia City to the territorial capital of Montana. There is located the famous Alder Gulch, a placer diggings of prodigious yield of free gold, and thence to Helena. The distance from Salt Lake was about seven hundred miles. It was late September 1866 when we rolled into Helena. The flour was sold, and Mr. Newman asked me to winter with him in Deer Lodge Valley, where his stock was to winter. His herder was a burly fellow named Fry whose chief diversion was operating a revolver, the care of which took up most of his leisure time, when not shooting it at jackrabbits and sometimes larger game. So expert was he in its use that he went mad if he missed his mark on a jackrabbit, to wit, one or both eyes—and he barely failed. We put up a log house of one room, rock chimneyed and side bunked, where the time passed with literature, hunting, and herding. It was three miles from the town of the same name, Deer Lodge. Choosing to be independent, I took possession of a smaller cabin a mile nearer the town, stocked it with necessaries, got some books at the town, and hermitted for the winter. I had a copy of Blackstone, Byron, and some other standards and, finding nothing to do in town, settled down to await the spring opening.

A little incident occurred to break the monotony. One very cold night while reading, I heard merry voices at a little run some several yards from the cabin and, going out, found that a sleighing party had overturned in a drift of snow. After righting up, it was decided that they would proceed no farther that night, and disposing of horses, they came into the cabin. There were two young men and two young women, and they were having no end of fun together, but it was plain to see that one of the men and one of the women were crosswise with each other, and their converse was tinged with a kind of acrimony. They kept up a fire of banter and small talk till near morning, the sequel to all of which is as follows; the facts I got at Deer Lodge in a day or two. It was a bridal party. The groom's name was W.A.C. Ryan, known all over the territory as "Whack" Ryan, the local editor of an Helena paper. The bride was a girl he had met at Blackfoot. It was a runaway affair, and by appointment, they were to meet at Deer Lodge and be married. Ryan was minus a clean shirt and so borrowed one for the ceremony, but the bride heard of it and called off the bans. Some interest attaches to this romance by what befell Whack Ryan later on. Ryan was a typical swashbuckler, in appearance a cavalier, and what was more, it was all genuine. He left Montana and joined the insurgency in Cuba, rose to general of their cavalry, and had charge the exporting of munitions of war from the States. With a cargo of these, he made a landing on the Island but was intercepted by the Spanish military and, with three others, was summarily taken out and shot. On his way to execution, he hummed some operatic air and laughingly received the penalty of his daring. It may be of interest the story told me by one M.P. Lowry (to whom I shall refer later), who went with Ryan to Montana in what was called the Peck Expedition in 1864 along the North Platte Route. The outfit was comprised of a large number of emigrants, women and children, as well as men, and for mutual protection against the hostile Sioux and Cheyennes banded together under the leadership of one Peck, to resume their individuality as soon as the hostile region was passed. On a day spent in resting, the energetic Ryan conceived the plan of a mock attack; getting a buffalo robe, he circled unseen out and around the camp, suddenly appearing over a ridge in Indian fashion swinging a rifle. The pack of wagons was put at once on the defensive, and things took on a warlike look. In the excitement, one of the women became wildly hysterical and, being pregnant, underwent a delivery so premature that it resulted in an illness that promised to be fatal, pending which, it was given to Ryan that her death meant his. She survived a day or two and Ryan was warned out of camp, but he defied them and put up such a game front that matters gradually quieted down.

An acquaintance in Deer Lodge gave me the cue of a stampede [mass movement to a newly discovered gold claim] about to come off in the spring of 1867. There were some two hundred of us with mounts that took an early start one morning for Cariboo—a discovery some twenty miles away.[36] The scramble was pretty active. The initial of a stampede is usually some individual discovery, the discoverer having the pick and a double portion of area—two hundred feet lengthwise of the gulch as discovery and the same as preemption. The remainder is preemptive only and is the mark of the vigilant stampeder. On arriving, the stampeders organize with a recorder, surveyor, and treasurer, and then locations are made and recorded by the payment of a fee of two dollars. Certain miners' laws and rules restricting area and promotive of dump and other features of rights and restrictions, these, when reserved, are given full faith and credit in all the courts, as much so as a legislative enactment.

OPENING AND OPERATING A PLACER

In placer or gulch diggings, the first step is to prospect it—in other words, to sink a shaft, usually three feet wide by eight or ten in length, down to the bedrock, testing the grit as the work is done and is commenced. When the soil or superficial surface is removed, a peculiar shaped pan, japanned, shaped thus [figure below] is filled with the grit and, in a still pool, shaken by a rotary movement that easily [leaves] the "color" or gold particles that remain at the bottom. While the balance is washed out, there is always a magnetic ore, very fine and very heavy, that remains with which the "color" is commingled, and when the gold is fine, quicksilver is required to amalgam the product. If not too fine, the said ore, called black sand, is carefully washed out the "black pan."

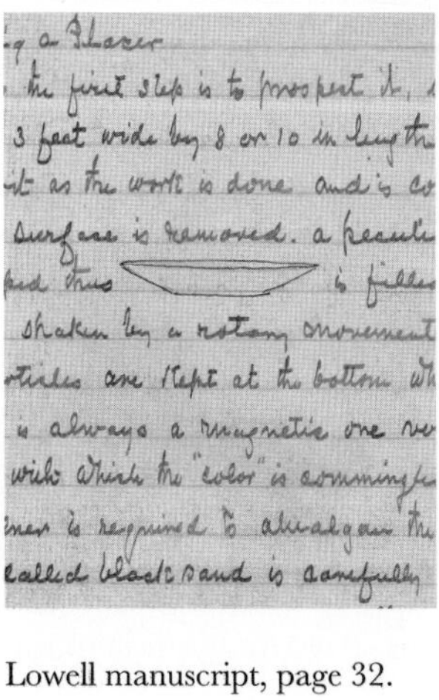
g a Placer
the first step is to prospect it,
3 feet wide by 8 or 10 in length th
it as the work is done and is co
surface is removed. a peculi
ped thus is fille
shaken by a rotary movement
rticles are kept at the bottom. Wh
is always a magnetic one ve
with which the "color" is commingle
ver is required to amalgam the
called black sand is carefully

Lowell manuscript, page 32.

A placer, generally speaking, is an alluvial deposit of varied depth down to bedrock and with a distinct gravelly formation extending lengthwise along the gulch between rim-rock and rim-rock that skirts each bar of the gulch in which resides the gold particles, and in miners' parlance is called the "pay streak." [A rimrock is the rock wall at the upper edge of a gulch or canyon.] Unlike quartz, there are no outcroppings. The gold is free and frequently in sizeable nuggets according to the wealth of the pay grit. Certain surface indicia usually exist where free gold is found, but gold is not near always found where these signs exist. Bedrock may be granite or may be decomposed slate or other formation. Gold frequently rests on bedrock only—at other times, is found in the compact above. After testing in one or more shafts and you are persuaded the find will justify it, a tailrace is dug. [A tailrace is a channel that carries away mine tailings.] This is allowable to be done on your neighbor's claim below, and the long opening is started far enough below to tap your lower boundary.

At bedrock, the bed of your tailrace has only sufficient fall to carry water and drain your claim; consequently, your opening tailrace gradually deepens as you approach your lower boundary. You now have a vehicle to drain your claim. The next step is to strip a pit at the immediate head of your race, which excavation extends to the pay grit. The next step is to build your sluice boxes extended along the race to the pit. A head box is set, and with a head of water, you shovel into the boxes the pay grit. These boxes vary in size. The smaller are twelve inches in width with side boards of eight or ten inches, open top. At the bottom, inside, are arranged riffles, thus [figure]:

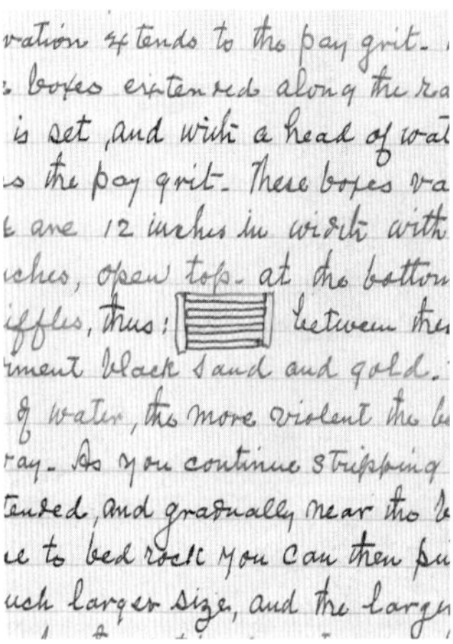
vation extends to the pay grit.
boxes extended along the ra
is set, and with a head of wat
the pay grit. These boxes va
are 12 inches in width with
ches, open top. at the bottom
iffles, thus: between the
iment black sand and gold.
of water, the more violent the be
ray. As you continue stripping
tended, and gradually near the b
ce to bed rock you can then pu
uch larger size, and the larger

Lowell manuscript, page 33.

Between these slats cluster the finer sediment, black sand, and gold. Give the work a strong current of water, the more violent the better; the gold will not wash away. As you continue stripping pits, your sluice boxes are extended and gradually near the bedrock. When pretty close to the bedrock, you can then put in a bedrock flume of much larger size, and the larger share of the work is done by the action of water and less by the pick and shovel.

The foregoing is, in brief, the method of ordinary open diggings. Where the bedrock is deep, a different system is required, by drifting, or where the pay grit is light and parsimonious, a Whim system is had on a much bigger scale. [A whim system utilizes a manual or steam-operated winding drum, or capstan.] In "cleaning up," a light head of water is used, all the riffles removed, the end of the boxes below blocked a few inches and the sediment gradually allowed to escape to the dump, and the collection of black sand and gold is taken out at the lower box in a black pan. An amalgam is made

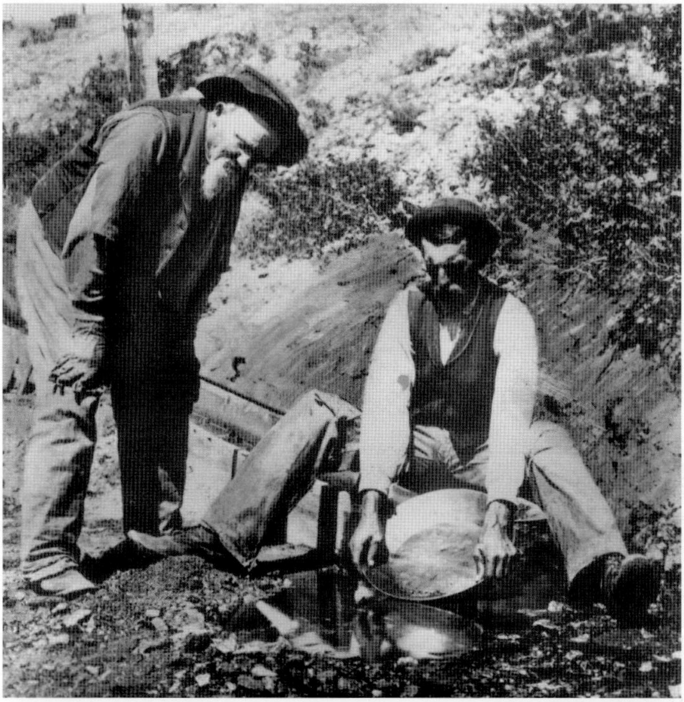

Gold panning in Nelson Gulch, western Montana. *Dan Dutro photograph reproduced by permission from the Denver Public Library, X-60187.*

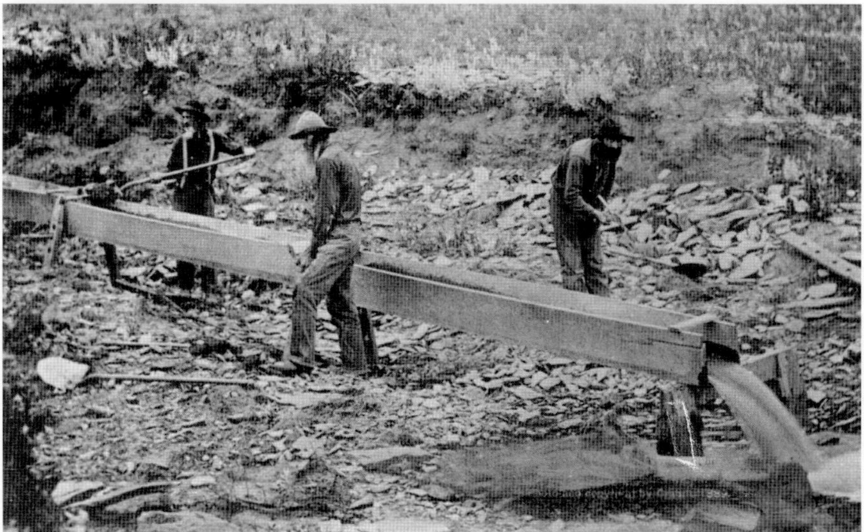

Tailrace, Dakota Territory. *Reproduced by permission from the Denver Public Library, X-60194.*

with quicksilver. When the black sand is washed away, and [the remaining product heated] over a blaze, the product weighed, you know something of the mine's value.

Independence Gulch was a tributary of Caraboo. It was there I learned the A.B.C. of placer mining. It carried the color, but measured by arithmetic, I went no further than to shaft it and condemn it. A California miner happened along, and differing from me, he offered a white nag and equipment for it, which of course was a good bargain for me. He spent quite a sum in development and a sluice test resulted in its abandonment. I could not afford to be idle and, with two others, opened a lumber trade, our stock being some fir trees out of which we rived shingles; however, as the Caraboo Mining District dwindled down to a half-dozen prospects that were worth operating, there followed a slump in the lumber trade.

DIGGINGS WITH WILLIAM HORACE CLAGETT

About this time, I came to know William H. Clagett, then in the law practice—later on, a leading mine lawyer of the West. We together looked over some of the deserted claims and each jumped one, both adjoining, and went to work to develop them as one company. We built a log house on the side hill bar, and when complete, he moved his family into it. I built a wick [wickiup domed shelter] up near by to sleep in but took meals with Clagett. They had two children; one was named Idaho. She was born in that territory while en route to Deer Lodge.

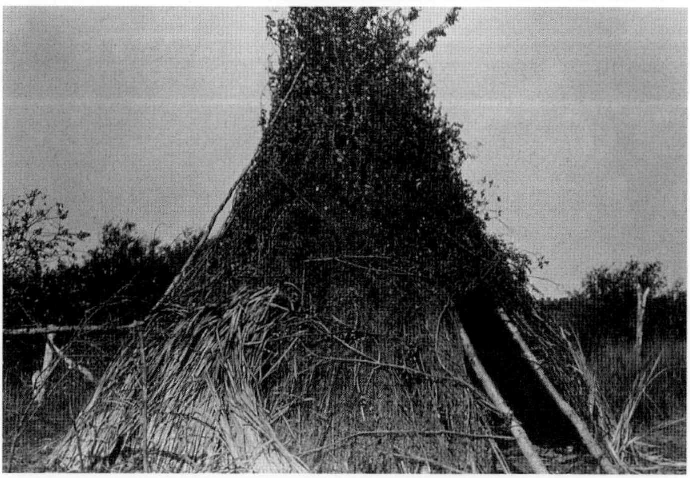

Bannock wickiup shelter, 1871. *National Park Service, 02730.*

Editor's Note: William H. Clagett

As a younger man, in 1861, William Horace Clagett (1838–1901) accompanied Samuel Clemens's party during a mining stampede to Humboldt County, Nevada. Clemens (Mark Twain) was an acquaintance of Clagett's from Keokuk, Iowa, and Twain mentions his friend on page 189 of Roughing It. *Clemens sent his publisher a photograph of Clagett, himself, and the Montana House Speaker A.J. Simmons, taken in 1864.*

In Montana, Clagett partnered with W.W. Dixon to form the Deer Lodge law firm Clagett & Dixon. The trading post located near Camp Cooke at the mouth of the Judith River was named Fort Claggett by the post's traders, who added an extra G to the spelling of his name. Elected Montana territorial representative for the 1871–72 term, Clagett introduced to the U.S. Congress the Act of Dedication bill in 1871 that ultimately led to the creation of Yellowstone National Park. Clagett Butte in Yellowstone is named in his honor. Clagett's oratory publicized Mormon practices and propelled the movement to outlaw polygamy. Despite Clagett being known as "the silver-tongued orator of the West," his friends said he was too uncompromising to be successful in politics. He lost two U.S. Senate bids for a seat from Idaho in 1891 and 1895. In tribute, his law partner wrote: "He will always be remembered as an historic character in the upbuilding of the great northwest, and when in future years, the west shall build a Hall of Fame for her immortals, in a niche where the sunlight falls softest there should be placed a statue of William H. Clagett." His motto was "Win honestly or die game."[37]

Mrs. [Mary E. Hart] Clagett was a niece of Governor Morton of Indiana, the War governor, and she was of a type of a class of womanhood I frequently met in pioneering. It was a constant puzzle to me how women could live contentedly in a wilderness amid such rude conditions, among rough and selfish men, preserve their tender femininity—keep themselves neatly and often gracefully dressed—and a mark sometimes of free compliments, women who could pass without apology to residing over and gracing a fashionable dinner party, or receiving in state at Washington. Mrs. C. was a linguist, an accomplished musician, and a noble specimen of woman.

In mining, you are always somewhere between a windfall and a catastrophe. This enterprise represented more nearly the latter, for it took out some hard labor that yielded no return and absorbed some money that never found its way out and left one of its projectors down at the heel. Beans were a staple diet, and we had a lot of amusement with a Flathead Indian who had the trick of leaning against the jam of the door on bean

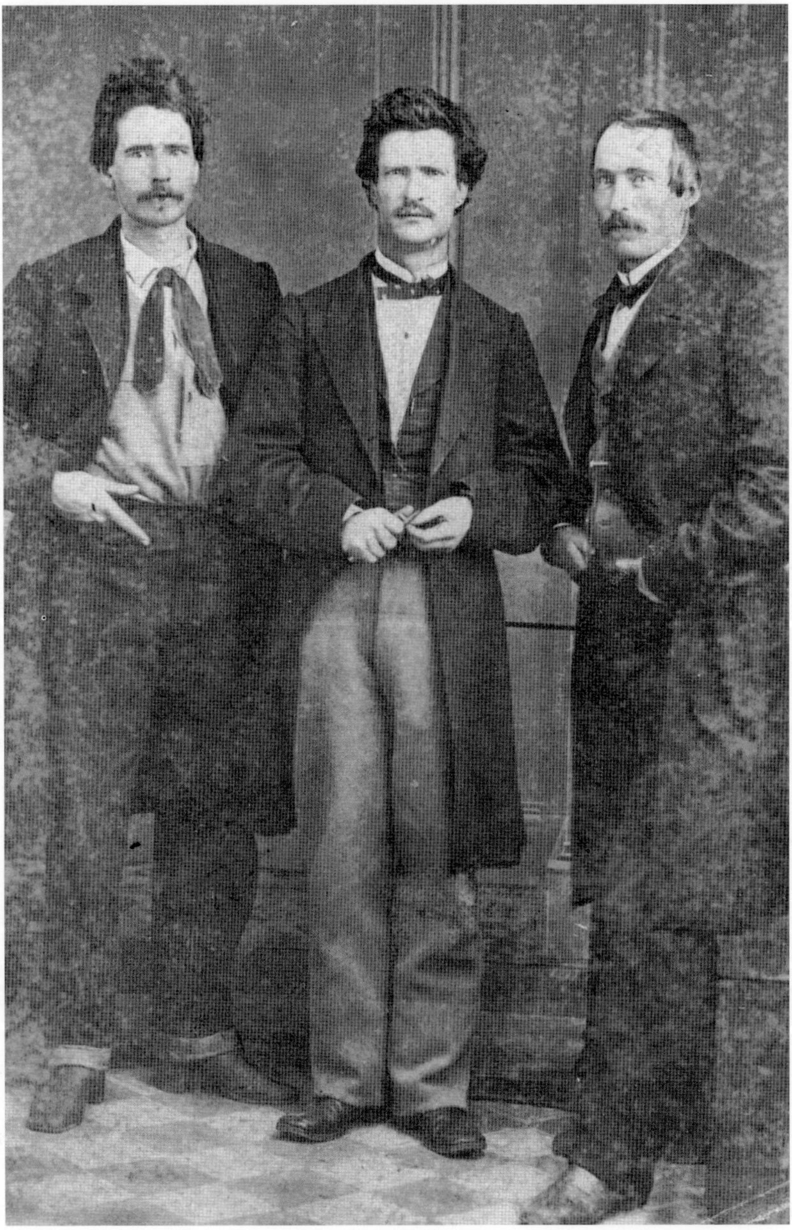

Left to right: William Horace Clagett at age twenty-five, a representative in the Nevada Territorial Legislature; Samuel Clemens (Mark Twain); and A.J. Simmons, Nevada Speaker of the House. Clemens, then twenty-eight, jokingly reported to his editor that they were horse thieves and captioned the photograph: "Three of the suspected men still in confinement in Aurora." *Courtesy of the Mark Twain Project, Bancroft Library, University of California–Berkeley, 00009.*

day, imposing on Mrs. C's hospitality, of which she had an abundance. One, two, and three plates, and then, like Oliver Twist for more parochial porridge, he would make the sign for more. A mess having got sour one day, the whole business was dumped into his shirttail and he took it off to his squaw and Papooses. For several days, he was unseen, but one day, he seated himself on the mine bar where we were working. Clagett asked him if he had eat up those beans yet. With both arms over his stomach he said, "Heap sick, heap sick."

On July third, Clagett and I got our mounts and rode to Helena fifty miles to celebrate the Fourth. We were miner outfitted and cut a picturesque figure among the City folk. The delegate in Congress, James M. Cavanaugh, Democrat, was to deliver an oration.[38] We were Republicans. The territory was overwhelmingly democratic. The delegate did make a good speech, but Mr. Clagett had been seen and his speech followed—the orator that he was—with telling effect. His ungroomed attire added spice to an inspiring address. The idol of democracy was shattered. This was the initial event that put Clagett in Congress as Montana's first Republican representative, of which I shall write later on.

HUNTING AND MINING WITH COGGSWELL THE FORTY-NINER

Things had now reached an acute state. Clagett returned to his law books at Deer Lodge, and I fell in with a singular character named Coggswell. We loaded up a small mustang with a pack and mounted, then plunged into unmapped recesses of the Mountains that lay North West. We coursed through virgin fastnesses stocked with wild fowl and beasts hitherto strangers to all appearance with human intruders on their territory. For several weeks, we spent the time in alternate travels and prospecting through this region thickly peopled with every species of wild game. Scarcely a day passed that did not reveal buffalo, bear, black and white tail deer, antelope, and an occasional mountain lion and wildcat pasturing either within the lofty mountain slopes or upon the valley between these gigantic abutments. Grouse, partridge, and the artless fool hen beat their wings in flight on every hand in the great woods of rightly named Montana. [The state name is derived from the Latin word for "mountainous."] The fool hen (not as good flesh as the partridge) is found sitting on a limb, often not more than ten feet high, and permits you to smack it down with a stick. It is about twice as big as a partridge and carries a lot of flesh grown upon a diet of spruce buds, which embitters it.

The plenitude of noble game in so barbaric a habitat is a great deterrent to the hunter instinct. Our needs only were consulted, flushing the one and molesting the other. The territory had been but superficially explored as Tim Campbell [D-NY], an ex-congressman, expressed it, there were "virgin forests where the hand of man had never set foot."

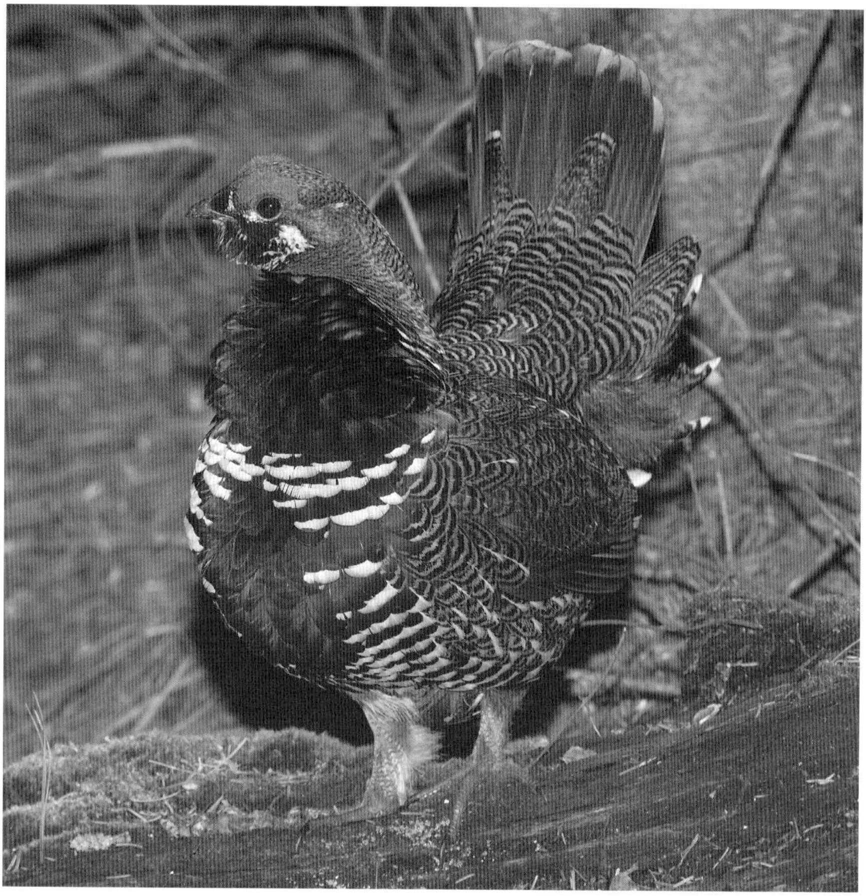

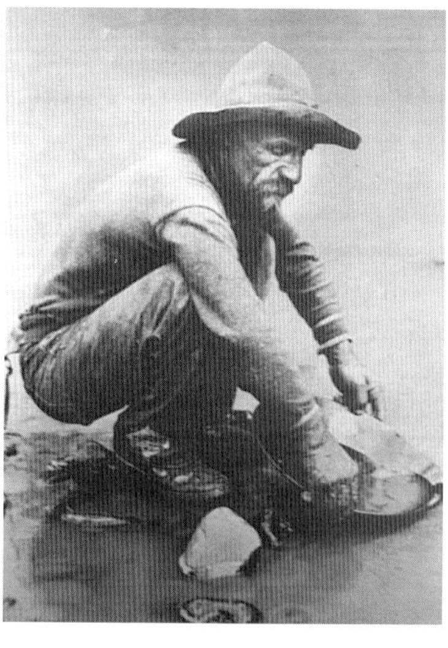

Above: Fool hen, or spruce grouse. *Algonquin Provincial Park, 2006, Creative Commons.*

Left: An old forty-niner (not Coggswell) panning the American River, California, 1850. *Photograph by L.C. McClure; public domain.*

William Coggswell was an old '49er who had come to Montana from California, where he had made stakes and lost them like many another. He was skilled in mountain craft, a superb hunter, and a past master in mining. A spiritualist, he could see intangible creatures. Morose, and if unhumored, was disagreeable. We got along fine together and grew to like each other. Under the stars at night, he was ruminative and Psychologic. The August election was coming on, and we turned toward Helena, as our supplies were getting low. I think the instinct of our animals more than any knowledge of our bearings got us out. One forenoon, we came in sight of a band of Broncos, a name given to untamed, unbroken, and almost unapproachable horse flesh of various ages under seven—beautiful, high-headed fellows. Our little Pack was a fleet chap and, trotting ahead, spied them and took after them, diamond-hitched pack and all. It was another Tam O'Shanter affair in which I got mixed up. My nag was a Spanish Buscaro, its flanks and shoulders all scarred up with Spanish brands, old and white. His early training was to pursue, as the word *buscaro* indicates, and his trainers had carried the lariat. He took on after the fliers and the bit also. The next thing I remember was Coggswell asking me if I was hurt. It

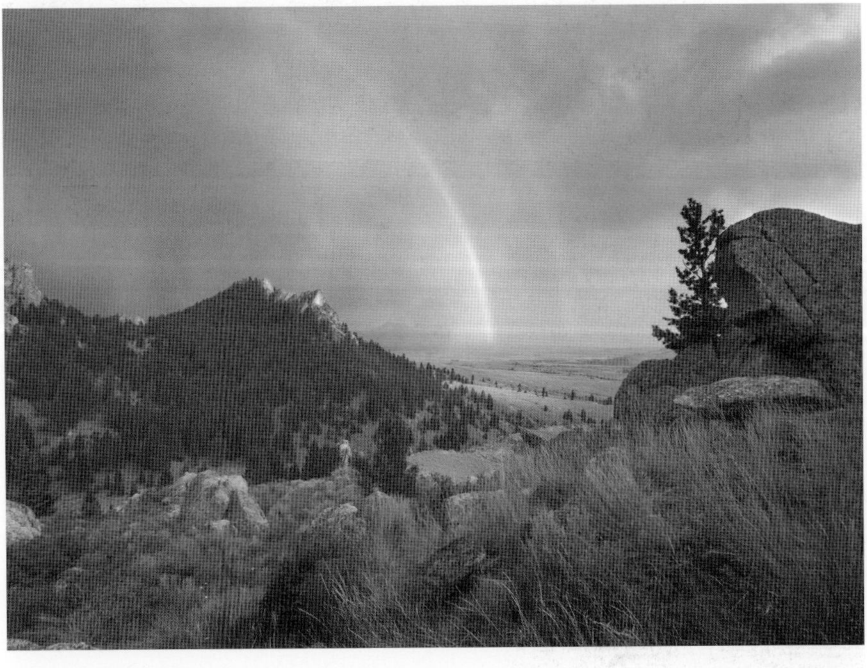

Photograph by Harold Ross.

seems that going full-tilt, the horse had stumbled and pitched over. Now, he was peacefully snipping the brush grass a little away. Just then, the herder came riding up, and leaving me to reinstate myself, the others went after the fugitives. I walked down to the herder's cabin, and toward evening, the others came in, but with none of the runaways. That night, after a long quiet spell, Coggswell spoke up and said he would look no further for our pack. I imagined he had consulted the Spirits, but nothing could persuade him differently, so the debate closed with my heartily concurring with him. The next morning, we took the mountain road leading to Helena and down Grizzly Gulch at whose outlet stands Helena. Going down the mountain, we came to a Quartz Stamp Mill, where I alighted, and stepping to go in, I saw aside the door our pack belongings. And I felt grateful to the spirits for saving us an unnecessary search for them, for our pony had wandered there the night before, and the workmen had undressed him and sent him to pasture on the hillside. This agreeable turn in the tide of our fortunes was most welcome, for our early possessions comprised in that pack would have been a hard thing to duplicate in the state of our finances.

HELENA

A Chance Encounter with Morrow P. Lowry

Helena was in activity over the election about to come off. It was a typical mining town; its streets were thronged with the adventurous class, freighters, whackers, hunters, grub-stakers, horse jockeys, and stockyard auctioneers; a few gambling halls, here and there a few pretentious buildings where the thrifty merchants harvested their bonanzas, and eating halls where for a dollar your appetite could get appeased; lawyers in abundance—the present Governor [Joseph Kemp] Toole was one of these.[39] A kind of annex to the town sheltered a drove of Chinese and was called China-town. Tough and bad men were much in evidence, yet there was a nucleus of steady, sturdy, and rightly disposed people whose public spirit raised the standard and made possible a well-ordered and prosperous community. Passing up the principal street to stretch my legs and see things, I came upon a crowd being harangued by an orator having strong democratic views. He was a pale-faced young man of evidently a studious habit and excellent education and about my own age. One glance at him, and I stood as if were riveted to the spot. I could hardly wait for him to close, and when he did, I followed quickly to him and touched him on the shoulder. He turned and gasped out, "Lowell, did you fall from the skies?" I had first met M.P. Lowry while on detached service in the army at Harrisburg, Pennsylvania, in 1863. He was connected with the paymaster's department and I with the mustering and disbursing. And we became very intimate. I last saw him in naval uniform as an officer and paymaster in that arm of the service, and we parted; he to the gunboat *Naiad* that was of the Mississippi Squadron and, except a few letters between us while in the service, I lost trace of him. He was in the law office of Shober & Lowry. The junior member was a brother, Jeff Lowry.[40]

CONFEDERATE GULCH, DIAMOND CITY, *1867*

At this time, Confederate Gulch was having a boom, and being ready to take up with most any thing, Coggswell and I provisioned up and in a day or two and left Helena for these diggings some thirty miles east in what seemed to be a spur of the Belt Range. The mines were remarkable in several ways, especially in their wealth of coarse gold. A miner's hamlet of log cabins was huddled together some four or five miles from where you entered the gulch, which to the summit of the belt was over twelve miles. This hamlet was mostly built upon the bedrock of an excavated series of bar mines and was and still is called Diamond City, and at that time (1867) had a goodly lot of idle mine owners—of necessity idle, for the reasons following. A good many shafts had been sunk to bedrock, which was at the depth of from forty to fifty feet, and enough was shown to demonstrate its value. Its being out of the question to mine it openly, a tail or drain race was started and pushed gradually to bedrock from a point below the demonstrated portion of the gulch. When this drain had reached pay grit or bedrock, the first owner could proceed to take out grit, which was hoisted through a shaft and dumped into sluice boxes on the surface in which it was washed out as before described. The tunneling was not interrupted but progressed with night and day shifts. This tunneling would permit but two or three men to operate it, as the face was only of an area to economically force the passage. This was paid for by an equitable assessment upon the owners in the gulch, and being necessarily tediously slow of progress, the upper owners, several miles above in the gulch, had

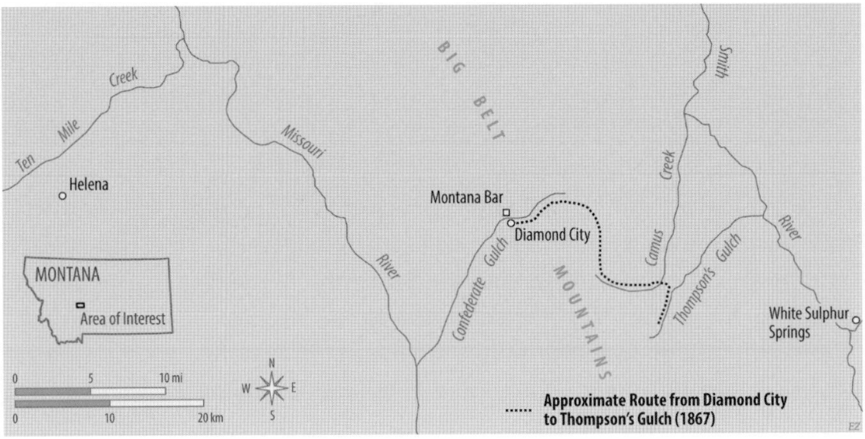

Map by Ezra Zeitler.

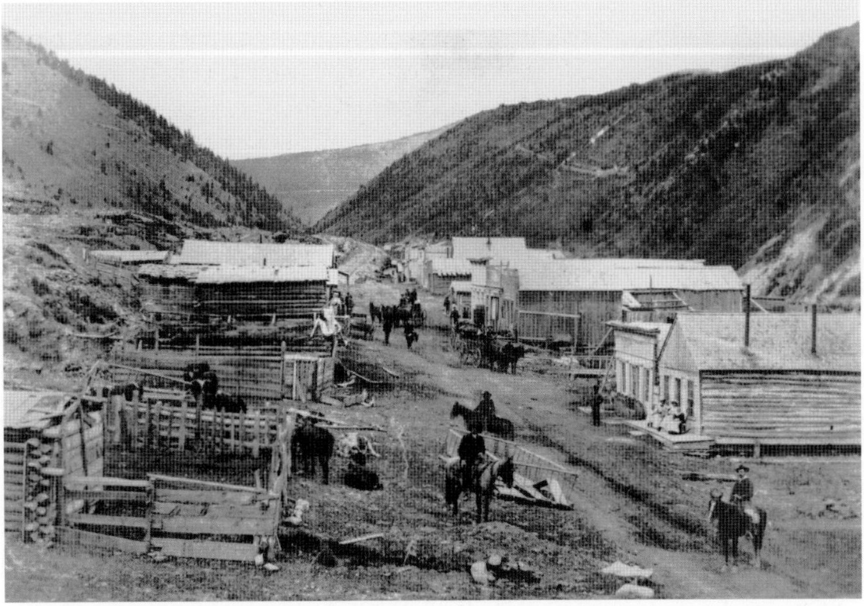

Diamond City in Confederate Gulch. *Reproduced by permission from the Overholser Historical Research Center, Fort Benton, Montana.*

a long wait. At Diamond was discovered the richest placer, except possibly Alder Gulch, at Virginia City. It was not in the gulch, but upon the bar of the gulch, and its operation was equipped with some remarkable natural helps. Bedrock was but eleven feet deep, the gulch afforded an abundant dumping place, and skirting the brow of the precipitous mountain slope at whose feet it lay was constructed a ditch carrying water to the hydraulic hose; this hose was used with telling effect in stripping off the surface to bedrock. The super-bedrock was of semi-decomposed slate that retained its forms and lay slanting at about forty-five degrees; between the layers of slate was the gold. This bedrock of slate rested upon a sub-bedrock of granite, about a foot in depth and easily worked. The name given was Montana Bar, and in one season, over two millions of gold was cleaned up, the season of 1866. Some little aftermath was worked out the season we first were there, 1867. It was an ideal placer mine.

THOMPSON'S GULCH

The Antelope Hunt

At Diamond, we got word of an abandoned mining district on the other side of the range, and thither we hiked, crossing the range divide in the month of September and descended into and across beautiful foothills peopled with colonies of deer and antelope to Thompsons Gulch, twenty miles from Diamond.[41] We explored the Gulch till we came upon an inhabitant—two of them—and learned that some of the prospectors had deserted the diggings while others had quit on account of low water, but they would return in the spring,[42] [and] that all the territory below their claim was open to prospectors. We learned they were doing well and taking out good pay and would remain there the winter. Work had ceased, as the head of water in the gulch had become low to admit of [allow] mining. That day, we staked off the adjoining claims below and, the next day, sunk a shaft to bedrock eleven feet from the surface. The first four feet held color and averaged fourteen cents to the pan—one pan going forty cents. It was in flakes and nodules and ranked medium as between coarse and fine gold and remarkably free of baser mineral. It is no wonder we slept that night beneath the firs, exulting in an El Dorado—a red-letter event! We had been rolling stones to the top of the hill only to see them topple down to the bottom again, but now—well, we will see! To further test our find, we sunk a second shaft laterally away toward the bar, with but little less showing, and at once commenced a tailrace. The work of development went on speedily, and some abandoned sluice boxes being set therein, a head of water was secured in a reservoir that had been confined some distance up the gulch. A pit was then stripped down to pay grit, and the eve of the pending experiment found our preparations complete for a trial of the mine the next morning. Coggswell was late in drawing the covers for the night, but I noticed nothing unusual except that he seemed moody and untalkative, which I attributed to the enormous work he had done with its fatigue. The breakfast fire was started in the darkness of predawn. The coffee and game steaks perfumed the air, but Coggswell lay covered in apparent sleep, a stiff jolt finally aroused him, and taking a pull at the coffee, he muttered, "I will never strike another damn pick in this gulch, so bridle your bucker if you want to see Helena to night." What could be done? Neither argument, persuasion, cajolery, pleading, nor swearing had the slightest effect on his purpose. Was it some such prevision whispered in his ear by the spirits that led him to abandon the pack pony at the head of Grizzly Gulch? Spirits that, like the Ghost of Banquo, "would not down?" I had stepped up the gulch and raised the gate of the reservoir, and as we saddled our nags, water came down full tilt to go to waste. I had saved a few black-pan prospects to take along to Helena. Our supplies were run low, and for that reason, the trip would not be without a personal purpose.

It was now nearly November, and during our stay together in the Thompsons Gulch, we had subsisted a good deal upon the product of the hunt. There is charm in the recalling these pursuits of the mountain beasts. Sometimes, a brief half day would stock us up. At others, luck would not so quickly smile on us. On one occasion, a doe elk rewarded a two-hour outing. We always shared with the neighbors above. On another occasion, we went some fifteen miles without a halt, intending to camp overnight and hunt the next day. While eating the evening meal, there came down the mountains towards us a hard luck and jaded chap so hungry that he cleaned up the larder. He was on his way to Helena, having left his party of Wolfers, and had run up against difficulties in getting through. This incident left us a morning and perhaps a day's hunt with an empty stomach. Nothing daunted, Coggswell trailed up the mountains for his favorite elk, I to go for antelope among the foothills not too remote from camp and our animals.

There was no trouble in sighting a band of these and, working to a leeward point of view, crawled toward the group. Now, as luck would have it, my caps someway had been exposed over night and proved no-explosive, and nothing was to do but to curse my carelessness and loaf around camp until Coggswell should come down from the hills. About mid-afternoon, he made camp and flung down his undischarged gun, adding to the gaiety

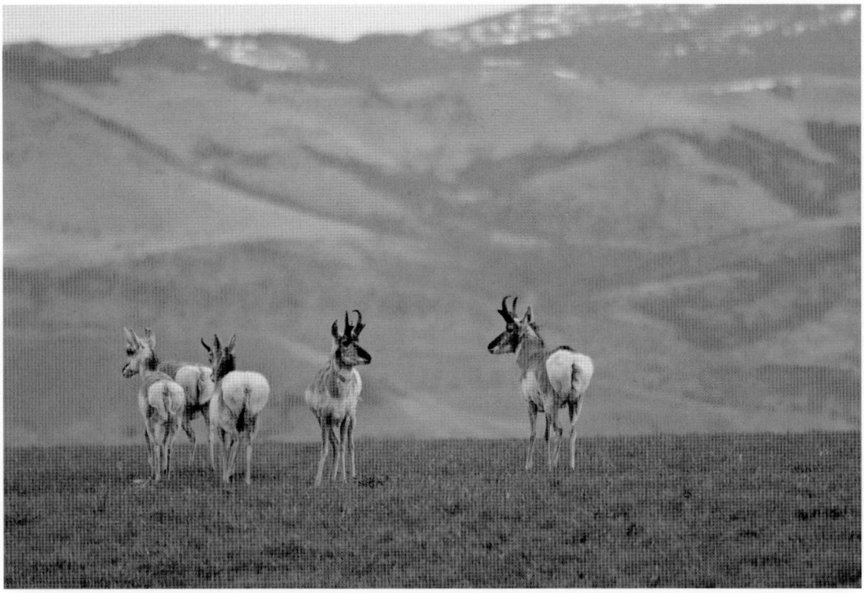

Foothills near Thompson's Gulch. *Photograph by Kelly Morris.*

of the occasion in comments that lacked no quality of malevolence against the world, the flesh, and the devil. Leaving him to fight out his humor, I took his gun (Colts revolving) and, a mile away, sighted a quarry of antelope. The boss method of gunning these creatures is by "Approaching." They flourished among the rising and falling foothills; their senses are acute to a feather edge—hence, craftiness is required to outwit them. Once their location is fixed, a leeward approach, or against the wind, is chosen that they may not scent you. Their habit is to feed in the dip between the crests, and the aim of the hunter is to get a range limit somewhere on the crest; however, distances in that rarefied atmosphere are very deceiving, and frequently, the chosen point to shoot is found to be unpractical. Then, another patient and laborious shifting and flanking is gone over, crawling belly wise through the bunch grass that half conceals the person and through which, when positioned, your eye sweeps toward the victims. On the occasion in question, the month being September, it was the mating season, a time when the bucks move lordily and daringly tender protection to the females and toward when they devote all their time in coquetting and blandishments, except when in jealous combat with brother bucks and rivals. In the idiom of the frontier, it is the season of "Curiosity" among the males. Of love and war, for during this period also is brought out all the quarrelsome proclivities of the Antlered sex. Having these things in mind—and my approach at long range, and having made the crest unobserved, there was nothing [to] it but to attract their curiosity, so springing smartly from prone to a sitting posture—gun at aim motionless, scarcely breathing, I awaited the result. The band was instantly heads up, and a retreat movement commenced among the does. One lofty buck, more hardy than his rivals, with a stamping step as if beating the earth with his fore feet, came up nearer and nearer to the silent decoy—whose every nerve was vibrant with the exhilaration of conquest. Turn, he surely would, and then was my time, when his form was broadsides. The turn was at two hundred yards, where his courage oozed out as he dropped. I ran down with my knife to make sure of him. It was unnecessary, as the bullet severed his jugular vein. Then occurred one of those singular happenings almost incredible except to the initiated. Going to a ridge summit less than a quarter of a mile where in plain view of camp I could signal Coggswell—some mile or more away—I sat down and waited for him, and together, on his coming, I confidently led the way to our quarry. One after another, we traced the slopes of the miniature hills, that:

In airy modulations, far away
As if an ocean in its gentlest well
Stood still, with all its rounded billows fixed
And motionless forever[43]
[William Cullen Bryant, "The Prairies," 7–10]

Until I began to think, as Coggswell did, that the whole business was an illusion, distances and locations in that marvelous atmosphere are liable to distortion and deception to any who did not fix upon some particular land or other mark to keep tab of them. But for all, the quarry was found, and its uncooked liver broke a day's fasting. No one's sense need be disturbed by the statement that the hot liver of an antelope or deer freshly killed does not require a hunter's appetite to enjoy it, as remarked in Biglow's papers:

Nothin riles me, I pledge my fastin word
Like cookin out the nature of a bird[44]
[James Russell Lowell, *Biglow Papers, Second Series, "Fitz Adam's Story," 267–68*]

Of course, you should reverently add a dusting of salt and serve without setting the table. The catalogue of unconventional meals was long, when contact with the red man, the relics of French Voyageurs, and the denizens of the Red River of the North developed their respective habits and traditions, as will be seen later on. It was now toward evening, and the hunt was called off and our course was toward the mines. While rounding a spur, a band of antelope took fright and was away in the dainty scamper so pleasing to witness; they crowned the ridge ahead of us, while we planned another Curiosity scheme. Coggswell was to pose as Curio, and I as an enlaureled Nimrod, hastily skirting around the ridge to where the tall, stiff grass shielded me, crouching down I waited for the shout to rise and fire. The call came presently, and by mistake—there being two bands—I fired at the most distant, not observing or supposing there was another to fire at. It seems that Coggswell had coached a different group than the one we saw disappear over the ridge. We thereupon hurried on to the mines and to bed, not however, without some bad-natured and, finally, some good-natured bickering and chaffing.

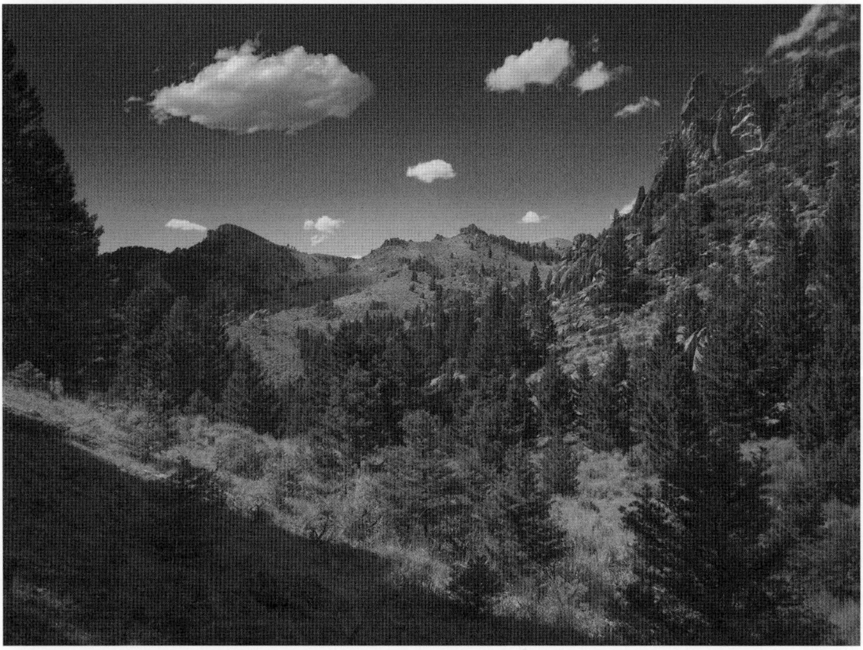

Montana foothills near Ennis, Montana. *Photograph by Harold Ross.*

Indian Summer in Montana

It is the ideal season: a season unrealized by denizens of the Atlantic Coast. Something approaches it in the Catskills and Adirondacks. Its realization is here. It is the lingering transition from summer to winter, and out of doors, life is at all times full of delights of which the uninitiated know nothing, a sort of world of solitude peopled about with primitive dumb creatures—dreamy in the tender heat—an ocean of faded yellow-green grass, a niche of God's Vineyard, which for long years after the Montezuma was shown as the Mythical Kingdom of Quivira.

A NEW DEAL

At Helena, I parted with Coggswell. We were genuinely friendly; he was an ill-tempered, hard man to get along with, so full of whimsicality and subject to his "Spiritual Controls." He was leaving an apparently good thing in leaving that mine because of that "Control" that powered him, and I asked myself, "Can his previsions be correct?" He was no toy frontiersman, with long, braided hair—particular about his nails, but a past master in placer mining and a crafty huntsman. He voluntarily gave me a deed to his possessions in Thompson's Gulch. I have never heard of him since.[45]

I looked up my friend M.P. Lowry, who, with his friend, examined the prospect of gold I had brought in. We got a third man—a tenderfoot—young and stout, and they together, outfitted with tools and provisions, hiked back to the gulch. We determined to open a new tailrace farther down, for now our preemptions and discovery gave us 1,200 feet lengthwise the gulch and also the two bars. We worked well together and with exceeding industry. The third man, Kieth [*sic*], we soon nicknamed "Sparks," after one of Dickens' characters, whom he resembled.[46] Lowry was a cultured and well-educated man, and the combination was a pleasant one all around. Our preparations were all ready Christmas Eve to open the reservoir gate the next morning. The weather had been ideal, but that night, a most violent storm came on: a freezing blizzard swept the mountain slope, with snow that the morning found piled up and still coming. We were unprepared to pass the winter there, and a brief parley determined us to cross the range before it was too late. Gathering our belongings, we hustled along the foothills to the pass over the divide. We were waist deep in snow for a long space across the summit, and a few hours only would have barred us from making the divide for that winter. As it was, we consumed the entire day till late at night to make the hamlet "Diamond" in Confederate Gulch—20 miles.

Gold Creek Mines

A Boston Yankee in Confederate Guise

On arriving at Helena, Lowry resumed his law studies, and "Sparks" and I sought and got a contract to dig a projected ditch in the Gold Creek mining district that lay northwest of both Helena and the intermediate town of Deer Lodge. Hell-Gate River was to supply the water for this ditch and a volume of water sufficient to operate a large area that prospected fine gold almost at the grass roots. The bedrock being quite shallow—a few feet, I procured this contract from Mr. Newman, the quondam freighter with whom I had been associated as before related. He was a shareowner in the ditch. His former wagon boss, Fry, was its blacksmith and general overseer. I went on ahead, leaving Sparks to bring on our tools and cabin furnishings. Arriving there, I ascertained the location of our contract work and, alone, leisurely rode over the district and towards night, along the line of ditch as staked out. Little work had been done, and night coming on, I drew rein before a log shanty, through the chinks of which gleamed an unsteady light. I summoned the occupant, a stout, broad-shouldered, stalwart-looking fellow, who eyed me with apparent disgust, which was in nowise softened when to his enquiry I replied that I hailed from Massachusetts. He shortly told me that his palace couldn't hold a rebel and a Yank at one and the same time. It did no good to tell him that the war was over, and this led to remarks pro and con, complimentary to neither, as soldiers for and against the lost cause. He declared himself a Georgian, unreconstructed rebel, and I thought it best—he being the biggest—to move away, but as I put my foot in the stirrup, he took the rein and, with some brag about Southern hospitality, led the horse to picket after putting the saddle and equipment in the cabin. Inside the cabin was a marvel of neatness. The floor was of slabs. On one side were two bunks, on the other were shelves and a rude cupboard; the first were furnished with books, the last, with canned stuffs. A few pictures adorned the walls, tastefully hung or tacked. Newspapers and periodicals, writing materials, the usual broom and other adjuncts of a thrifty housekeeper, a few ingeniously made chairs, a table, on which was spread a clean cloth—all were spic and span and everything in apple pie order; his tools, sledges, picks, and shovels in one corner, articles of toilet, and a general appearance of culture, an air of refinement pervaded the place. All this I inventoried as he quickened the fire in the corner rock fireplace and took up the business of getting a meal. By the fire's light, I got a better look at the man, with a square, open face full of resolution, softened with a kindly light. As he mixed up a sort of batter of self-rising flour and ingredients, it struck me as an anomaly that this man could be a Southerner. If not, he had disguised the vernacular of a Northman. He said nothing but proceeded to make and fry some slapjacks in absolute silence; this last act knocked me down, and I felt sure I had been guyed. He presently enquired if I was ever in Boston, and Yankee-like, I asked him what street in Boston he hailed from. He laughed, and we at once exchanged greetings. The fire-eating Georgian was displaced by a jolly, frank-eyed, modest, co-native of Boston. He told me a syndicate of ex-rebels owned the ditch, and their contractors were generally of that persuasion. These contractors had it in for him as a galvanized Yankee and were making life as intolerable as possible, and they would sit down where he was at work and engage him in bitter controversy over the lost cause and its incidents. He detected me as being of his kind at first and invited me to stay with him till Sparks should arrive, and together, we might rout the annoyers. To make a long story short, I did as he requested and with good results. Our contract was an extension of his, and we passed a very pleasant winter with this Mr. Hopkins.[47]

Our job lasted all the winter, and at the earliest, I left for our mines in Thompson's Gulch, leaving Sparks to clean up things and follow later. On my way out towards Deer Lodge, I fell in with an elderly, genteel-appareled man, obviously a tenderfoot; the perfume of the drawing room still lingered in his wardrobe. He was of the class of prim and cultured dignity and of exact English in speech and altogether an entertaining co-traveler and welcome relaxer of solitary journeying. As we approached the town of Deer Lodge, on the opposite side of the river of that name—a river at that point, some 150 feet in width—instead of crossing at a ford a trifle above the town, he, against my warning and deceived in the distance from the bank surface to the bed of the stream, undertook a passage directly opposite the town. He had some trouble getting his horse's forefeet over the bank, but when he did, the toboggan became so acute that he gradually slid over the pummel of his saddle and the neck of his nag plump into the river. As he realized the outcome, or rather the *in go*, he exclaimed in precise phrase, "I perceive I am falling." Some of the denizens of Deer Lodge witnessed the maneuver, and soon, the opposite bank was lined with men who offered a good deal of advice as he shook and blowed and struggled waist deep and more in the water. Some of the men recommended one thing, and some another, and one called on him to get a boat, another a balloon, and so on. There was no danger, as he could wade out, which he tediously did, his horse following. He took the chaffing with good nature and insisted on my spending the night between sheets in the town of Deer Lodge at his expense. The early morning found me stretching in luxurious abandon in a real bed, smiling at the walls and ceiling with infinite appreciation before getting up to make a leisurely toilet before a framed mirror hung above a store washstand, bowl, and pitcher; then to wash, to comb, and brush in a room in a mushroom tavern with its wooden frame and board partitions furnished with a table with turned legs and chairs and things. It struck me as luxury. The fatted calf looked not more seductive to the eye of the husk-fed prodigal than these in the early spring of 1868, after nearly two years of total abstinence.

Two Seasons in Thompson's Gulch

No one would question but that the mines we were returning to were extremely promising. The fact that credit was tendered for tools and material emphasizes this view, and it takes money to equip even a placer mine and put it in operation. Lowry furnished a man to represent his working interest, and we determined to enlarge our tailrace and put therein a bedrock flume; hence, we early got to work. Our lumber was brought over the range by oxen over a government built road, the contractor of which succeeded in shortening it by an ascent more precipitous than any known to the oldest frontiersman. A bedrock flume such as we made was two feet in width and eighteen inches high, and instead of stripped riffles to place at the bottom, we cut down fur trees two feet through and sawed them in four-inch-thick blocks with an x-cut saw; their being round, of course, it left the intervening unoccupied spaces for the gold deposits. In due time, the owners of mines came in, and newcomers took of the claims below us, and when the water came from the melting snows, we were ready and at work in the ground sluices. Two shifts were run from six to six. One half the season, I had charge of the night shift, from which I would emerge in the morning soaked to the skin. Measures were discussed in the miners meeting to lengthen out the water season, for one must have plenty of water to placer mine. We decided to bring in water from a neighboring gulch, and a four-mile ditch was projected for that purpose, to the construction of which each mine contributed in labor. On our mine were hired three miners. Each shift having three at work, the new ditch was speedily dug in the way stated by hiring additional men. Wages were five dollars per day. There were some fifty mine owners on the gulch that year, 1868. High up the range, at the head of this ditch was a broad and extensive Amphitheater forming a wide catchment area, welled in by a rampart of the comb of the range. Into this natural basin seeped the melted snows from the vast watershed that encompassed it. Where the ditch had its source was a narrow defile with precipitous sides. The bed of this gorge or basin was of sufficient fall to carry water, and the whole formed an ideal site for water storage by building a shallow barrier of earthwork across the narrow neck of the defile, or exit. In this basin were numerous beaver dams of great length. Thus equipped for water storage and supply, the miners worked the season til pretty late. There was stretched along the bank near our work a huddle of log shelters, a kind of store of limited stock, and a blacksmith shop, but generally, these huts were built along the gulch where convenient to the mine owner. Measures were taken for rallying and consent of action in case of the sudden appearance of war parties or predatory Indians. Under these hopeful conditions, we called a cleanup after a thorough trial of some two or three weeks. We removed the riffles, or blocks from the flume, and with a low head of water, we reduced the gravelly mass to a block pan of black sand and amalgam; removing the sand and evaporating the quicksilver, our product remained. There were nuggets that would weigh four dollars and five dollars and lesser weights to a tiny flake, but the result was trying on the nerves, and no one could understand or give a reason why a prospect that promised so much should yield so little. It was evening, and having slept on it, we went to work to unravel the mystery. Turning off the head of water, we let the dump get thoroughly sun dried, and this dump then revealed the cause of our discomfiture. There were the globules of a most tenacious and adhesive clay holding within them the coveted prize. Hopefully, we shaped up again, steering our pits zigzag in hopes to strike a freer soil or grit until the end of the season, with the result of paying expenses and debts incurred in the creation of the plant. The mining season ordinarily closes early in the fall, but spasmodic operations continue so long as water storage in the reservoir continues.

A Diversion

The operations spoken of were in a virgin scope of territory. Ranchmen were not then in evidence, except in the three Great Valleys—Jefferson, Madison, and Gallatin—and these were fugitive and often temporary. Outside of the mining camps and a few towns, business was of the adventurous and primitive stamp. Miners, wolfers, and trappers operated the infant industries of the territory; it was only natural that in a region so fruitful in wild game that hunting furnished the chief subsistence of these several crafts, that most everyone was learned of the use of the gun, the habits of the prey, and that a love of sport became a passion. While mining in Thompson's Gulch, we had, at times, what were called "Killings." A portion of the miners would saddle up and, with extra packhorses, go out for meat. I have been along. We would ride to a camp fifteen or twenty miles away where there was water and fuel and prepare for the following day's hunt a bark log with small fuel strung along it, and fired, it would light up the domicile. Along the log, the fresh cuts from a deer or antelope would be cooked on the red coals. The initiated only know the luxury of such a feast—sharpened in the bracing altitudes and enlivened with the witticisms and banter of the banqueters. Early morn, and the camp stirred with the bustle of inspecting guns and equipment and the quick meal. Soon one would steal away in the dark of the thicket, then, another, while one or more would take to the open for antelope. There were elk and buffalo, mountain sheep, black and white tail deer, bear, and possible moose. All these have been catalogued at one of these killings as the assets of the hunt. Having a weakness for antelope, this was the chosen assignment of the writer. The big game men carried some extra garments, even a handkerchief, along to attach to the carcass as a protection against the approach of wolves or coyotes, who will, unless emboldened by hunger, avoid the odor that clings to a human garment. As the evening approached, the several Nimrods stalked into camp, one after another, and the day's exploits were gone over and discussed as the great feast tickled the hungry palates and the tired limbs were stretched out for the night. The next day was given to going the rounds with the packs a-gathering the spoils of the chase; there was good work to be done and often flavored with dangers. Upon returning to the mines, an impartial division was made of the plunder among all the denizens of the Gulch, and the hunt was adjourned till the larder was again depleted.

A QUEER VACATION, SOLITARY WINTER 1868–69

The vacation intervening the close of the mining season and its resumption in the following spring is a period of months, and how to occupy it becomes a matter of interest. The miners usually quit the gulch to avoid the dense idleness of it. All except a half dozen in Thompson's Gulch went away to more populous centers such as Helena or Virginia City. About half dozen outfitted for a wolfing expedition distant towards the Sun River Country. I had some books and volunteered to remain and keep camp. At the time to which this tale relates, the smaller peltries—beaver, mink, etc.—had but small market demand, and this character of industry centered upon wolf skins they brought, undressed, at the shipping center at Fort Benton at seventy-five cents per hide, head and tail. Despite the hazards of the hostile Indian country, it became an occupation for many during the winter months. The method of wolfing was to fix a temporary camp in the vicinity of buffalo, dropping [a buffalo] here and there within a radius of eight or ten miles. When killed, one turns the animal on its spine, splits along its brisket, opens and disembowels it, and stretches the gap so that the exterior forms a basin. In there, one pours a solution of strychnine and, with a paddle, splashes the solution to every part of the inside. These carcasses are visited every morning by the operations with tools to skin the poisoned wolves or horses to drag them, if frozen hard, to the camp. When skinned, they are tightly stretched and dried, and in that form, they are ready for the market. I have seen four hundred skins, the product of two baits, though bigger hauls have been reported. Care is taken to get a good head piece. Large amounts of these skins were exported especially to France during the period. Wolves were incredibly plentiful on the vast bench lands, the ranges, and the plateaus, and along the Missouri bottom, or wherever buffalo ranged.[48]

The half-dozen miners with two large wagons and equipment for the winter left Thompson's Gulch in the month of November 1868. The departure of this outfit gives me an opportunity to inventory the realm of which I was now Chief Magistrate and Sole Administrator. The two structures that took up the most skyline were a log store and a smithy. Inside the former stood a few boxes containing the stock in trade left over, chiefly of fabrics suited to the patrons of the merchant miner. Flanking these were a dozen cabins, so aligned as to make a tolerably even and straight roadway in their front and all facing the diggings that stretched along up the gulch, all of logs. This comprised the City proper for more than a mile up the canyon. Other abodes of like character contributed to make up the mining district. Near the business center, a small cabin (chinked and having one-half window sash, a rock chimneypiece and fireplace, bordered on one side with a bunk, a few books, and handmade chair and table) represented the chief functionary's staying place. Below the hamlet opened out a broad expanse that marked the borderline of hostile territory, and all walled in from the world by frowning ranges. No newspapers, letters, telegrams; no book agents, overdrafts, paydays; no tattling, backbiting, or quarreling. A smile had no return; speech, no response. Neither doctor, lawyer, nor preacher. The chatter of blue jays summoned the solitude to matins; the winds whistling down the canyon's aisle called the vespers. The warden at the pen of Lansing says that convicts who labor at the trades above ground become eager to go below to work in the coal pits, because in the former, they are prohibited to converse, while in the latter, they are licensed to talk with one another, but this is only one phase of complete isolation. Compensation cannot be had either in the generally coveted recreations of hunting and fishing. The outlook for the winter was fatiguing to contemplate, and shortly, I worked up an excuse to go to Diamond City on the opposite side of the range. This was quite an undertaking at that time of year, but I got over the range and, returning, got in the middle of a furious snowstorm that nearly barred the mountain passage. Night came on, and the slow progress gave me a stop on the slope. Picketing my nag and clearing away a space to domicile, I built a fire and amused myself as best I could till daybreak—it being out of the question to sleep.

A little hunting now and then and a daily traipse of several miles, with books to read in the evenings, made up the program for several weeks. A surprise came one evening when there came in view a horseman followed by a large greyhound—so large that from a distance away it seemed a horse, or at least the foal of one. It was easy to see that the man needed assistance to alight, and while I got ready a hasty bite to eat, he gave an account of himself and how he happened there. He carried four gunshot wounds—one of which had passed through a lung. He related how he belonged to a party of wolfers who operated some seventy miles distant. When out one morning to look up the result of a bait, and seeing a chance to get a shot at some deer, he managed to get away some ten miles from his camp when his hound made signs of trouble. By the time he got himself together, a volley of bullets whistled around him, one of which killed his mount, which he now used as breastworks. From behind this carcass, he claimed to have killed or crippled four Indians. He rose to fire his last cartridge when he received a shot through his body. The Indians now pulled off behind a cresting, and guided by the dog's intelligence or instinct, our man drew away and, by tacking and keeping in cover, dragged himself over the distance to camp. His hurts would ordinarily have laid out a stout man, but he made no fuss and helped with cheerfulness when I dressed them for the night; his splendid physique and long inurement to hardy, open-air life in that climate contributed especially to recuperate the ills. His was but one of many of the experiences of that sort. In a day or two, he got ready to finish his journey to Helena to consult a doctor, and I thought I would go too and get a law book or two. It was some fifty miles, and we started back after completing our errands. Meantime, a Chinook wind had mellowed the severity of winter so that the ice on White River had thawed and broken up, and the ferry we were to cross was impassible because of the float ice. We were in a dilemma, as we knew of no other ford or ferry, and the river is quite wide. We rode along its bank for some hours for a chance to cross; the current was swift and carried blocks of ice and compact slush, but for all, we determined to get our nags in and try it. With difficulty, the animals were forced in, and then came the tug for the opposite shore. We had selected a crossing where, on the opposite side, there was a cabin and signs of occupancy. A wild struggle ensued in which progress was slow and trying to the brutes. We gained at last a compact of ice stretching along the goal shore. Extending some ropes from the landing on some of this, we could bear part of our weight, for we left the saddles to ease the spent horses, leaning partly on them and our weight partly on the compacts. By urging, the animals, whose feet now touched the bed of the stream, would rear and make a length. In this way, they labored out to the landing, where with ropes, the ranchman had lent a hand. "A passage perilous maketh a port pleasant," and the pleasure was none the less that in the cabin we were met by one of those wifely women whose presence seemed so incongruous in a wilderness. Our belongings at the crupper of the saddle, my books, had not escaped a wetting, and our wearing gear a drenching. All this was attended to and our shivering bones jacketed, so that by morning, my foolhardy friend and his equally foolish companion were headed toward Thompson's Gulch. Where, a few days later, they separated.

From this on till spring, the sole occupant of Thompson's Gulch had it all his own way. The wolfers came in from their winter's stint rewarded with a big haul of hides and, with the early freshet, began the summer's work in the ground sluice. It was midsummer of this year of 1869 that we disposed of the mine, settled all bills, and—with a small capital—looked around for an opening. I had concluded to go to Fort Benton, where my friend Lowry was located and was practicing law, and it was arranged between us to become partners.

Editor's Note

The chronology is confusing here. Lowell makes the decision to join Morrow P. Lowry, the Pennsylvania lawyer he befriended in Harrisburg during his army days, but then Lowell delays his trip to Benton to earn cash by guarding the mining camp at Thompson's. Curiously, he barely mentions Lowry again in the manuscript, nor does he mention the law firm Shober & Lowry. Morrow P. Lowry's brother Jeff (Thomas Jefferson Lowry) successfully practiced law in Helena with John H. Shober during this period.

At this time, the miners offered me the job of managing the reservoir that supplied the four-mile ditch before alluded to, and to increase my exchequer (for the pay was liberal), I moved my traps to the basin high up in the mountains and settled down to the arduous task of raising a gate to let the water into the ditch at three o'clock in the morning and shutting it down at three o'clock in the afternoon. This duty did not interfere with an amusement found in studying the habits of the beaver and of undoing the mischief they created through the night by their damming the flow of water along the stretch of the great amphitheater that nature had constructed there. The rising steeps from this basin would reverberate in the night with the crash of a monster

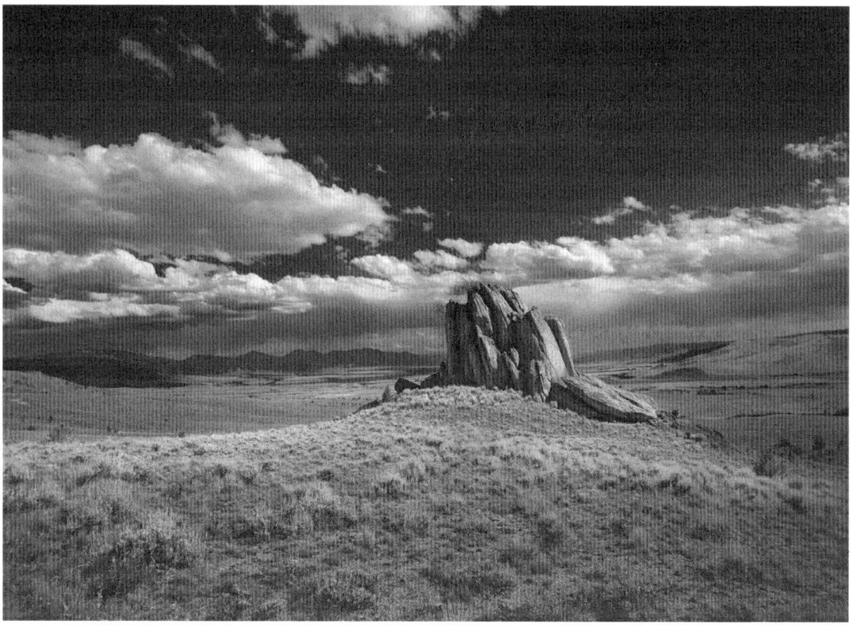

Near Ennis, Montana. *Photograph by Harold Ross.*

tree felled by these varmints. Into this bowl of the mountain came, now and then, nature's creatures to feed and water—the deer and, more rarely, the elk. Their advent was too common to encourage sport, and alone, how distasteful to indulge it! The inured, while habitant of the plains and the mountains, no less than the Indians, deplored the wanton destruction of the noble brutes that gave to the habitation its unique picturesqueness. I had become somewhat accustomed to being alone, but it was by no means being alone there. It had no suggestion of banishment or restraint, nor was it, for the time being, tame. The four-footed, horned visitors, and the expectation of others to come—perhaps a moose, or a mountain lion, a buffalo, or elk—may denote a wilderness, but not necessarily solitude. The diminished flow of water ended my third and last season in Thompsons Gulch, and I think in October 1869, I bade farewell to it and some noble fellows there with whom I had associated.

FORT BENTON AND ENVIRONS, *1869*, ALEXANDER CULBERTSON

If I had been early trained to a literary trait, it is possible that I could have made the topic of Fort Benton and its accessories interesting. I have met the Voyageurs of an early time; one, over ninety years of age, with faculties bright and disposition communicative, of this latter I shall speak further on. I met Major [Alexander] Culbertson, as we called him, full of reminiscences of an early era, whose half-breed daughter, an educated lady, I shall also refer to. In a small collection of books at Fort Benton, I read a manuscript I found there in pamphlet form written by an educated white man who seemed to have accompanied one of the earlier fur trading expeditions to Fort Benton.

Of Major Culbertson I will say he was very solicitous that I write his experiences of many years in Montana: Oh! That I could have felt capable. Of the book in pamphlet: Oh! That I had stolen it, as I did in part, and walked back, conscience stricken, and restored it to the library on my departure from Fort Benton. Culbertson's condition—addicted to strong drink and, being like old men, reminiscent when mellow—excuses me somewhat, but I have no excuse for not stealing the manuscript. It spoke of the journeying laboriously up river from the settlements, how the voyageurs cordelled the heavy boats against the current, wet to the neck—shoulders chafed—the song, the jest when respited from work at the campfire and the other details that made up the daily life on water and land through the years that compassed this diary. Of the tradings with the different tribes: the Gros Ventres, Blackfeet, Sarcees; of the long

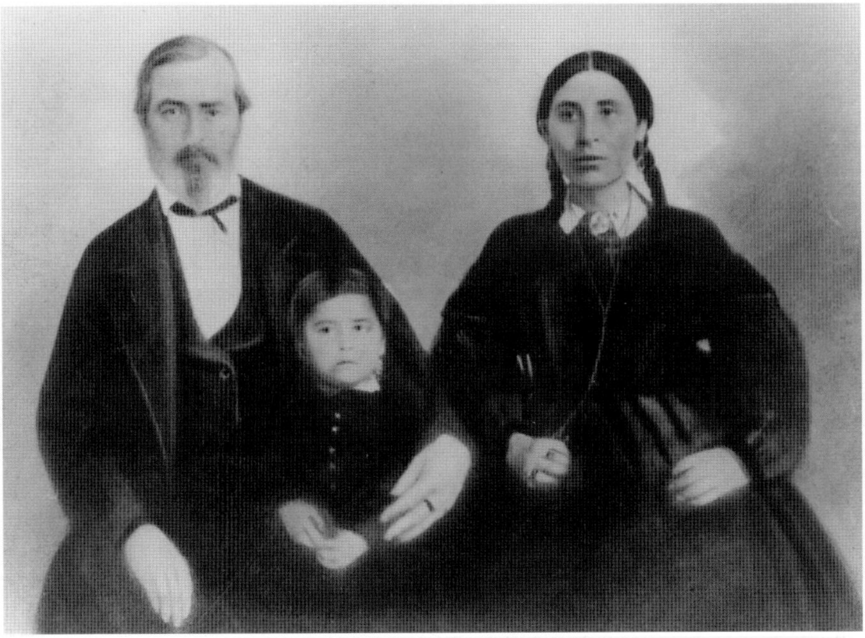

Known as King of the Upper Missouri, Major Alexander Culbertson acted as the post agent at Fort Benton for thirty years. His second wife, Natawista Iksana, was the daughter of a chief of the Blackfeet Nation. She played a critical role in tribal negotiations with the federal government. *Reproduced by permission from the Overholser Historical Research Center, Fort Benton, Montana.*

warerooms stored with robes and furs; of the coming of spring when these products were sailed down river, state bound. Mixed with these and more, this diaryman wove in the thread of human conduct that prevailed in the little community of less than a dozen men of different nationalities with whom his lot was cast. But this is a digression.

It was in August 1869 that I went to Fort Benton, or more correctly, Benton, for the Fort was over a mile below the town. From Thompson's Gulch, I stopped at Helena and there exchanged my "dust" for the circulating medium—only recently circulating—currency. It was a strange thing to divest myself of a pair of pocket scales, a buckskin bag, bologna size, and figure out my finances from crisp paper money. To Benton was 150 miles, probably a little more. It seems that the day before I booked for a stage, a Piegan outfit had surprised some herders between Fort Shaw and Benton, scalping a few and running off a lot of horses.

In consequence, I had but one fellow traveler who cared to venture the trip, and I am quite sure that it was because his duties as telegraph operator

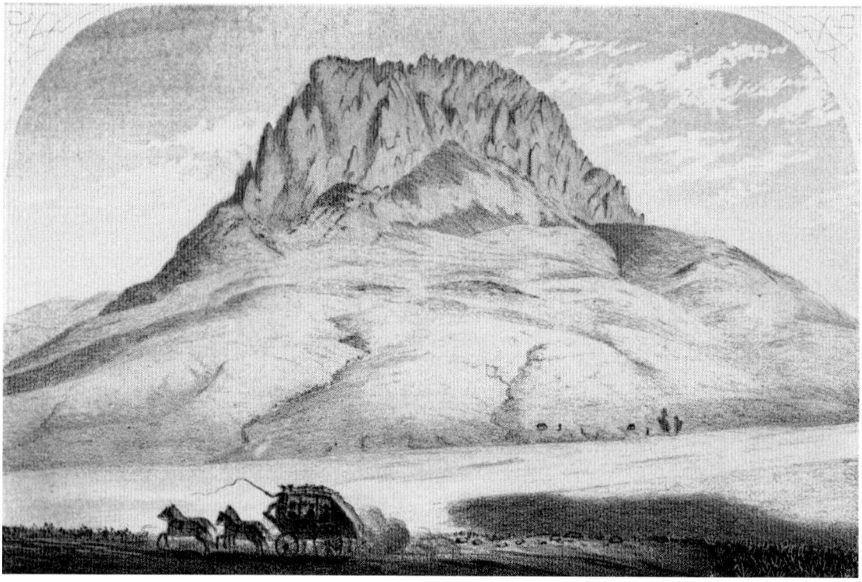

Birdtail Butte, situated midway between Helena and Fort Benton. This 1868 A.E. Matthews drawing was published a year before Lowell's journey on the same stage road. The mountain was so named due to the summit's resemblance to the tail feathers of a bird. *A.E. Matthews drawing reproduced by permission from the Mansfield Library, University of Montana–Missoula.*

at Benton demanded of him the trip that accounted for his going, but as I reasoned it, no securer times could be chosen than just after a massacre. We were both well armed, as was also the driver, and proceeded merrily along by relays day and night. At night, after passing Fort Shaw, the country is a stretch of lonely plateau; the driver suddenly checked up and gave the signal to be ready. Sure enough, directly ahead of us, a quarter mile away, were figures plain to be seen. Having cleared the deck for action, the driver plied the whip, and in a few minutes more, we were dashing through the open ends of a corral of wagons, saluting the sentries at each end with a whoop. After a little badinage in which Mr. Clevenger—the telegrapher—was worsted, we settled down for the home stretch, which we reached early morning in time for breakfast. The descent from the high plateau to lower bottom, broad and wide, opened up the vista of two rows of adobe structures, tallest among which, was the courthouse—all one story. Treeless and verdureless save the brown coverings of bunch grass and the low, lean sagebrush, and at the water's edge just back of the levee, stood the town of Benton.

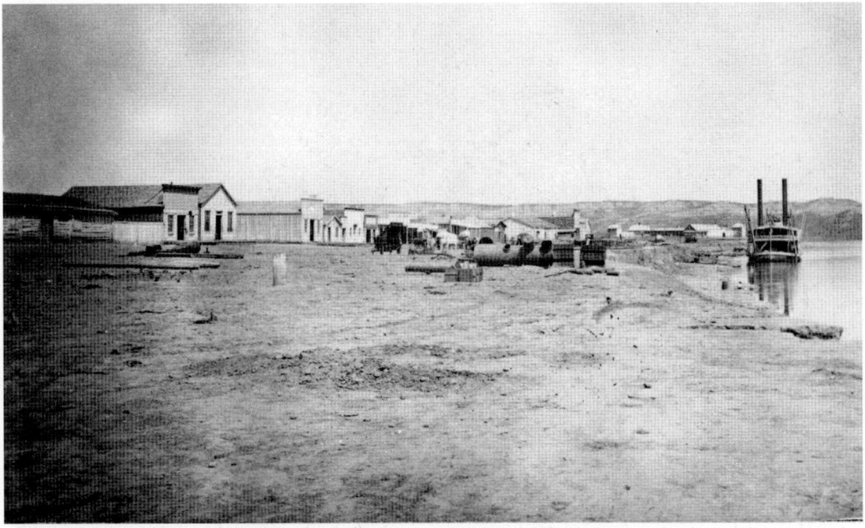

Fort Benton levee, August 1868. Fort appears in the distance (*right*). *Photograph by C.R. Savage, reproduced by permission from the Overholser Historical Research Center, Fort Benton, Montana.*

The town was the head of navigation, the gateway to the mountains and valleys of the territory where navigation ceased and through which gateway was passed and distributed the commerce brought by the stern-wheeled steamboats during the months of high water, freighted chiefly at St. Louis, and to be discharged on the broad levee to be thence sent to the mercantile centers by bull and mule trains. The town consisted of the two rows of adobes, above-mentioned, paneling the river and the courthouse, a small-bodied affair with a wing at each end.

TOMAHAWK JURISPRUDENCE AND VIGILANTE JUSTICE

I had come there at the solicitation of my friend Lowry, who was in practice there as a lawyer, and although not at first admitted to practice, I was to break in upon the somewhat tomahawk jurisprudence then in vogue. It was something more than an ordinary pioneer town. Its principal industry was freighting. All other legitimate callings centered on the steamboat and distributing business. Benton was a theater alluring to that class known as *bad man*, and the abandoned and the bull and mule drivers were of the dissolute kind that hover the frontier. There were, too, indomitable men of character to leaven the human kind: Tom C. Power, afterwards, Montana's first senator; the Bakers, of I.G. Baker & Company; Carroll & Steele; the great freighters of the Diamond "X" [Lowell misremembers the freighting company name, Diamond R]; and a few others. The great drift, however, were the whackers, the wolfers, the plainsmen—most of whom were gamblers—and their time while in Benton was spent in the two or three long halls dedicated to the hazards of gaming, chiefly short-hand and Faro. [A card game played between a banker and players winning or losing according to the cards upturned.] So far removed from the rigorous administration of the law, it was a sanctuary for the bad man.

Benton was the county seat of Choteau County. There was one court in active operation, probate court. It had jurisdiction of all sorts of cases, civil and criminal, within a limit of $500. It had authority of all criminal cases that did not require the intervention of a grand jury, and it had binding over jurisdiction of the latter. No lawyer, or incipient lawyer, wore the ermine while I lived there, and that is why I characterize as "tomahawk" the procedure and practice into which I blossomed on my arrival. The personnel of the district court, which had its source in Lewis and Clark County at Helena, was largely fictitious, for the district judge never sat in Choteau County while I was there, so that the title conferred on me in July 1870 of Clerk of the District Court was, in effect, equally fictitious.[49] For political purposes, this was simply to keep up the political organization of the county. Later on, I received the appointment as deputy district attorney. I regret that this written appointment is lost, and I am not sure that any record is preserved of it, but I remember that there were several cases in which parties were bound over at Benton by me as district attorney acting. It is of no special importance and may have been for aught I remember a special appointment, for it befell that afterwards, I took on the defense of cases. But there is one instance where I acted as prosecutor that is impressed indelibly on my memory.

One wing of the courthouse, as I have said, was occupied by me as a sleeping apartment. One morning, I was awakened by the sing-song lamentations of Indian squaws immediately in back of my quarters. The intonations defy description. It will awaken the soundest sleeper. An official is, or was, regarded as a Chief by our redskins. These women pointed me to a dry well that contained the cause of their trouble, to which we all went. It was located a little way off in the yard of a stable. There was an Indian or two there of the Piegan tribe and a few white men. The body of an Indian could be distinctly seen at the bottom of the well, which then was dry.

It is the nature of an Indian to have a superstitious dread of the underground, and it would have taken a key, yet unmade, to unlock the superstition, but this was made easy when there came to the well a man who frankly said he had put the Indian there and was not too proud to accommodate his relatives by taking him out. Of this man, I will speak later. A rope let him down, and in the course, both corpse and man were hoisted to the surface. The death of an Indian at that time was of little consequence. It was an incident—nothing more. The vindication that follows the law regarding the sanctity of life, of living, of property, and the pursuit of happiness was of little worth to these persistent violators of obedience to law and the behests of humanity. The exertion to put into operation the machinery of the law to punish the doer of this crime was feeble and abortive, and the prosecution failed, as might have been—and really was—anticipated.[50]

On the other hand, an incident occurred in which I took the part of defending. The coach that made the run into Benton—like all end relays,

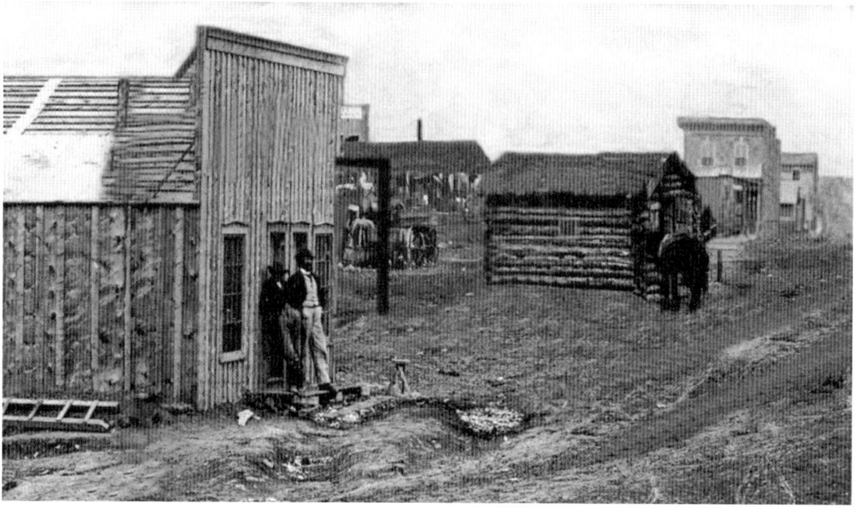

This collection of log structures, including the jail and gallows pictured here in the 1860s, was known as Benton's HooDoo Block after the 1868 execution of a self-appointed sheriff, Billy Hensel. The locals considered the block cursed. It was the scene of murder, destruction by wind and fire, and sudden death. The well Lowell describes was near this block. *Reproduced by permission from the Overholser Historical Research Center, Fort Benton, Montana.*

was the best equipped with horses, and the whirling in of this coach as it traversed the levee front was a sight. The driver's long lashed whip curved through the air, the high-stepping loftily checked nags showed off grandly, the expectant mail and the news from inland points aroused the waiting populace. On the box sat the driver, a splendid specimen of lusty manhood. His wide-brimmed sombrero flapping in the breeze, altogether jaunty, invited the admiring glances of womankind. With one or two exceptions, there were no females unmarried. There was one, the wife of a gambler, whose eyes caught the infection of knightliness in the Irish lad that mastered the whip, and there, of course, the trouble began.

I was playing billiards one evening in a small hall adjoining a hotel—so called—a row of low sleeping rooms stretched to the hotel—so called. While playing, the gambler aforesaid walked in and called for drinks at the bar. He was pretty full even then, and I could hear him breathing vengeance on somebody. A few minutes after he went out, we heard shots fired, and I went to the low built apartments where the gambler and wife lived. On the entry platform where his quarters were, the gambler was lying bleeding and unconscious. We called for help and took him into the billiard hall, where he soon died. I take great pride in remarking that at the very

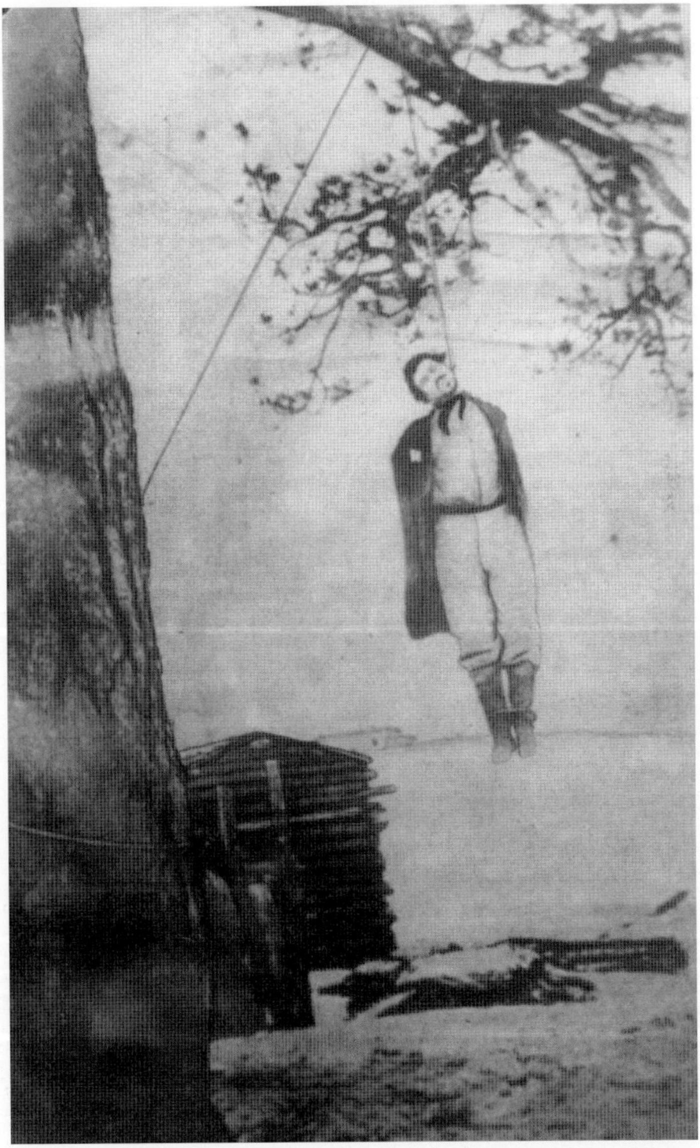

The body of James Daniels strung up in Helena, 1866. A Virginia City jury convicted Daniels of killing a man with an eight-inch knife over a card dispute, but Daniels won a temporary reprieve from the acting governor and returned to Helena, the scene of the crime. He died in a noose with the reprieve in his pocket and a note pinned on him by the vigilance committee; it promised a similar fate for the governor if he were to do the same again. Sixteen months later, Acting Governor Thomas Francis Meagher disappeared over the edge of a boat moored in Benton. Montana vigilantes lynched more than fifty men between 1864 and 1870. *Reproduced by permission from the Overholser Historical Research Center, Fort Benton, Montana.*

lonesome grave of this abandoned man, I read the Episcopal burial service to a handful of warm-hearted attendants—the sole rites that occurred. On the other hand, I take on something like remorse that I was persuaded to appear at the preliminary hearing of the slayer of that man and procured his discharge—what became of him I do not know. These are samples of my first introduction to the administrations of the law.

One other incident, both dramatic and tragic, is very vivid to me. One evening, late, I was reading in my den when I heard the loud screams of a squaw about a block away. On arriving, I found in the street a woman squaw holding in her arms a papoose, which she had brought over on her shoulders, with a bullet hole across and through its temples. It took quite a bit of arguing to learn how it happened, and this is the story. This woman and another were in a cabin, and a drunken half-breed entered and, after frightening remarks, drew his gun and fired. I was then acting deputy district attorney and filed with the probate court an information against the man whose name was the French one of Pipeneaux Wypert.[51] [Lowell varies the spelling of the first name in the manuscript.] He had taken to the brush and for more than a year was not within our jurisdiction. He turned up one day, and I got out a warrant and he was put in the jail. This jail was some three hundred yards in the oblique rear of the courthouse and was made of staunch logs. It was probably a few nights after, and after commitment, that I heard sounds from my quarters in the wing of the courthouse coming from the direction of the jail. Stepping out into the shadow, I noted a body of men at the jail door. I recall, as yesterday, the rising of the moon and lighting up the scene. I saw the leader and heard the conversation. The jail door was broken open, and Pipeneaux was led out. The father of the slain papoose, whose name I have forgotten, was there. The preliminaries were talked over and arranged. The Master of Ceremonies prescribed with much ability what was to be done. Pipeneaux was given a certain number of paces, which the Master stepped off, and the parent was given free scope to follow him. Pipineaux asked for a pair of moccasins. This indulgence was granted. The pursuer was given a Henry Rifle, and at a given signal, the Master, who had placed Pipeneaux, called the word. The moon had risen and lighted the level of mingled sagebrush and low thorn that stretched a mile and more toward the fort. It was not a duel; it was a gauntlet run. Thrice wounded, Pipeneaux sunk down and expired within a quarter mile of his start. The men moved away to the halls, save one, I saw him—the Master—go alone to the body of Pipeneaux and fire his revolver into him. The crowd had dispersed, and following this last function of the Master of Ceremonies, I walked to the halls to see him and the confederates as easily and demurely plying the vocation there as if nothing of importance had interrupted the game at the tables.

The incoming and outgoing of bull and mule trains at the levee strewn with merchandise; the boats, some moored to the shore, some out and some ingoing; the roustabouts jumping the boats; the nightly dances at the halls where Cyprians graced the festivities in furbelowed attire [prostitutes with ruffled dresses]—all these and some more heightened the activities of Benton, and the scenes ranked well up in the hierarchy of fantastic and delirious recklessness. And there saw you graceful and nonchalant riders: saddles, double cinched; guns, each side the saddle cantle; the silver spade bit, the crowned sombrero rakishly cocked, buckskins on his shanks with embroidered fringe and tinkling wheel spurs. This was the Master of the gauntlet running, courtly and polite to all. These were flush times when life was held by an uncertain tenure and eked out as recklessly as it was yielded up. The leathery-faced freighter whose business it was to lash bulls and mules across arid and scorching wastes was in evidence, with his earnings, and his searcher there in waiting. As Kipling says:

> *And honest Jack who sold them slops*
> *And harvested their pay*[52]
> [Rudyard Kipling, "The Ballad of Fisher's Boarding-House," 35–36]

It is not to be denied that order and a respect for the law were not entirely ignored. No indeed, the crucial point between lawlessness and order may have been overstepped, but not for long. Benton was never dangerously overridden during my stay there, I mean, unredeemedly so. A vigilance committee was thought necessary, and its organization comprised a resolute minority; an executioner of the committee's decisions was a member. He was the Master of Ceremonies where Pipeneaux Wypert was given a chance for his life.

It happened this way. The winter of 1871 had nearly depleted the town. Off on hide and fur quest and a large party to the British dominions had diminished the residents. They were away to make a stake, as it was called. The town was practically dead—the boating season over—and nothing really to do. Our hangers-on levied tribute on the merchants and got a subscription of $200 per month to parade and night watch the town. It was during this period that an incident occurred. On the range, some small herds of cattle—few in number compared with the herds of later years—sometimes these small herds were the prey of marauding Indians. In one of the herds, the owner noticed a loss of three or four taken one at a time. This was considered a White Man's business. Below Benton and near the Fort was a slaughterhouse and, anchored in the river near its beach, held down by rocks, were found the hides of the missing beeves branded and certain of identification. This meat plant was owned and operated by one named W.S. Stocking, with whose family—a most estimable people—I boarded. One evening, entirely ignorant of the circumstance related, I was passing a corridor where the telegrapher, Clevinger, held forth, and my attention was arrested by sounds in Clevinger's office of loud talk. This was then the rendezvous of the order of Vigilantes. My knock, though recognized, admitted me with some forcible insistence on my part. The reason was quite plain. These were some men of character standing there, but my landlord, Stocking, was to all appearances to be victimized, the evidence against him seemed to have no defensive feature or the basis for a plea on his behalf, except the hearing was ex parte. On this point, I took up the cudgel and, to my surprise, moderated the feeling as against the "Executioner," who had seemingly got hold of those present with his extreme notions of dealing with accused persons; the result was that I was appointed a committee of one to warn Stocking to leave town within ten hours. I have a letter from Stocking written in his hiding that followed the order of the Vigilantes. It is only fair to remark that Stocking claimed that an enemy of his planted the hides in the river at the junction of his slaughterhouse, and I have no reason to disbelieve his statement. That night after the adjournment, I went to my quarters in the solitary wing of the courthouse after leaving the house of Stocking, where I delivered the message. I could not rest or sleep and watched from the windows—gun in hand—for the man whom I had denounced in plain terms at the meeting of the Vigilantes. The next day, passing up the riverfront, came towards me the man; he offered a gentlemanly greeting—and more, he proffered assistance should I ever need it from him. It is needless to say that a microbe was taken out of me. He was skilled in the art of immediately presenting an absent gun. Among his maxims was, "If you see a man looking for trouble, accommodate him." I stood once at a bar with him and others; he raised his two forefingers apart and said, "Hills never come together, but men may," then brought his fingers together.

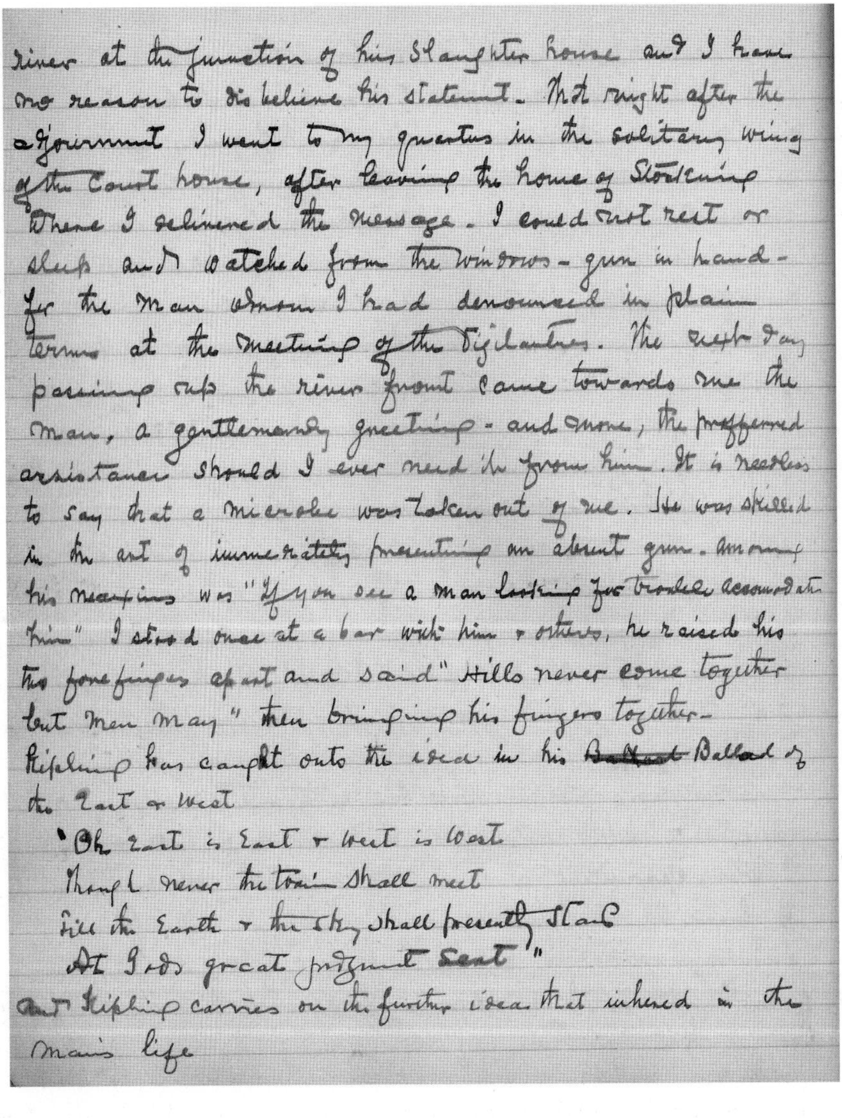

river at the junction of his Slaughter house and I have
no reason to disbelieve his statement. That night after the
adjournment I went to my quarters in the solitary wing
of the Court house, after leaving the home of Stoeckling
where I delivered the message. I could not rest or
sleep and watched from the windows - gun in hand -
for the man whom I had denounced in plain
terms at the meeting of the Vigilantes. The next day
passing up the river front came towards me the
man, a gentlemanly greeting - and more, the proffered
assistance should I ever need it from him. It is needless
to say that a misnake was taken out of me. He was skilled
in the art of immediately presenting an absent gun. Among
his maxims was "If you see a man looking for trouble accommodate
him" I stood once at a bar with him & others, he raised his
two forefingers apart and said "Hills never come together
but men may" then bringing his fingers together -
Kipling has caught onto the idea in his ~~Ballad~~ Ballad of
the East & West

"Oh East is East & West is West
Though never the twain shall meet
Till the Earth & the Sky shall presently stand
At Gods great judgment seat"

and Kipling carries on the further idea that inhered in the
man's life

Lowell manuscript, page 80.

Kipling has caught out the idea in his Ballad of the East and West:

Oh East is East and West is West,
Though [sic] *never the twain shall meet,*
Till the Earth and the Sky shall presently stand,
At God's great Judgment seat;

And Kipling carried on the further idea that inhered in the man's life:

But there is neither East nor West,
Border, nor Breed, nor Birth,
When two strong men stand face to face,
Though they come from the ends of the earth!
[Rudyard Kipling, 1889, "The Ballad of East and West," 1–2, 96–97]

One versed in the springs of human conduct has said, "For the achieving of a desperate deed, a man should not select thy agent merely because of the fierceness of his nature, but one who has had his hands formerly in blood." Reasoned out, you may find in this truism an explanation of why the dead body of Pipeneaux Wypert received the bullets of one whose hands were red with the blood of his fellow man. The Master of Ceremonies was no dime novel desperado; no more courtly gentleman was there. He had none of the airs of the bully; his antecedents were unknown, and in that little community, he was held more in fear than in detestation; and as far as I know, he was never guilty of striking down any who did not deserve it. White, nor Indian. In the tragedy of Pipeneaux Wypert, he gave the accused moccasins and distance between him and the fatal rifle that followed the well incident. He had to him a justification as a promoter of the peace. The Poet Homer sang the ruffian Achilles into renown. I am not sure but the man of whom I write deserved as stately a history. Ivanhoe, who killed the neighbors "for love of God and Lady," lacked some of the good qualities of our bad man. But be it remembered, "That he who sups with the devil must have a long spoon."

Hamlet says [of the king, his stepfather]:

Carrying, I say, the stamp of one defect,
Being nature's livery, or fortune's star,—
Their virtues else—be they as pure as grace,
As infinite as man may undergo—
Shall in the general censure take corruption
From that particular fault: the dram of base eale
Doth all the noble substance of a doubt
To his own scandal.
[Hamlet, 1.4.31–38]

As might be supposed, the Master's death was tragic. I have heard that while about to execute the decree of the Vigilantes upon one whose guiltiness was in doubt, he was seized and executed.

Editor's Note: Lowell and the Law in Benton

Without Lowell's recollection, one can only speculate as to the identity of the "Master." Contemporary sources from Benton during the late 1860s and early 1870s are rare. Fort Benton historian Joel Overholser identified the sheriffs during the period as J.D. Weatherwax and H A. (Fred) Kanouse, but elected sheriffs at the time generally mediated merchant disputes rather than personal disagreements. That duty fell to the so-called vigilance committee. Fred Kanouse was the ne'er-do-well son of Jacob Kanouse, a respected attorney, but Lowell noted the Master's antecedents were unknown. Another possible candidate for the Master would be deputy marshal John Xelpho Beidler, known as "X" Beidler. The famous Montana marshal appeared in and out of Benton during the period. In some respects, his vigilance activities resemble those of Lowell's "Master," but Beidler survived to a ripe old age and was not considered a "bad man." Lowell described the character as dying by the hand of his former mates.

Vigilante Billy Hynson (a.k.a. Billy Heusel or Hensel) resembles Lowell's Master in a few respects, but Hynson died in 1868, hanged by his fellow citizens for rolling drunks. Lowell's vigilante was still around in 1871.

Another possible candidate for the Master is Dennis Hinchey. Hinchey was a troublemaker who was executed by a saloonkeeper in 1872, five months after Lowell left town, so that piece of biography hits the mark. The Helena Weekly Herald *proclaimed Hinchey's demise:*

> *On Sunday morning, about four o'clock, one of those unfortunate occurrences that frontier towns are not unfrequently subjected to, occurred in Marshall's billiard saloon, resulting in the death of Dennis Hinchey, formerly a citizen of Galena, Ill., but for the last three of four years of Colorado and Montana, and a somewhat notorious character of the border. Hinchey was on one of his sprees, and apparently determined to wipe out some one; when, for his own preservation, and probably that of others, Mr. Marshall, one of the proprietors of the saloon, shot him, and he is sustained by all good citizens in so doing. This affray brought to light the strange fact that the only officers of the law present in Chouteau county are two Commissioners and the Assessor; no Sheriff, no Coroner, no Justice of the Peace, no Constable. I am informed that a full set of officers was elected at*

> *the last election, but most of them are at present out at Whoop-up trading with the Indians.* [Whoop-up was a whiskey trading post.] *Now, Mr. Editor, this may be all right at Benton, but I hardly think that is what those officers were elected for....*
>
> *Since writing the above, the Coroner's jury found that Dennis Hinchey came to his death from four pistol shots from the hands of L. W. Marshall. A jury of twelve men, summoned by subpoena from the Probate Court, pronounced Mr. Marshall justified in the killings of Hinchey....Hinchey is supported by one man, who is confined in the county jail, charged with the crime of forcibly entering the house of George Croft (who is at present absent) and destroying his furniture, and grossly insulting his wife. I do hope that the citizens of Chouteau county will now see to it that persons and property of law abiding citizens of their county be protected in future.*[53]

Hinchey fits the bill as Lowell's "Master."

While Lowell hadn't passed a bar examination, he appears in Overholser's history of early law enforcement in Benton as an attorney and county official. The historian referred to Lowell's three-year struggle to collect his pay as Choteau County assessor:

> *Perhaps the first professional* [attorney] *to practice in Fort Benton was James H. Lowell, wide ranging traveler and unsuccessful miner at Diamond City, who came to Fort Benton from the latter camp in August 1869 with intent to return east, instead, lingered for two years. Lowell had been wounded at Antietam in 1862....Lowell was deputy district attorney and county assessor, as well as lawyer in Fort Benton, for kicks and cash traded with Indians for T.C. Power near Cow Island.*[54]

Likely, kicks were not the primary motivator. Lowell himself wrote that his goal in moving to Benton was to join his lawyer friend Morrow P. Lowry and further his studies. Lowell met Lowry in Harrisburg while he was recuperating from wounds suffered at Antietam and working in mustering and disbursement. Lowry hailed from Conneautville, Pennsylvania, and was working as assistant paymaster for the sternwheeler USS Naiad (1864–65). Suffering from lung disease and seeking a healthful mountain climate, he followed his brother Thomas Jefferson "Jeff" Lowry out to Helena after the war, where Jeff partnered with John H. Shober in the successful law firm Shober & Lowry. As Lowell recorded earlier in the memoir, he bumped into his wartime friend in Helena in 1868 while M.P. Lowry was giving a stump speech. He recalled the same chance encounter in a letter to Kate Mary.[55]

Strong drink got the best of M.P. Lowry, but at this point, in 1868, Lowry was elected to the Montana House of Representatives and resided in Fort Benton. He appeared in the 1870 census as the county assessor. So both men lived in town for about a year before Lowry returned to Pennsylvania in 1870. Likely, Lowell practiced law under the auspices of M.P. Lowry in Benton before receiving any formal legal training and continued in this role after Lowry quit town. We know Lowell was prosecuting and defending cases and teaching school.

Lowell demurs from recording his friend's decline, but a long, public record in the form of his widow's pension application demonstrates that Lowry's drinking rendered him unable to write for himself when he returned to Pennsylvania in 1870. Likely, he suffered from tuberculosis.[56] *Neither of the Lowry brothers appear in the narrative after Lowell arrived in Benton. The most plausible explanation for M.P.'s sudden absence from the story is that he wasn't practicing much of anything in Benton at the time other than lifting a glass.*

BENTON *1869-71*, THE KANACKERS

In the summer season every year, Benton received a various kind of visitors. The Kanackers—of mixed Indian and white, French white—came down from the Red River of the North in the British possessions.[57] In a long cavalcade, they journeyed the tortuous way through the mountain fastening of two hundred or more miles and by the sweet grass region so devoutly regarded by the Indians. Their wheeling was in carts, two-wheeled, made entirely of wood—not a thing of iron about them. They were laden with the skins of animals: buffalo, beaver, minx, otter, and peltries of all sorts. They brought also pemmican in jars of primitive manufacture. Pemmican is a concentrated food of maximum nourishment and minimum weight, dry and of small bulk. It is a compound of saw-dried beef, then buffalo meat, ground fine, and with other ingredients of tallow and a small fruit grown on Red River—modernly substituted by raisins with some acid, like cranberry. The mixture is pressed into molds or the jar. It requires no cooking and is ready in all seasons. They brought also another article of diet called "Depuyah," in French, "Deponille." On the base of the boss ribs of a healthy fat buffalo is a growth, a layer of (I have seen) four inches of a consistency of the lard of a hog and cheese. This is "depuyah." This rare product was then the fatty ingredient of pemmican, and on long tramps, the easily portable character of pemmican, or depuyah alone, made it the sustenance of adventurers. A town in Montana, I am told, now bears the name of Depuyah.[58]

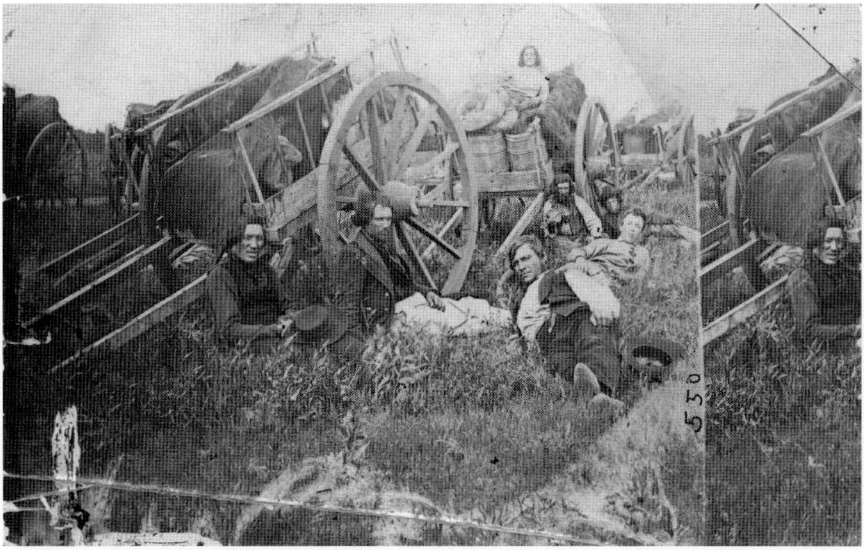

Métis drivers (Lowell called them Kanackers) with Red River ox carts. *Photograph by Benjamin Franklin Upton, reproduced by permission from the Minnesota Historical Society, 97537.*

The Kanackers in their annual visits brought with them a racing horse, which they never stinted to back against any hoof on the course southwest of town. They would stack up their robes and peltries on this plain and invite the denizens to bet against them. No pains were spared to procure in the territory a rival beast for this tournament, but in vain. The race of 1871, carefully prepared for, was beaten by the semi-nude Indian who rode the Kanacker mount, and with ease, and when the visitors had left for the Dominions, they were followed and traded out of their nag. But to the amusement of all, the beast would never repeat the performance.

STERN-WHEELED BOATS

Pierre Choteau was a son of a Madame Choteau, who was the wife of a baker of New Orleans. Their humble people and their descendants romantically figure in the annals of the great Northwest. Pierre Choteau and Regis Loisel engaged in the great fur trade and carried their operations to Fort Benton and the tributaries of the Missouri. Regis Loisel, less plebian, figures in the titles of many tracts of land in Kansas and elsewhere. These two carried their operations to the headquarters of the Missouri and the extreme fastnesses of the Rocky Mountains. It is not the purpose of this writing more than to point out the primal impulse given to transportation up the Missouri. From the start, thus given by Pierre Choteau and Regis Loisel, developed the sternwheeler trade that plied the Great River at the time of these memoirs. It was a holiday occasion to witness a sternwheeler rounding the point just below the Old Fort Benton under full steam in the spring and the levy thronged with its hungry crowd for a sight of real-live States people. The legal dynasty had its innings too, for, on landing, came to our office a throng of roustabouts who now had jumped the boat and gave in for collection the account of their earnings on the boat from St. Louis to Benton. The collection of these claims was done under a territorial statute providing for the tying up of the boat as a hostage, or attachment. The warrant issued by the probate judge enabled the sheriff to take possession of the "Defendant," that is, the boat, as a security for the payment of the claims for wages made by these roustabouts. It was very effective, and unless the captain could show contract papers known in admiralty practice as [he leaves a blank, but Lowell refers to "shipping articles"] the writs were enforced, a sheriff or deputy occupying the wheel room of the boat—night and day if necessary. The captains were great bluffers and, as a rule, held out until the last minute but invariably gave in during my time, and a more genial, hospitable, and jolly class of men than the captains of these sternwheeled boats would be hard to find after the stormy tide had run them down.

Along the shores of the shifty river were wood yards—as called, where the boats would moor and take on fuel in the shape of cordwood. These fuel stations were separated in distances to enable safe and sure propelling power to the fifteen to thirty boats that then plied the river from St. Louis to Benton. This cordwood was carried up the landing plank by the roustabout on his shoulders from the ranks of the owner of the yard, and this was one of the industries, and a valuable one, to the yard owner of early times. The distance over which these boats have been plied between Fort Benton and the mouth of the river was 2,285 miles. For ninety years, this river was navigable, and the amount of traffic was enormous during this period of non-railway service. From 1840 to 1870, the staunchest boats—some with cargoes of five hundred tons—have carried from St. Louis to Benton this enormous freight.[59] All of this business was upon the steam in its natural condition. The many restrictions and drawbacks, which are inseparable from the navigation of this river, have, at least, for the present, placed it behind the railroad as an efficient highway to commerce, but it is not at all certain—shrewd viewed—that this disappearance is a permanent thing. The steamboats may come back again, just as they survive in usefulness in the densely populated countries of the Old World. But today, the river, as commerce, is practically nonexistent.

The region traversed by the sternwheeled boats was, in a sense, Titanic. The vast land lying on either side of the river harbored the fierce Sioux. The shifting sands of the river made navigation perilous. This led to the selection of water-wise pilots, but they were not always so. Misadventures occurred through the error of pilot. On one of these sternwheelers, the captain said to me, "I am helpless," because, as a rule, the captain had no authority over the pilot. This captain, livid with rage, kept a calm demeanor. On the sand bars thrown up by the river's current, this same captain gritted his teeth but made up order. The pilots were well paid, and to prolong the cruise only increased their pay. Thus, on one occasion, our boat was sand-held for three whole days, and the continued "sparring off" failed to release the grasp.

The easing of a boat loose from a sand bar was both provoking and entertaining. A tall spar was dropped butt end down on each side of the

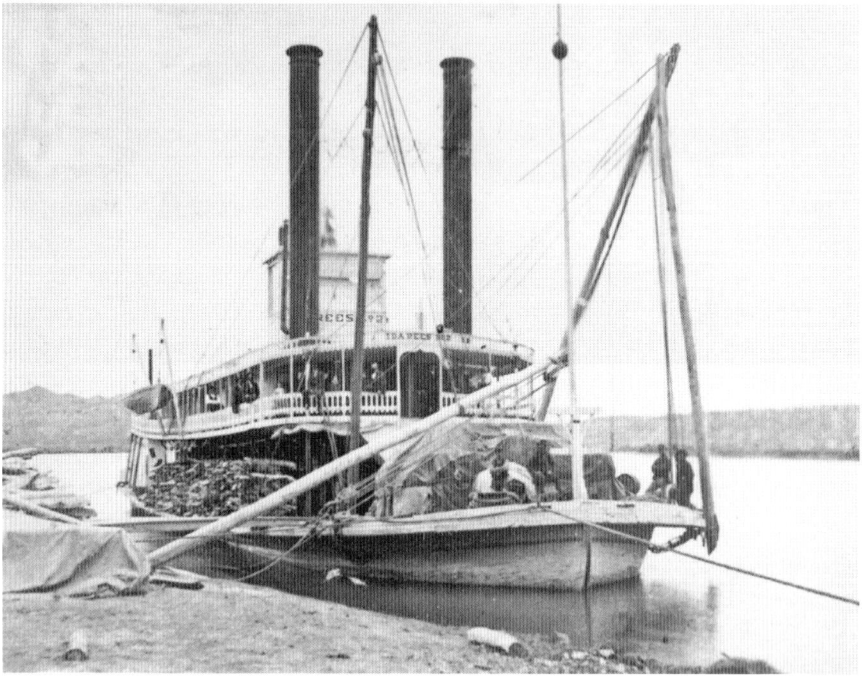

Ida Reese No. 2. *Reproduced by permission from the Overholser Historical Research Center, Fort Benton, Montana.*

boat and so connected at the top as to form a kind of derrick to which was attached block and tackle. A small engine called a "Nigger" operated the contrivance. [A contemporary term for a sort of capstan engine.] The tackle was secured to the boat, and at a given signal, both the engine above deck and the engine below struggled, the one to raise the bows and the other to back out. On the upriver trips this shifty watercourse was beset with dangers to the freightage by reason of contact with these sand bars, and wrecks did occasionally happen. The writer remembers seeing the *Ida Rees*, or its wreck, broken in two as its bows heaved onto a bank. This was a favorite craft at that time, and a photo of it moored to the levee is owned by the writer.

The evolution in transportation, beginning with the "bull boats" made out of the sun-dried hides of Buffalo, has served to carry many million dollars worth of fur over distances which would seem long to a walking man. The keel boat and the sweep-the-sail and the tracking line figured early in this commerce—later, the Great Mackinaw boats, fifty feet long with twelve- and fourteen-foot beam, with some of fourteen tons capacity.

Each of these latter boats took a crew of twelve men and took six months of the hardest labor: towing, tracking, poling, and rowing, to get the clumsy thing from St. Louis to Benton; the down run took thirty days. The first sternwheeler, the *Chippewa*, was specially built to overcome the difficulties and got through to Benton in 1859. [Editor: July 2, 1860] The vanishing of both stern- and side-wheelers occurred about the same time and shortly after the writer returned to the States. Two causes are assigned: the falling off of the pelts and buffalo hide freight that made up largely the return cargo, and the creation of the railways across the continent. The passing of these steamboats is recalled with sincere regret by all who have witnessed their coming and their going. The Lordly Pilot who was a great man wearing a diamond and defying the captains, and the be-cursed roustabout have gone also, and there comes over one an emotion akin to that felt by the hunter over the disappearance of the buffalo.[60]

THE BAKER MASSACRE

During the winter of 1870, a considerable band of Piegan Indians teepeed on the Teton, [Editor: near the Marias] a small river ascending westward from the fort, just below which it emptied into the Missouri.[61] All the different upper river tribes during that period hedged against the common enemy, the feared Sioux. Some of these bands, like the Crows, were really seceders of and of common origin with the Sioux, but for long had lived apart and under another distinctive name. Before recalling the facts of what was called in the States of the Atlantic a massacre, it will be of interest to say something of the condition of these Piegan Indians. They were ostensibly peaceful and chose the Marias because it was so near the Fort, then garrisoned by U.S. troops. But the Piegans had behaved so as to require discipline. They had ravaged the herds of cattle in the vicinity of Benton, they had killed herders and others in doing so, and they were doing these outrages in a treacherous fashion while hypocritically professing friendship. They leaned upon the whites and the military to protect them, as they were not numerous, nor were they enabled through their weakness to dwell in the more remote quarters where game and grazing were more plentiful. They were therefore in a state of mild terror of the Sioux and even of other bands or tribes, such as the Crows, Gros Ventres, Bloods, Crees, Blackfeet, and others—all of whom were friendly in word, if not in spirit, with the government and the pioneers. That winter, the deadly smallpox invaded that portion of the territory, and Benton itself was a hospital for the white and the red. Many of the writer's acquaintances were stricken; and some good friends among them, and having once, while in the army, had the smallpox, the writer found work for his hands in the town.[62] At the Fort was a surgeon named [Archibald B.] Campbell,[63] an old, accomplished physician, scholar, and gentleman with whom the writer was very intimate. He was surgeon of the post, and together [we were] in constant attendance on the afflicted. The disease got into, or originated in, I don't know which, the Piegan camp. There were some thirty to fifty of these who were living in adobe huts in the town, some of whom were diseased. We got from Colonel Baker [Major Eugene M. Baker was often referred to as "colonel." Wylie, 239] or the commandant the promise of quarantining the Piegans in their camp on the Marias and also that all Indians able to go should return there and rid Benton of them. This was done, and they were given to understand that they must keep away. Colonel Baker's headquarters was at Fort Shaw about fifty miles distant [twenty-eight miles west of the modern Grand Rapids]. The injunction was disobeyed, and a few of us went to the fort again and another more vigorous warning was given the Indians. Even that was not wholly regarded. Relatives would sneak in to see the afflicted ones. The camp at the Marias was rife with the contagion. Some chiefs came in and offered Dr. Campbell and the writer hundreds of ponies if we would go there and doctor them. Their camp was a pandemonium making medicine, and their remedy, prescribed by their chief medicine man, the writer can state from actual observation. They would cut a hole in the ice-covered river and dump the patient under good and plenty. This, of course, would drive the fevered disease to the vitals, and death would shortly ensue. The remains would be wound up tight in a buffalo robe and hauled on the ground by a pony to a ravine some miles away. There, it would be placed up on a frame open structure for transportation to the happy hunting grounds. Small parties of the camp continued invading the herds of stock, and it was unsafe to be caught out. And this was the state of affairs when, under Baker's orders, the troops at Fort Shaw and Fort Benton made an early morning descent upon the Camp on the Teton [Marias]. The punishment was severe and a complete surprise, although forewarned.

Dr. Campbell, who was along, told me of his experiments with the virus of smallpox when administered internally. General Harney's estimate of a "good Indian" was exemplified there with powder and ball.[64] This affair was kept quiet as possible, and its details, I presume, were omitted from the official reports. It was known, however, by all Indian tribes on the upper

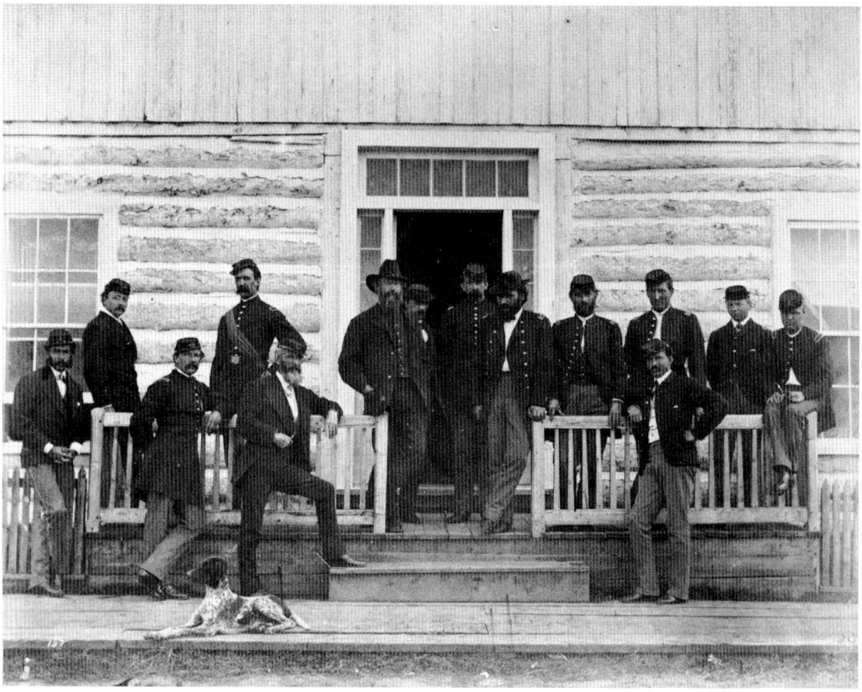

Major Eugene M. Baker and the officers of the Second U.S. Cavalry at Fort Ellis in 1871. *Baker is standing ninth from left in the doorway with his left hand on the rail post. Library of Congress.*

Missouri, and its results were of great value to the pioneers in creating a profound fear of the government soldier. It brought down upon Baker the maledictions of Eastern philanthropists and preachers.

Editor's Note: The Baker Massacre

In the late 1860s, Indian depredations in Montana had intensified as the bison populations diminished and the government crowded the Indian tribes into smaller hunting grounds. The publicity surrounding the murder of frontiersman Malcolm Clarke on August 17, 1869, further roiled the settlers, who were already seething with anger and demanding protection from the army. The following editorial published in the New North-West *at the time of Clarke's death gives a sense of their indignation:*

> *We believe that the Indian Bureau should be transferred to the War Department: that the whole of our Indian Territory should be divided into*

> *convenient districts and placed in charge of military Governors, invested with plenary powers and with a military force sufficient at once to protect and restrain the Indian; and thus protected and restrained, let him have such instruction as he is willing to receive, and let his future treatment be such as he deserves or seems to require. Under the old system* [under the Indian Bureau] *the Indian has been a robber and a murderer until his power has been broken and his spirit crushed. He has then become a thief and a vagabond, listless and worthless, hanging around the outposts of civilization until drunkenness and disease have put an end to his miserable existence....* [L]*et extermination by fire and sword be immediately begun, as a cheaper and more humane alternative.*[65]

The author of this column, editor James Hamilton Mills, launched the *New North-West* in July 1869 from Deer Lodge, Montana, after editing the *Montana Post* for several years. The killing of Clarke and the wounding of his son Horace served as a tipping point in the increasingly hostile relations between the whites and the Blackfoot Confederacy (Blackfeet, Bloods, and Piegans). Native American accounts characterized the murder of Clarke as a revenge killing for Clarke beating the Piegan warrior Peter Owl Child in front of his peers and for Clarke raping Owl Child's wife. The whites' version of events has Clarke beating up Owl Child as a punishment for horse theft. Amplifying the perceived wrongs, Owl Child's spouse was a cousin of Clarke's native wife. The chain of events was intensely personal, but in 1869, the entire white community felt threatened. Less than five months later, Malcolm Clarke's son Horace, who barely survived being shot in the face, accompanied the Second Cavalry in its pursuit of the Blackfeet on the Marias, the pursuit that devolved into the Baker Massacre.

Regardless of who originally carried the smallpox contagion into Indian territory or who was illegally supplying the natives with whiskey, in 1869, white settlers perceived the Indians as a problem that required a fix. Indeed, whiskey fueled much of the violence, but whites who profited from the illegal whiskey trade hesitated to relocate the Indians to remote places where trading would be inconvenient. Already, much of the commerce had taken place at Fort Whoop-up over the "medicine line" in Canada. Of course, the tribes had to learn from white settlers the significance of the boundary line between the U.S. territories and the British possessions.

After the Baker Massacre, local press accounts lauded the army's firm hand in dealing with the Indians, and Lowell was no different. According to the official report, the massacre left 173 Piegan Blackfeet dead, including 53 women and children. An estimate by a mixed-blood scout who witnessed the attack, Joe Kipp, put the body count much higher, at 217. Joe Kipp was the son of an early

Montana fur trader, James Kipp, and a Mandan chief's daughter. While history will never record the exact casualty figures, other witnesses testified that the official army count was low, particularly in the number of women and children who died. At the time of the attack, most of the able-bodied men were out hunting. Only one cavalryman died. Many of the sick suffocated in their teepees when soldiers intentionally fired upon the supporting lodge poles, causing the enclosures to deflate upon cooking fires. Most were shot, but some victims were slashed or axed to death.[66] Not included in Baker's first military report was the key fact that he had attacked the wrong village. The intended target, Mountain Chief's band, was camped ten miles away. Baker's attack on Heavy Runner's camp served as a diversion that enabled Mountain Chief to escape over the forty-ninth parallel into Canada.

Much was made later of Baker's heavy drinking as a factor in the error. One of the guides recounts it was "an undeniable fact that Col. Baker was drunk and did not know what he was doing."[67] Witnesses testified that many of Baker's troops were fortifying themselves with drink for night marches through snow in temperatures that dipped to forty-three degrees below zero. By the time they reached Heavy Runner's camp, the soldiers were spent.

In later years, evidence emerged that a second scout who accompanied Baker on the raid, the trader Joe Cobell, intentionally picked off Chief Heavy Runner as he ran toward Baker with a note of safe passage signed by Lieutenant Colonel Alfred Sully. An Italian immigrant who had come west in the 1850s, Cobell married a sister of Mountain Chief and might have been anxious to keep the Second Cavalry occupied with the wrong village while his in-laws escaped.

One participating officer called the Marias Massacre of 1870 "the greatest slaughter of Indians made by U.S. troops."[68] At the time, he was right. Lowell's account of the slaughter hedges by excluding details of the brutality, many of which came to light during subsequent investigations, but this firsthand account of the prelude to the massacre reveals how white townspeople perceived the threat of deadly smallpox from the local Piegan camps. (Lowell had suffered a mild case of smallpox after Antietam and was immune to the virus.) When details emerged, "the maledictions of Eastern philanthropists and preachers," as Lowell says, deterred Congress from transferring control of Indian affairs to the military. Thus, the Baker Massacre played an important, though lesser-known, part in the history of American Indian affairs. Eleven years after the massacre, the army court-martialed Baker for being intoxicated on duty.[69]

In this section, and in his letters, Lowell betrays an attitude toward Native Americans that is both ethnocentric and contradictory. He laments the end of their way of life, then ruthlessly denounces the Indians as savage brutes. His views were not atypical for his day. The following passage from a description written by Colonel Richard Irving Dodge, an aide-de-camp to General William Tecumseh Sherman, gives a sense of how white settlers and military men perceived the native tribes:

> *In order to attain a true knowledge of the North American Indian, it is necessary that he should be described as he really is—A stony adversary, an in human wretch, Incapable of pity, void and empty From every Drachm of mercy. One of his most striking characteristics is the ferocity and cruelty which he displays against his enemies, be they red or white.*[70]

For full accounts of the Baker Massacre and its consequences, see: Graybill, The Red and the White, *105–51; Wheelan,* Terrible Swift Sword, *251–53; Wylie,* Blood on the Marias: The Baker Massacre.

INDIAN MEDICINE

I have spoken of Medicine as administered by an Indian. The term *medicine* as here used has been caught up by hosts of quacks, and concoctions called Indian medicine have been offered to the ailing as specifics for almost every malady. How the term originated as applied to Indian pharmacy is probably unknown. As a matter of fact, it is a substitute, or in opposition to, our way of handling a disease or ailment, but it is something more and embraces every phase of evil and good. It is worked by a specialist to produce the welfare or ward off an evil that threatens the community or the individual savage. There is a variety of "medicine men" among the Indians, each a specialist in a certain department. War, peace, scalps, horse stealing, buffalo, epidemic, change of domicile, and many other topics have its specialist. The *materia medica* is the simplest form of medicine, hardly within the definition. It is more a system of seerage, or forecast and prophecy. Are the Indians short of meat? At once, a council is held, and squatting in a circle in a teepee, the pipe is filled and handed in by a squaw. One of the number—the specialist—sits in apparent stupor, oblivious to all things mundane. Trance-like and dumb, he "makes medicine." It may be hours—a day or more till the revelation arrives—he arouses and announces the territory where abound game. The camp is alive, the ponies saddled, and away they go, followed by the squaws with travois, knives, darts, etc. It is common for the specialist to fast before

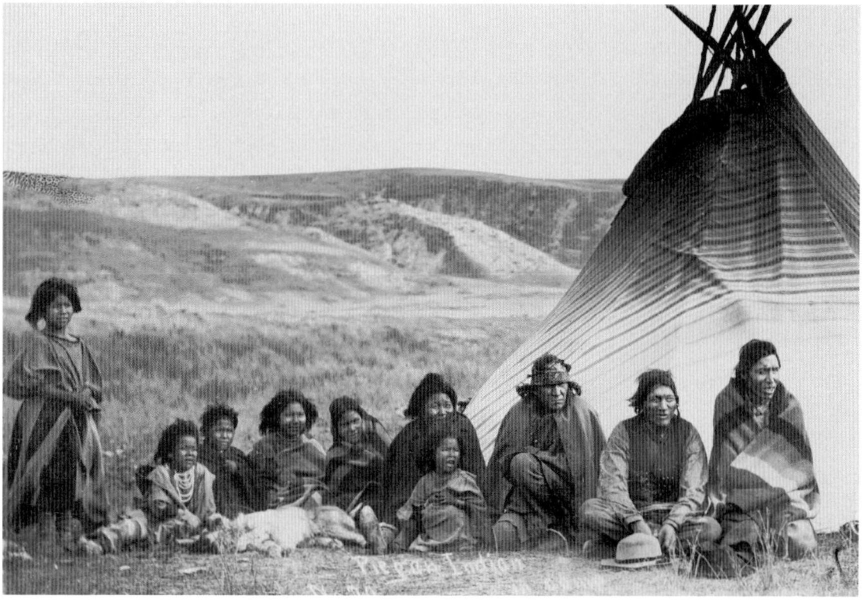

Piegan Indians on the Missouri River, one mile above Fort Benton, 1884. *Photograph by Dan Dutro, reproduced by permission from the Montana Historical Society Research Center Photograph Archives, Helena, Montana, 955–517.*

the council until gaunt with emptiness, but while the seated council lasts, a wrong movement will break the medicine. The writer once went innocently into a teepee to see a chief and broke the medicine by making a few steps the wrong direction around and got roughly handled in consequence. This briefly is making medicine, the method mattering very little whatever the purpose of orgy.

The American savage is a Polytheist. They believe in, and in their thought, worship, a large variety of remarkable and mysterious beings, calling on these for assistance, attributing to them all good and evil, and striving by such ceremonies as here given to promote good or avert evil. Among these beings thus propitiated are animals, sun, moon, stars, and fire. Fire is prominent, and its flaming is to a savage a phenomenon. A faker once gave an exhibition at Benton. He threw knives and did sleight-of-hand tricks. The writer was present and noticed how the few Indians present regarded these stunts. The faker gave the trick of blowing fire out of his mouth, and that was enough for the Indians. With scowls and horror, they broke for the open. To them, the faker was possessed of the Evil Spirit.

THE OLD FORT BENTON

I have spent many pleasant hours in this historic structure, now a mass of crumbled ruins. It was built in the year 1846 by an expedition acting as agents of the American Fur Company who named it in honor of Senator [Thomas Hart] Benton, who was a member of that company. Near its site, as early as 1805, Captain Meriwether Lewis and a number of his men, while temporarily separated from his main command, camped and set about to determine whether the Missouri, or the Marias, was the main stream. His co-officer, Clark, joined him later, and they together fixed upon the former as the principal waterway. Without doubt, they were the first white men to set foot there. More than forty years elapsed after the Lewis and Clark invasion till the town site of Benton was selected by an expeditionary party as an eligible trading point to mark the head of navigation. The same fur company projected the enterprise and an adobe fort was then erected in 1846. This fort was about two hundred feet square and, having been built on the bank of the river, was protected on the riverside from rifle shot from any of the neighboring heights, the broad valley extending northward more than half a mile. The officers' quarters were furnished with huge fireplaces, and separately, in each room above and below the west wall, those walls were three feet thick and sixteen feet high. Completing the quadrangular enclosure, in the middle of this wall was an opening for gateway, the walls overlapping to make protection more complete. The gate was massive as hewn logs could make it, framed together crosswise and swung on a post sunk deep in the earth and locked to a second post of the same build. Two

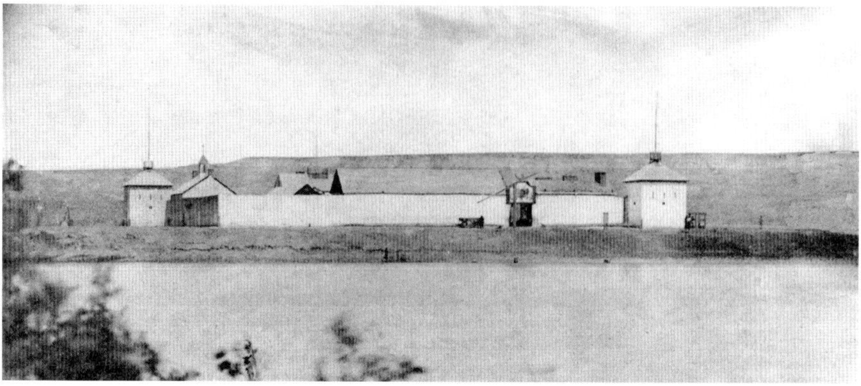

Fort Benton, 1860. *Reproduced by permission from the Overholser Historical Research Center, Fort Benton, Montana.*

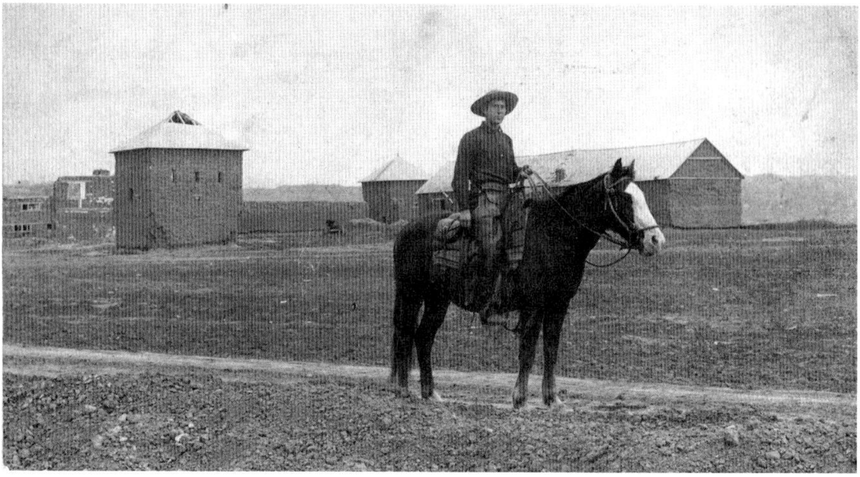

Fort Benton in the 1880s. *Reproduced by permission from the Minnesota Historical Society.*

bastions were connected with the corners, one the northwest and one the southwest, which projected several feet from the connecting walls. These bastions extended upward higher than the rest of the enclosure, with portholes at short intervals, which completely swept the approaches in every direction. It was completed in 1850 and was dedicated by a grand dance on Christmas Eve of that year. It was used by the fur company as a defense against Indians and as a storehouse for supplies and peltries until about the time of the Civil War, since when, until its demolition by time, it was used

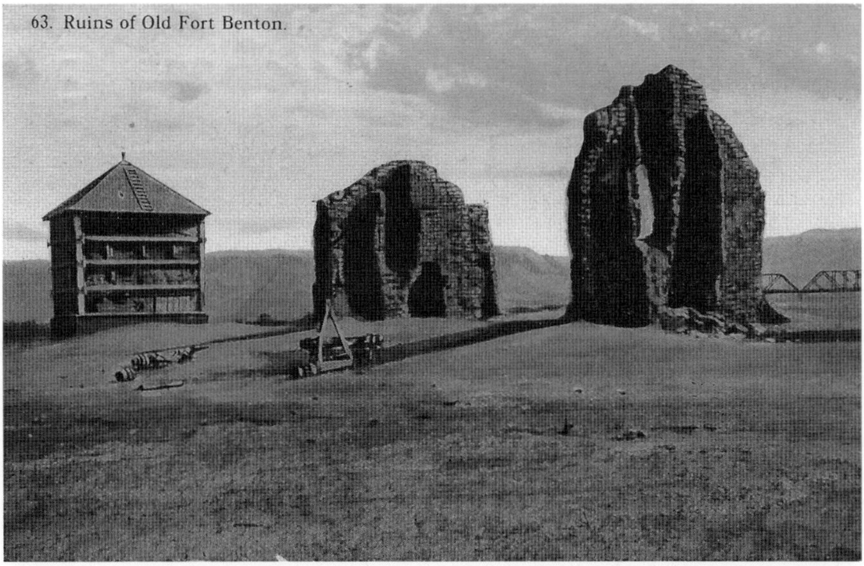

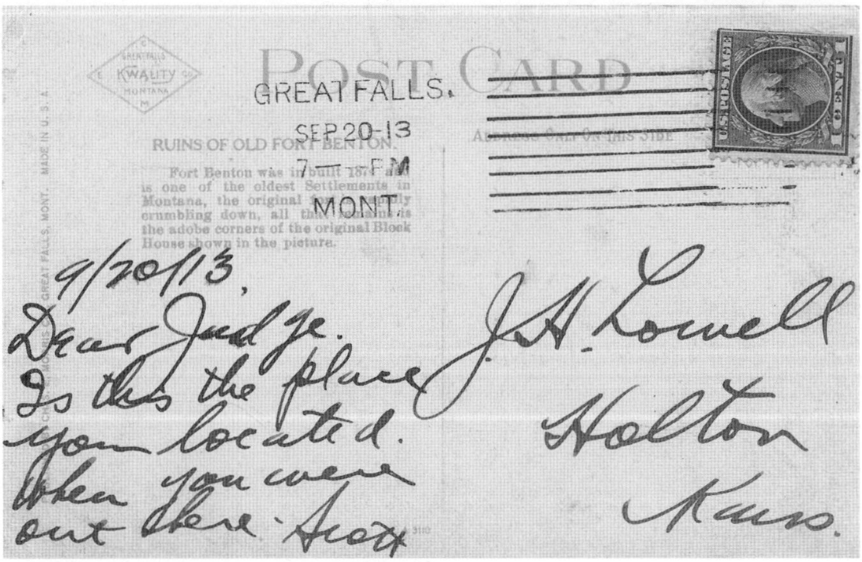

Ruins of Old Fort Benton. Postcard sent to Lowell in 1913. The fort was a crumbled ruin until the Daughters of the American Revolution spearheaded the restoration of the northeast bastion in 1908. *Author's collection.*

when required by the government troops. It was adobe work throughout, reinforced by massive beams and timber. Some repairs were made by the government troops, and at the time I became familiar with it, 1869–1871, it was in a ruinous condition except one of the structures, where two companies or troops of soldiers domiciled. But one bastion now remains.

The surgeon with this detachment and myself became intimate. He was an elderly man—much traveled—an epicure and a gourmand; his quarters occupied the entire upper story, and his cuisine abounded with canned stuffs, especially meats, and relishes, spices, flavorings, and pungent condiments, the names of which I do not know. He did his own preparing and used a large chafing dish. He was too much given to eccentricity to find congeniality with his fellow officers but was extremely entertaining to one who was a good listener and who found enjoyment in oddities. There was an attraction in sharing this man's hospitality in that dimly lighted, spacious loft, enclosed with adobe and roofed with ponderous timbering, watching him grope around to find this and that to add to the concoction that bubbled in the chafing dish, talking as he worked, perhaps of some escapade of his in the capitals of Europe or of his amours elsewhere.

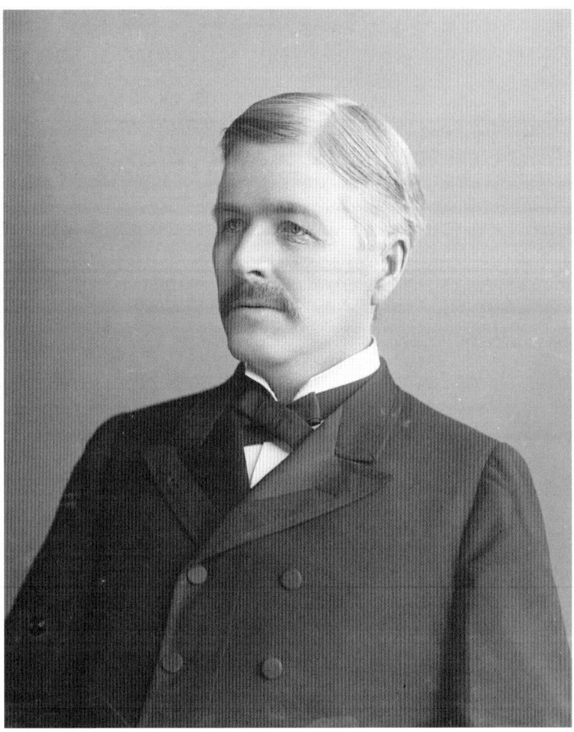

Senator T.C. Power funded Lowell's trading venture with the Crow and Gros Ventre tribes at Camp Cooke at the mouth of the Judith River in the winter of 1870–71. The army abandoned Camp Cooke in 1869, and post traders rebuilt a structure on the grounds and renamed it Fort Claggett, after Lowell's mining partner, William Horace Clagett. The men added an extra G. *C.M. Bell photograph, Library of Congress.*

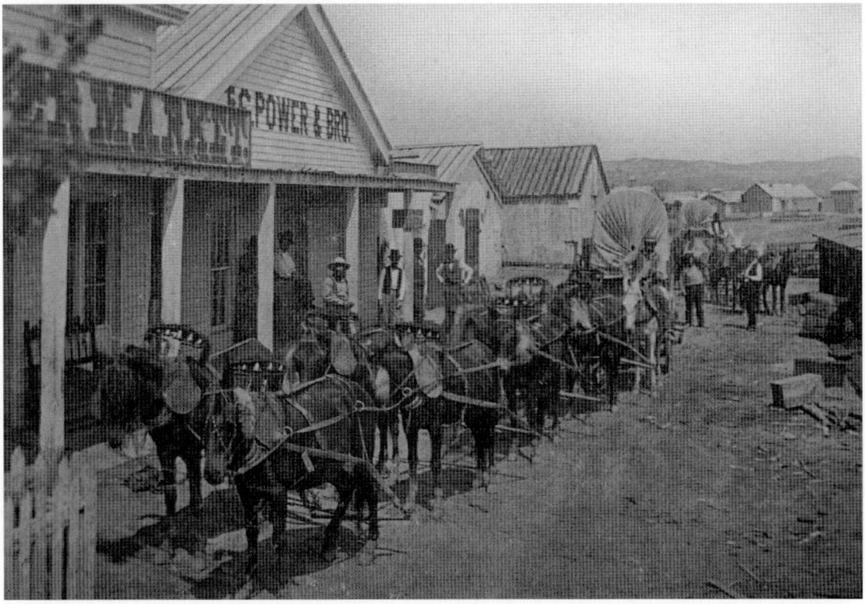

Mule train at T.C. Power's trading company at Benton, circa 1880. *Reproduced by permission from the Merrill G. Burlingame Special Collections of the Montana State University Library–Bozeman.*

INDIAN TRADING AND ADVENTURE

Senator Thomas C. Power, Courtenay's Wood Yard

In November 1870, through Tom C. Power, the merchant at Benton, and afterward, Montana's first senator in Congress, I procured a permit to trade with the Crow and Gros Ventre tribes, then camped about Camp Cooke two hundred miles below Benton on the river. Mr. Power had a trading post at Camp Cooke operated by a Mr. [Joseph Hempstead McKnight] Knight.[71] The point covered by my permit was some distance below his camp, perhaps seventy or eighty miles, at a wood yard owned by one Gordon and partner.[72] I purchased of Mr. Power $1,000 worth of trade material: flour, beads, calico, lead powder, sugar, tea, coffee, and a variety of blankets, which were classed according to size as points, and so marked thus, "11"–"111" points, among other items. And as transport, I built a mackinaw thirty feet in length—with ten-foot beam—having a medium sharp bow, and into this boat was loaded the trade stuff. It was about the middle of November that all was ready to push off from the levee at Benton. We made ready, Gordon and I, for an early start, and the evening before, we went to a billiard hall to play a game. With an awkward move of his cue, Gordon hit the butt against a hanging lamp, breaking it, and in struggling to save it, Gordon got a bad gash slitting across the back of his hand, as if cut with a saber. I sent for Dr. Campbell, who did up his wound. This was a serious misfortune in rendering Gordon so crippled as to throw upon me the oar work of our craft, but delay at that late season was out of the question, and we had to hasten on the long and tedious cruise before the ice formed. We had between two hundred and three hundred miles with a low river that merely moved its current, with night halts moored to the bank; for the passage was not without peril from predatory parties of Indians, and the constantly shifting current required daylight to the most water-wise navigator. Gordon was married, in a fashion, to the daughter of a Gros Ventre chief—the tribe's horse-stealing chief—and was familiar with the Crow and Gros Ventre tongue and sign to some extent. He had come to Benton to get employment of me as interpreter and locate the trade. He had the promise of both Crows and Gros Ventre to give me two or three trades during the winter. We made an early start and, of necessity, slow progress, merely floated with the stream except when the oars were used. The river bends one way or another about every two miles. These stretches are called "points," and frequently, a land walk of a half a mile would be accomplished by water in ten or more miles. We were eternally going and coming back. In course of time, however, we reached one evening "Courtenay's Wood Yard," which was about two miles above Camp Cooke.[73]

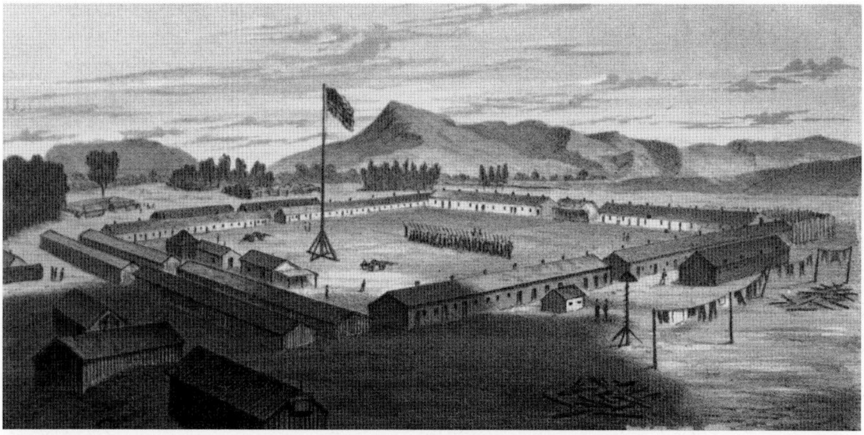

Camp Cooke was Montana's first military post, built in 1866. The fort withstood Sioux attack, but the remote location and rat infestation led to the army's abandoning the post in 1869. *A.E. Matthews drawing reproduced by permission from the Mansfield Library, University of Montana–Missoula.*

There were two reasons for tying up there. Just below Courtenay's was Drowning Man's Rapids, a perilous passage even in the day.[74] Then, we wished to time our passing the Crow Camp so as to avoid the annoyance of the Indian kids who love to experiment in target practice with bow and arrow—in other words, to steal past them in the night with Courtenay as pilot. Besides, it seemed best to lay by a day and rest myself, as I had borne the laboring oar.

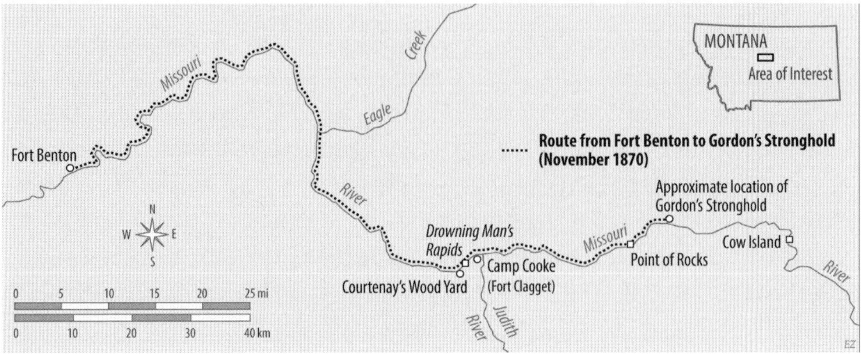

Map by Ezra Zeitler.

I was well acquainted with Courtenay, and our trading goods were removed to a log cabin adjoining the one he occupied. Hearty cheer awaited us under cover with buffalo tongues, and a capital bread of Courtenay's making met our hungry eye. It was commonly reputed on the river—and not denied, but so stated to me by Courtenay—that he was a younger son of an English lord, but to see him that night, you would say that he had just stepped out of the blessed story book of Robinson Crusoe, bearded, bronzed, and hardened. Clad with animal hide—his hairy and peaked skin cap—all that was needed was a man Friday to fill out the picture. Inside was neatness and thorough housekeeping. On shelves were books in plenty on topics philosophical, polemic, scientific, travel, and history, and this short, stocky, red-headed gentleman was furnishing wood to the steamboats that plied the river at this point and wrestling with the solitude of a wilderness.

We staid over till the following night and yearned to stay longer, but December was near at hand, and ice began to thinly form on the river edge. Our plan to pass the Drowning Man's Rapids was laid to accomplish two things: to get past the Gros Ventre camp just below the rapids—and quietly. Now Gordon's squaw was in that camp, and we had gotten word to her to get across the river, and Gordon would meet her—he going from Courtenay's afoot for that purpose. This left the management of the mackinaw to Courtenay and me. A little before midnight, with Courtenay as pilot and I as oarsman, we pushed out into the stream and soon were nearing the roaring, rock-bedded swirl of waters. Whether because of the dark, or because he lost his head, at any rate, Courtenay had the boat centered upon a rock and impaled there. I looked to see the thing break in two. Giving Courtenay an oar, I got out into the water and found a footing, and by our united working, the boat was made afloat, but our gladness was to suffer another shock, for instead of keeping the channel, Courtenay had run us down a chute—that is, the wrong side of a sand bar. As soon as we discovered this mistake, we pulled to the shore, and now we had some work. The boat had to be towed up (you couldn't row it against the stream) and so far up that we could head off the bar. When this was done, with bow toward the other shore, some hard pulling at the oar was the next caper, and rounding the bar, we dropped into the channel and, presently, were in sight of the fires of Camp Cooke.

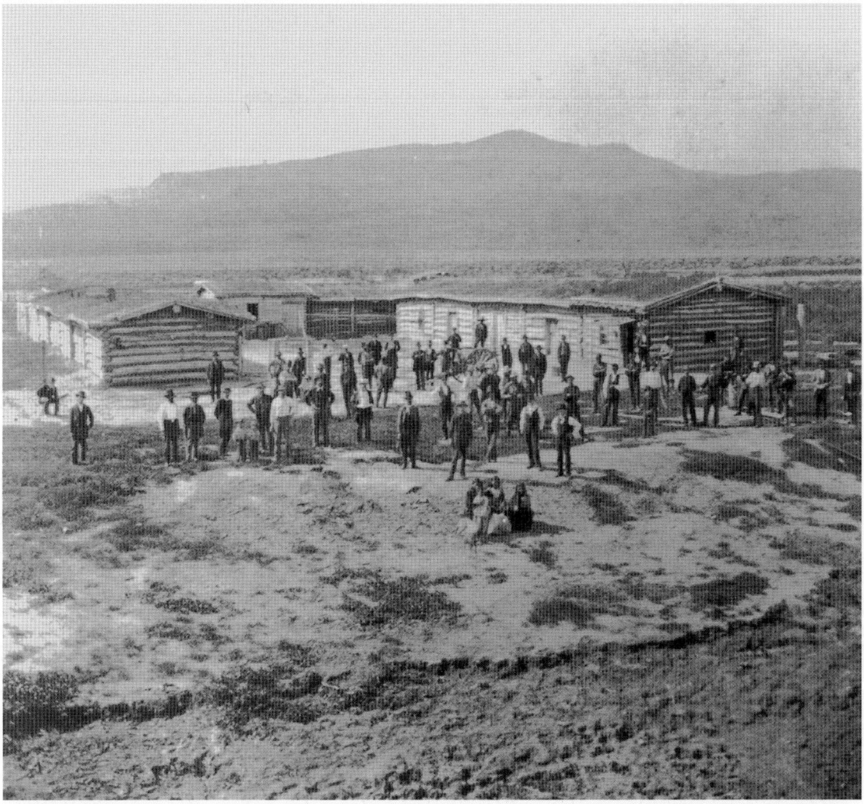

Fort Claggett, built on the site of the abandoned Camp Cooke at the mouth of the Judith River, served as a T.C. Power & Son trading post manned by James H. McKnight in the winter of 1870–71, when Lowell was there. *Reproduced by permission from the Overholser Historical Research Center, Fort Benton, Montana.*

A thousand dogs set up a chorus as we slid along, and the camp became animated. The fires were stirred up and rekindled, and concealment was impossible. The wolves set out to outdo the dogs, and with this serenade, we passed around a bend and shortly pointed into a cove in response to Gordon's invitation. There we moored up for the night, or rather till morn, for it was nearly the latter, as I pulled off my breeches and wrung out some zero moisture and shivered in a blanket the night out. Gordon had become pretty alarmed at our delayed appearance and, leaving his squaw, had gone up the river dreading but we had met our fate in the rapids and had spied us by the light of the camp, safe and afloat. Courtenay bade us goodbye and made for his wood yard, considerably crestfallen, for I had by no means spared him for his blunders. After all our precautions, some red chaps were with us as we left in the morning, and some young urchins let fly a few arrows at us for pastime as we glided towards Cow Island. The nights now grew colder and ice formation more pronounced, and we hastened to the limit of endurance. The last night of our journey we went by the stream with Gordon, now familiar with the water—at the tiller.

GORDON'S STRONGHOLD

The Sioux, Assiniboine Sioux, claimed by frequent visitation dominion here. Gordon had a partner, and they together had made provision against attack. There were three heavy log structures connected together and formed an L. One was a living room and quite large, one was the private room of Gordon and squaw, the other was for tools and to hang meat in; the living room on one side had three bunks. On the opposite side [stood] a huge stone fireplace, here we lived, cooked, and housed, and Gordon's partner and I slept here. This house plant was some five or six rods from the edge of a bank that descended sharply to the river's edge a distance of some forty or fifty feet, so precipitous that a pathway tobogganed obliquely to the water below. Inside the living room was a trapdoor; beneath it was an excavation about waist deep to a floor of soil, thence another drop that led into an open passage that zigzagged to a chamber some ten feet square. Here a cross-planked massive door opened out a little above high-water mark of the river. A hole had been dug in the soil floor of the chamber down to water to be used as a well. The room was supplied with jerked or dried meat and hung in festoons from the cribbing. There was kept there bread, which was replenished when staled, other stuff in cans and ready for use without cooking; stretching from the chamber to the landing at the trapdoor was a fuse kept in place and ready for business. If required, a keg of gunpowder was also stationed where it could quickly be placed on the said landing. The devious passage presented any probable inconvenience to an occupant of the chamber further that what little smoke might circulate riverward. It may be surmised that should the enemy gain entrance to the cabins, or be reasonably near to them, the explosion of a good-sized keg of powder—enough to shatter the structures—would be injurious to such enemy. In the cabin where the tools etc. were kept, there was hung up a good many animals skinned and quartered; there was choice, young, fat buffalo, white and black tail deer, antelope, elk, and bear, and it was the practice to keep a quantity of bread on hand for emergency. We were well armed. Gordon and partner had each a Henry and a Colt rifle. I had a Spencer. I don't know how many revolvers completed the armament. I am disposed to say right here how vain this preparation turned out to be, for the winter following, Gordon and partner (whose name has escaped me)[75] were both caught out of this stronghold and tortured and scalped. What became of Ca-but the squaw I never learned, but old John Gordon, who was a merchant in Holton [Kansas] for so many years, was, I discovered, an uncle to my Interpreter, and he related to me the facts of his nephew and partner as above stated. This squaw, Ca-but, had been taught by Gordon to speak our language some. He was as devoted to her as any man to his wife that I have observed. Here is the romance:

Ca-but

The name means in Gros Ventre "I walk," or "to walk," or "walk." Like many other Indian utterance to express an idea, it is comprehensive of many phases. She was born on the train while the camp was moving; her mother was afoot in the file, hence the name. She was quite short and very comely in comparison with others of her kind. The previous winter, her father had led a horse-stealing party out of Camp Cooke and wandered down the river twenty miles below our posts to Point of Rocks, a little collection of Wolfers cabins, where Ca-but, who had been taken along, got sick, and the party returned to Camp Cooke without her. When she thought she was able, she undertook to return to Cooke alone, and on the way, while crossing a trail, she was overhauled by sixteen (so she says) Indians, of what tribe she did not know, who were out for some devilment. One after another ravished her; as she supposes, the whole party had a hand. When she regained her reason, her pony was gone, but plucking up, she made her way up the river and, in the night, sunk down at the door

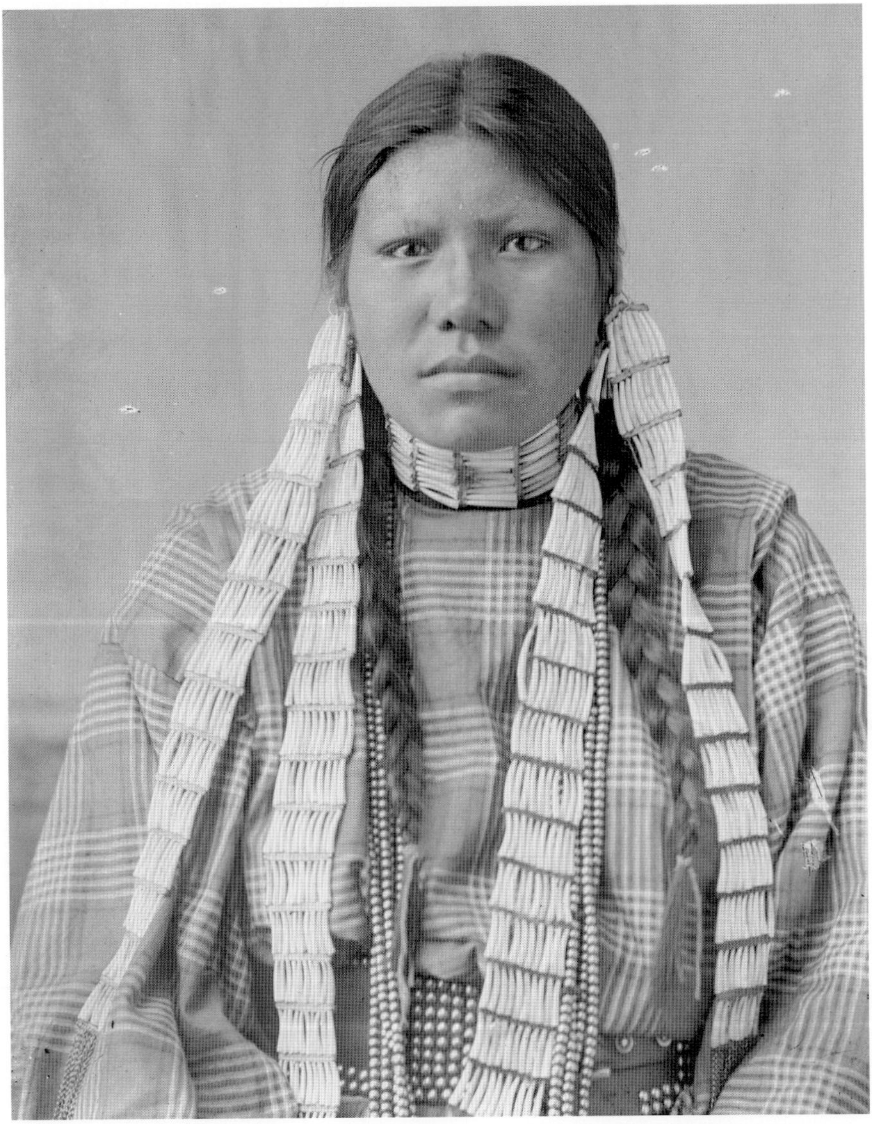

Unidentified Crow woman, 1880s. *D.F. Barry photo reproduced by permission from the Denver Digital Library.*

of Gordon, who discovered her and took her in and nursed her to health. She forsook her people and made a companion to Gordon. She was handy about the household, quick to pick up our ways, and it was a pleasure to drill her to speak our way.

Editor's Note

In a letter written less than a year before Lowell's trade, Lieutenant General Philip H. Sheridan argued for government assistance for the very same River Crow and Gros Ventre people. Famous for his brutal suppression of native tribes, in this instance, Sheridan champions their cause:

Headquarters Military Division of the Missouri.
Chicago, Ill., July 1st. 1870.
Bvt. Major General E.D. Townsend.
Adjutant General U.S. Army.
Washington, D.C.

General:

In passing down the Missouri river, I met a band of the River-Crows, and feel it incumbent on me, if for no other consideration than that of humanity, to represent the condition of this tribe to the Government. They have always been friendly, and on that account have been legitimate prey for the Sioux on one side, the Blackfeet, and the roaming bands of Yancton Sioux on the other, until there is but little security left for them. They receive scarcely anything from the Government either in the way of support or protection, and the burden of their complaints is that they are being killed off by hostile Indians because they will not kill white people.

They should be placed on a good reservation at some point along the Missouri, or a little South of it, at the Judith Mountains, and well fed. They are broken down and can be easily managed—the difference between a broken down Indian and a wild one is the difference between a wild horse and one broken to work.

The Gros Ventres of the prairie, another small band, have been driven in to Bear Paw Mountains by a war band of Yanctons from Fort Randall, assisted by the Santee Sioux from Lake Winnipeg, who now hold the Milk River country.

These Gros Ventres have never killed a white man, and war is now made upon them for that reason. They have a Mr. [Henry W.] *Reed for an Agent, who holds forth at Fort Browning on the Milk river, who does all he can, and seems to be a good man, but has not the means to do much for them. They should be located on some permanent reservation where they could be protected. The burden of their complaints is the same and that of the River Crows, that they are all being killed off because they are friendly.*

Very respectfully,
Your obedient servant,
[Signed] *P.H. Sheridan*
Lieut. General.
Adjutant General's Office.
Washington, July 8, 1870.

Official copy respectfully furnished for the information of the Commissioner of Indian Affairs.
Thomas M. Vincent
Asst. Adjutant General[76]

A FEAST AND A TRADE

Revenge, Murder, and Siege at Camp Cooke

The Sioux were active that winter, and word reached us of several having been caught out had received the usual torture and fate. These tidings coming from Point of Rocks and still further down the river had become known at Camp Cooke, and the promised trade at my post was consequently postponed. Meanwhile, there was nothing to do but make excursions for game. It was very plentiful, and our ammunition was therefore spared for choice specimens. I frequently went alone, and on no occasion was there absence of the creatures; indeed, from the low level that stretched way from our post, but up and down river, we could always see on the mountainsides buffalo and often elk and deer, and antelope were in evidence everywhere. A severe storm of winds and snow brought at one time to our very door antelope in countless numbers. They swarmed along, heedless of our presence, and crowded our buildings as they moved along the low level. We shot quite a lot of them and secured the fattest for our larder. At another time, we three were out and corralled several black tail deer on an island in the river and got them as they took the ice to escape the pursuit. All this game-getting was in anticipation of a trade. On one hunt, Gordon brought in a wildcat that we carefully skinned and stuffed and put on a crossbeam of the living room in crouching attitude, but it became such a terror to a huge domestic cat of Ca-but's that she took it out of sight.

One morning, I took a pail and went down the path to the river for water. On my return up, I raised my head on reaching the crest of the bank to look into the eyes of a mounted Indian, hardly two steps away. For an instant, I thought it was "Good bye John" Sioux! I said, "How" and leisurely moved toward the home. Inasmuch as I got there alive, it dawned upon me that this was the advance agent of my Indians, and so it proved to be. Gordon and partner were out, and I called Ca-but, who knew our visitor, and found out that one hundred strong of mixed Crow and Gros Ventre were en route and due to arrive an hour to sunset.[77] Before they arrive, I will remark that there is but one thing to do at the start with Indians, and that is to make them believe that you are Master, however timid you might be and however you are shocked when you encounter them suddenly. It was Hamlet who appealed to his mother to "Assume a virtue if you have it not." An Indian will respect firmness and decision and seize upon the least sign of timidity and take advantage of it. It is then all over with you. It is better to risk offense than to incur their derision.

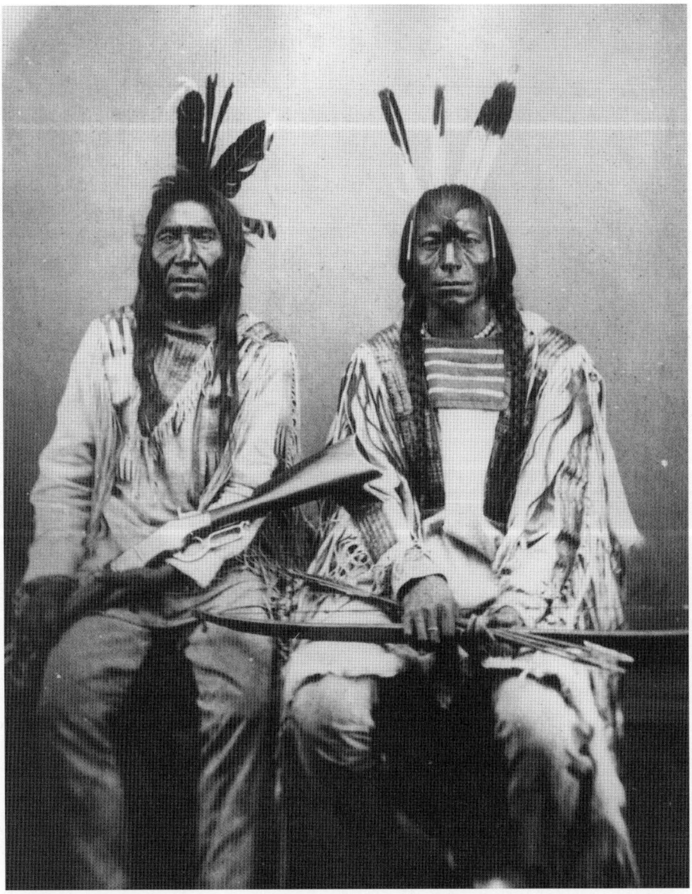

Atsina (Gros Ventre) chiefs, 1872. *Reproduced by permission from the Denver Public Library, X-30959.*

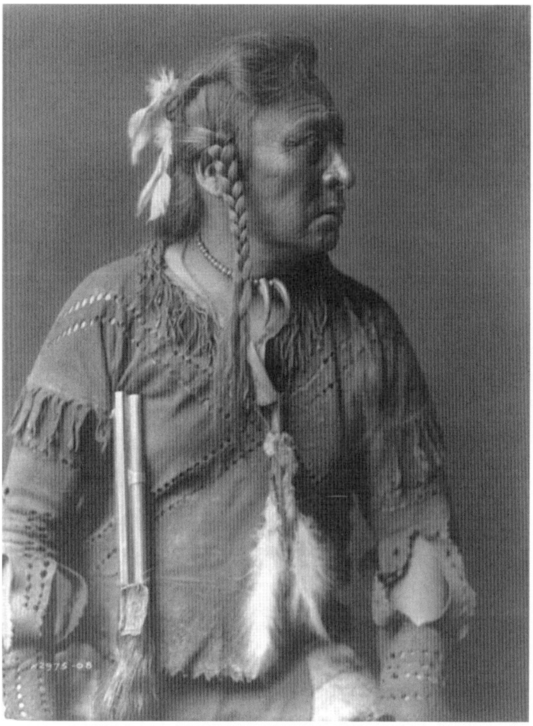

Left: Horse Capture, Atsina (Gros Ventre). A famous horse-stealing chief of the period in Montana. Possibly the father or grandfather of Ca-but. *Edward S. Curtis photo, Library of Congress.*

Below: Moving camp–Atsina (Gros Ventre). *Edward S. Curtis photo, 1908, Library of Congress.*

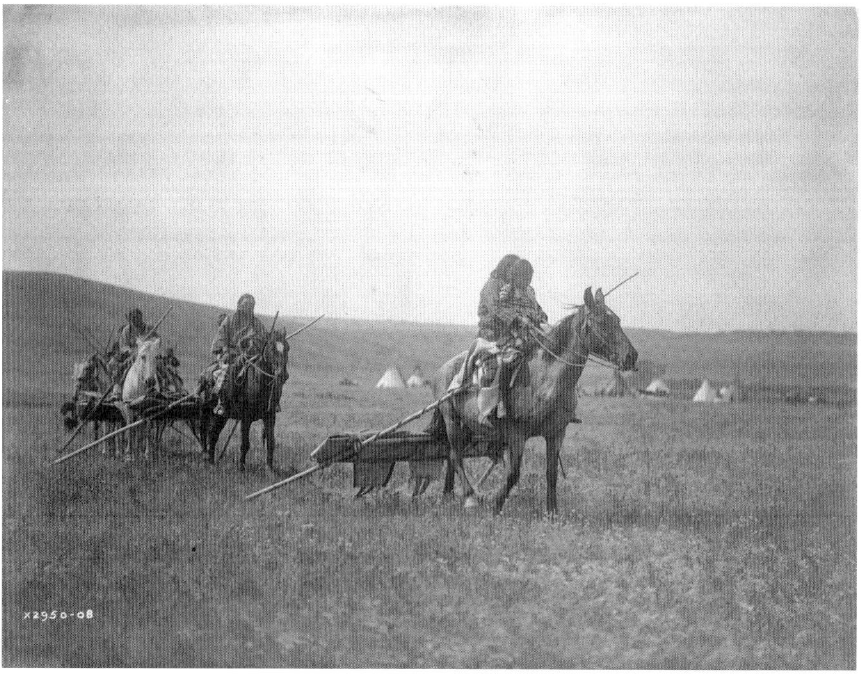

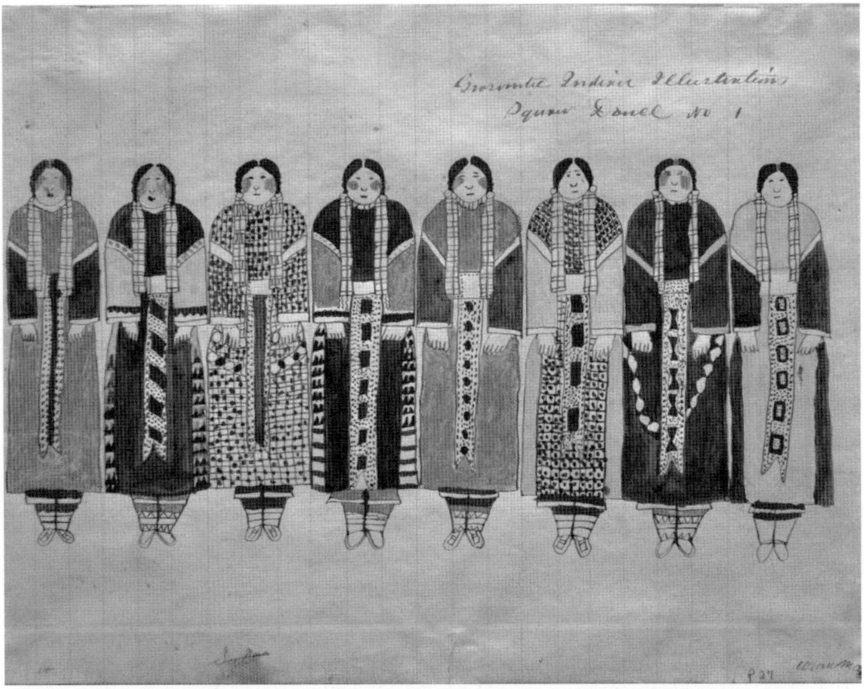

"Gros Ventre Women at a Dance," ledger drawing by Gros Ventre artist New Bear, 1883, Crow Agency, Montana. *Reproduced by permission from Montana State University–Billings Library Special Collections, Charles H. Barstow Collection, 1930.66.*

Gordon returned from his wolf traps before the visitors swarmed in, and preparations for their reception were hurried up. They made quite a racket and helped as they bore down upon us, Ca-but's father in advance—a tall, splendid specimen—and bearing himself like a cavalier.

He was followed by a motley crowd of bucks, squaws, and papooses; the latter on travois trailed in, chattering like magpies. "How-Ha," shouted the leader, and the bucks alighted. The squaws jumped to the ground and, with the younger ones, proceeded quickly to make camp. A few of the more prominent gave their reins to the squaws and boys and, in state, approached headquarters and impudently advanced as if to crowd into the cabin. But they found the line drawn, and Ca-but's father was only allowed in. This discipline had a good effect to start with and taught them their place. They were told, however, that later on we might invite a few others in. Meanwhile, the squaws were busy. It is usual for the older to both strike and raise the teepee. In taking them down, they dismantle the tent poles, wrench them out of their earth sockets and lash them, two on a side, to a subdued pony;

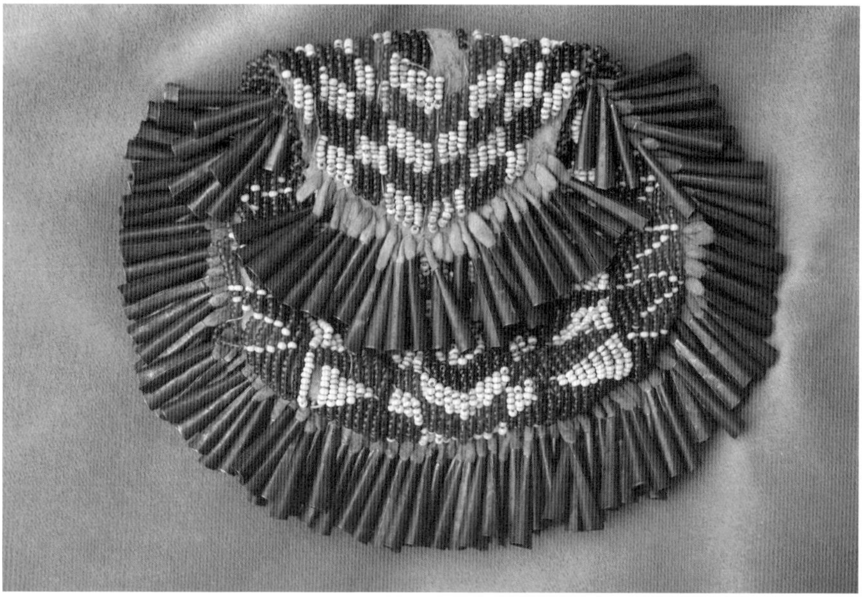

Pouch collected by Lowell possibly used for carrying flints. Anthropologist Tim McCleary, former chief historian at the Little Bighorn Battlefield National Monument, identified the origin as possibly Apache. *Author's collection.*

the folded tent cover is fastened between the poles makes a comfortable nest for the enfeebled or infantile and for the rawhide packs. To strike teepees is simply to undo this, and the ease of changing, and acquiring a domicile is done. This done, and the squaws primped up—with brushed and braided locks, painted faces, dressed in their best gear—the open universe their toilet room, and each other's eye their mirror.[78]

Shells, beads, and feathers are the finery. The young bucks were resplendent in embroidered leggings and shirts, with ornaments glittering in their braided scalp locks, snapping necklaces, and ear pendants. High Priests of Nature! An indispensable preliminary to a trade is the feast. Meal mush and molasses makes up the first course. Meal is furnished by the squaws, who cook it in their pots; when ready, a parade of tin plates is sent out to them, which, with the spoons, they are privileged to keep as souvenirs. Meats also are produced in abundance and variety, for there is huge feeding going on with the dilating powers of an anaconda. The rite was one prolonged festival. Inside, as guests, were a half dozen of them, a few of the elder, and the balance were the beaux-painted and in their best attire who sang songs of love and war and who carried their hijinks to the utmost limits.

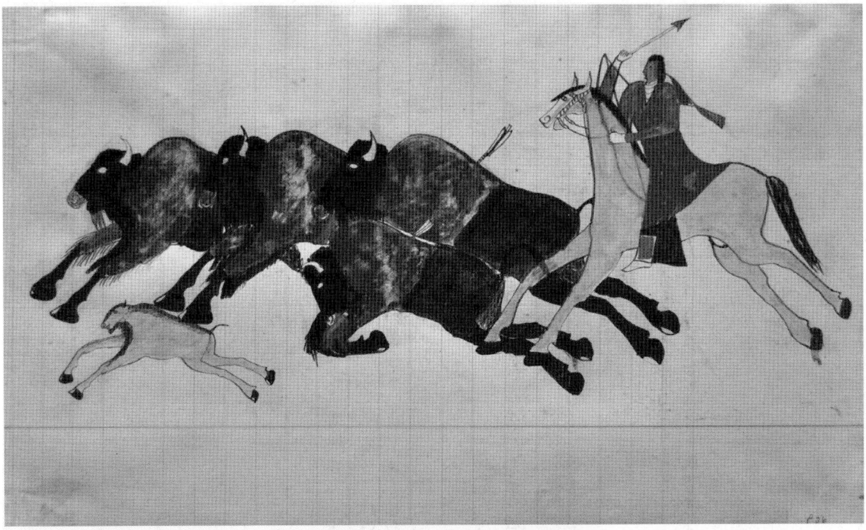

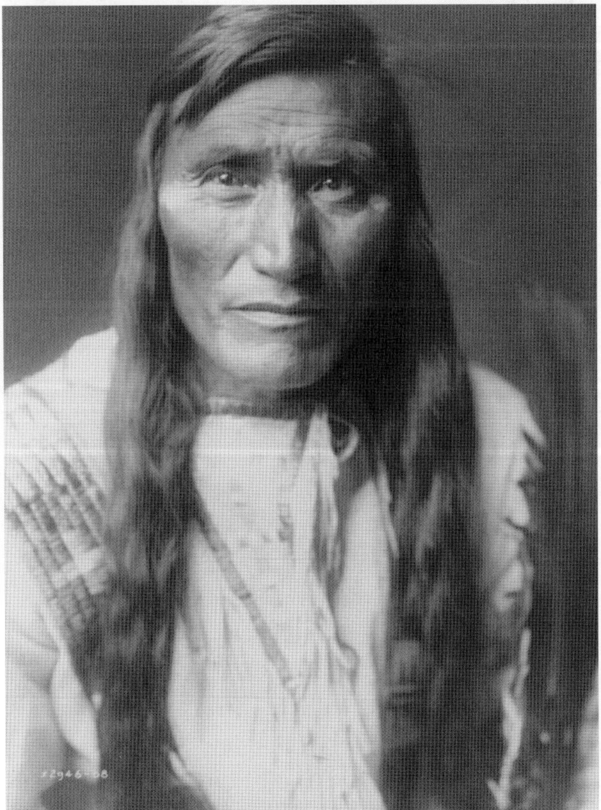

Above: "Indian Chasing a Buffalo," ledger drawing by Gros Ventre artist New Bear, 1883, Crow Agency, Montana. *Reproduced by permission from Montana State University–Billings Library Special Collections, Charles H. Barstow Collection, 1930.60.*

Left: Portrait of Atsina (Gros Ventre), Montana. *Edward S. Curtis photo, 1908, Library of Congress.*

One night, I have forgotten which, we had a buck who, with his tools, painted figures on a fine robe. These figures of horsemen in repose, or in action, may commemorate some drama or event in the life of the artist; the style is as distinctive as are Chinese pictures. There is little perspective, and the allegory needs an interpreter to catch the meaning, but an Indian will make a long and sometimes dramatic incident out of a small amount of scenery. It seems that Gordon had intimated to this buck that I could draw pictures and accounts for his asking me to make a horse. I thought I did a pretty good job for him, and it was hard to understand why he should treat the effort with such scorn and derision.

If this writing were not a recital of events current during a period of early pioneering in the great territory of Montana personal to myself, I would be tempted to enlarge upon some of the characteristics of these children of nature. Not as seen in reservations, but in the free air of their native dominions. His teepee is as much his castle as is the house of any white man, with the difference that it is without locks or keys. It is of importance in estimating or contrasting his character to remember there is an entire lack of privacy in the household, open at all times to the searchlight of observation. There is no concealment of follies, methods, criticism, and ridicule, which are a common privilege, and it is very self-evident that out of these traits has grown the self-restraint and reserve so often taken as sullenness. They live upon the ground, sitting, sleeping, and eating there. By deep-rooted custom, they have each their place in the family group. They so pitch their tents as the entry will be easterly—a visitor should always turn to the right entering a lodge, and if a guest, he will take his seat opposite the opening. Nothing is owned in common, and each is respected in his ownership. The bucks sit upon their heels or cross-legged—not so the squaws. She sits sideways, gathering her feet well under her, and thus makes a broad, smooth lap. It is a good point in etiquette to rise without touching hand to the ground. The cradleboard is about eight inches wide and nearly thirty inches long, covered with a layer of some soft skin or calico. When asleep, the papoose's arms are under cover, when awake, released.

I was very anxious to have a good trade with the Indians, but Gordon told me to not manifest anything of that sort or they would best me at the game. A long table or counter was stretched from side to side of the living room, and the fracas began. Such traders! You hardly knew how to take them. One thing especially is to keep in mind—to deal, as the populists talk, "special privileges to none." We found out that one got a brighter tin plate at the feast than another and one missed getting a spoon; hence, we had been partial,

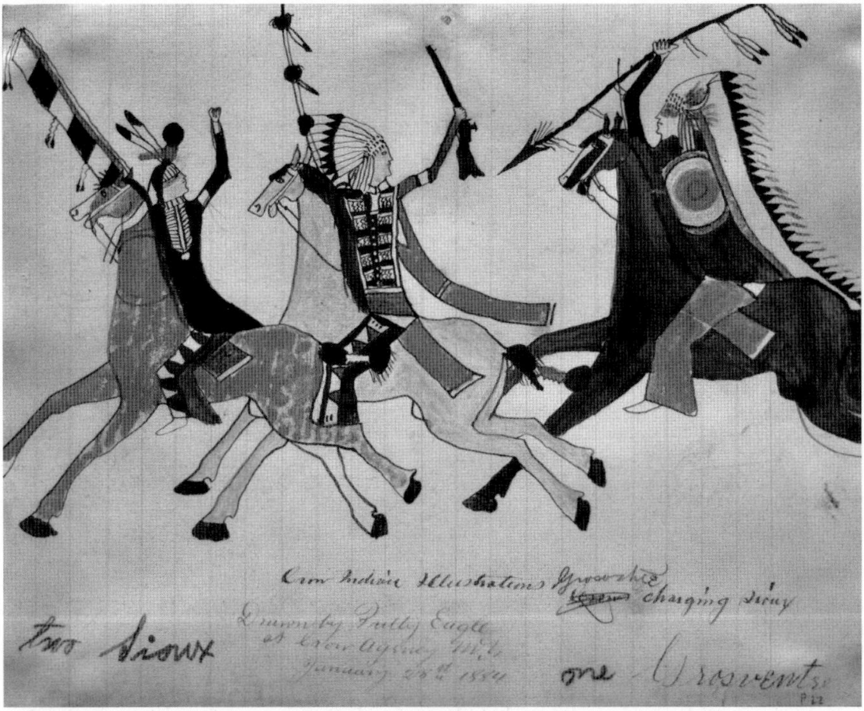

War record drawing with handwritten caption: The word Crow is crossed out, Gros Ventre is penciled in, charging Sioux (written in a different hand), two Sioux, one Gros Ventre. Ledger drawing by Pretty Eagle, 1884, Crow Agency, Montana. *Reproduced by permission from Montana State University–Billings Library Special Collections, Charles H. Barstow Collection, 1930.37.*

and a sulky trader was the result. The most surprising grounds of complaint had to be met, and they would yield neither to evidence nor reason. At times, it was desperate, but for three days, the trade went merrily on.

It collapsed when an outrider came in with "sign" that the Sioux were on the warpath down the river. The striking of teepees and a hasty bolt for Camp Cook [Cooke] followed. The nomadic gathering about the Post dispersed in panicky haste at the ominous word, Sioux, and left it to an interval of solitude and inaction; the robes and peltries were baled and stored away to await the downriver navigation the following season. I went down to "Point of Rocks" to stay a bit with the trader there and found it true that the Sioux had visited that vicinity. Three wolfers were caught out but a little way from the Post, stripped naked, and tortured, apparently while alive, by cutting their members, which were found in their mouths. The post-atrocity was quilling the bodies with arrows.

While at this place, the days were given to hunting and buffalo killing Indian fashion, by running with the herds. Farther down the river was a small settlement composed of wolfers and woodyard men named Copperopolis, where, the year before, was enacted the following incident, and this tragedy will explain, probably, the excess of demonism practiced upon the three wolfers above mentioned, as well as upon many another that winter and since. These cabins were built upon a considerable elevation sharply rising almost perpendicular from the river's edge. These venturesome denizens were driven to the most alert measure to maintain their footing in that rich field for wolves, and one morning, one of them came in from downriver in a hurry with tidings that a war party was coming up and that he had retreated to camp unobserved. An ingenious plan was formed and carried out to do business with these redskins. Leaving their animals and everything else, they went in a body upriver to a "point," crossed on the ice, and, under cover, retraced in parallel back to opposite their belongings and deployed, hid from view and on their bellies, awaited the visitors. There was a cut and graded foot walk leading from the river edge up the mentioned bank. Below this walk, the river had washed the bank during the high water so that it had become straight up and down and, at intervals, had washed recesses that took the form of small caverns. The Indians' plan was to make the footway and rush the camp, climbing up and falling onto the surprised victims. It was a case on both sides of consummate strategy. Ten or twelve whites were of the one party, and the forty or more Indians carried out their plans so far as to reach the footway—none of whom, however, escaped the deadly aim of those toughened pioneers, who soon reduced their enemy to a few crouching in the shallow caverns. These found brief asylum there, but the slayers did not stop there. The brute instinct that quickens with the spilling of blood of (especially) a hated and ruthless foe was given vent by beheading their victims, boiling till the skull was unclothed, and taking them to a point down the river a few miles, where these skulls were ranged along the huge trunk of a fallen tree and there left. Later on, a wolfer going to the place discovered aside each skull a pair of papoose moccasins. The significance of this act of the Indians can as well be imagined as told.[79] One purpose, the main one, in visiting Point of Rocks, was to get an idea regarding the future purposes of the Sioux from the people there. The killing of the three men mentioned showed that the tribe was active and their designs unfathomable, but nevertheless, on returning to my post, I sent word to Camp Cooke that the way was clear for a safe trade, but it was unavailing. A few weeks were spent in the house routine, when an incident happened to change the order of things and break routine and monotony into little bits.

A burly wolfer of Point of Rocks went to Camp Cooke to get a squaw wife and, after much banter, bargained for the daughter of a chief named Lone Tree. She was quite young and immature, but he took her to Point of Rocks and established her in his cabin. Her immaturity brought on trouble, and presently, he kicked her out one night in the cold. She found a way to get to her home at Camp Cooke, and a wrathy father and his brother together went to Point of Rocks and, after boozing up late at night, broke in the door of the son-in-law and entered, single file—Lone Tree behind. His brother was armed with an axe that broke in the door and was holding it uplifted. The wolfer was in bed, but he had apparently mistrusted the errand of his assailants, for he immediately fired a gun; the bullet passed through both arms of the axe holder and thence through Lone Tree, who expired almost at once. I think I have stated that the post trader there was operating a branch of the Camp Cooke Post [McKnight]. He saw at once how serious a trouble this affair would produce and, loading up his stores in two wagons, started for Camp Cooke via the ice-covered river, reached my post the first evening, bringing along the "remains" of Lone Tree and also his brother. They spent the night with me. Dressing the wounds of the brother, I observed and he demonstrated just how he held the axes to be hurt so curiously.[80]

It was now February 1871. The previous year, I had been elected County Assessor of Choteau County, and my duties began March 1st, so I made hasty preparations to go with the party to Camp Cooke on my way to Benton. I had to be there, trouble or no trouble—and surely it looked like trouble—toting an Indian chief, cold, right to his teepee and relatives, but no other way was open. A number of Indians and one old French Voyageur were with the party. I found the old Frenchman (he said he was one hundred years old) entertaining, and we rode together our horses during the slow trip. As we neared the camp, I asked my companion if he had any suggestion to make as to how we should enter the camp. We discussed the matter, for we both thought it a very serious situation. The result was that when about five or six miles of camp, I pushed rapidly on ahead and rode to the stockade, where I saw McKnight. "There is serious trouble, let us put things in defensive attitude." Without a word, McKnight gave the necessary orders; the bales of blankets were ranged along the interior uprights of the stockade, rifles were mustered, and a quiet putting of things in order commenced. Meanwhile, I told enough to the force to explain the situation. When the wagons drove quickly up, in a jiffy, we had them unloaded and turned our animals over to some kids to take to the herds. The massive doors of the stockade slammed to and were bolted when the music began.

I looked through the peepholes to witness the drama now coming to a head. A thousand figures burst out from the lodges, as the wail of squaws proclaimed their bereavement. Mingled with lamentations were the shouts rising to war cries, while the orators strode along the avenues between the lodges toning up the anger and savage excitement of the multitude. Male and female, young and old joined in the orgies, soon made hideous by the flames of burning teepees of the relatives of the dead chief. One, at least, of the squaws slashed her breasts and arms with a knife; others piled upon the flames the furnishings of the destroyed teepees, and from their gestures, it was plain to see that the nine men garrisoned within the stockade were marked, in their unreasoning wrath, as an avenging sacrifice. "They are going to attack us, they are going to fire on us," so said Jim Fox, the interpreter. Now Fox was an adopted Crow and had lived with the tribe since boyhood. The transforming effect of climate and nomadic life, with its exposures and vicissitudes, had made Fox over into an Indian. He claimed to be a brother of the Fox sisters who made such notoriety in the world as spiritualists and mediums. The warning he gave put us all on a war footing. All had the Henry rifle, except I bore a Spencer. A number of rushes were made, and the stout timbers of the stockade clattered with the punt of bullets. This, and the pandemonium of the enraged assaulters, continued for a while, but no shot was returned; we simply bided our time, being reasonably well protected. Besides, it became evident that a few old heads were venturing to counsel the younger element against such hostility, and by night, the tumult had quieted considerably. It was a sleepless night for besiegers and besieged; the former was in constant harangue, and the rise and fall of their conference indicated the state of their pulse as a whole.

It was towards morning and during a lull in the ceremonies that McKnight asked Fox to go out and call for a peace; Fox hesitated and sat silent. McKnight ordered the bolts drawn and, without a word, in a moment, stood outside in the glare of the huge fires that lit up the scene and loudly spoke to the surprised audience that stretched to a distance into the darkness, inviting to a peace council a few of the old counselors, and returned inside the stockade. It was only after a second like invitation, more determined in language (for he could talk their speech), that three old men were admitted. They told of their own friendship and of the difficulty of

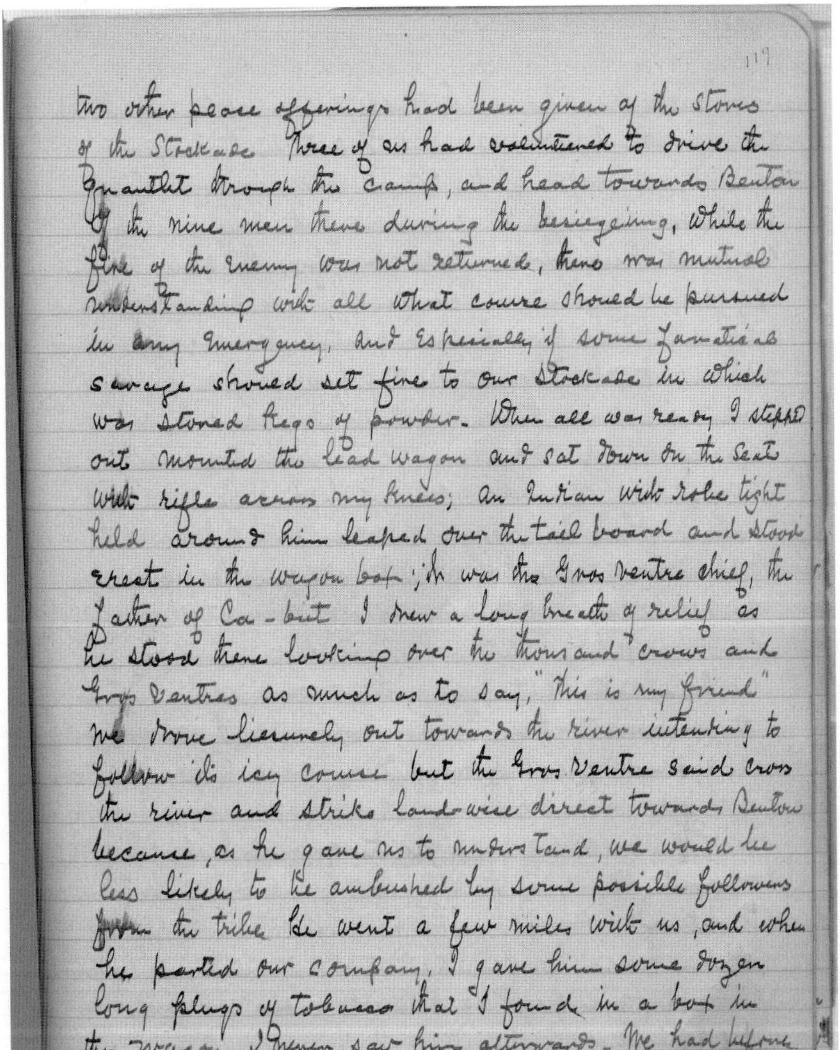

119

two other peace offerings had been given of the stores of the Stockade. Three of us had volunteered to drive the gauntlet through the camp, and head towards Benton of the nine men there during the besiegeing, While the fire of the enemy was not returned, there was mutual understanding with all What course should be pursued in any Emergency, and Especially if some fanatical savage should set fire to our Stockade in which was stored kegs of powder. When all was ready I stepped out mounted the lead wagon and sat down on the seat with rifle across my knees; an Indian with robe tight held around him leaped over the tail board and stood erect in the wagon box; it was the Gros Ventre chief, the father of Ca-but I drew a long breath of relief as he stood there looking over the thousand crows and Gros Ventres as much as to say, "this is my friend" we drove leisurely out towards the river intending to follow its icy course but the Gros Ventre said cross the river and strike landwise direct towards Benton because, as he gave us to understand, we would be less likely to be ambushed by some possible followers from the tribe He went a few miles with us, and when he parted our company, I gave him some dozen long plugs of tobacco that I found in a box in the wagon. I never saw him afterwards. We had before

Lowell manuscript, page 119.

controlling the young bucks, that the relatives of Lone Tree had destroyed all their belongings, that the time was not ripe to appease the vengeful spirit that was kept alive by their orators. Nevertheless, McKnight promised to bestow a peace offering from the store of trading material to show our good will and sent the old men out to work a quietude in the camp. The offering was given, and during the following day, the demonstrations of hostility subsided so that at about midafternoon, we secured some young kids to get our animals from the herd and hitch up our two wagons. Meanwhile, two other peace offerings had been given of the stores of the stockade. Three of us had volunteered to drive the gauntlet through the camp and head towards Benton. Of the nine men there during the besieging, while the fire of the enemy was not returned, there was mutual understanding what course should be pursued in any emergency—especially if some fanatical savage should set fire to our stockade, in which were stored kegs of powder.

When all was ready, I stepped out, mounted the lead wagon, and sat down on the seat with rifle across my knees. An Indian with robe tightly held around him then leaped over the tailboard and stood crest in the wagon box; it was the Gros Ventre Chief, the Father of Ca-but! I drew a long breath of relief as he stood there looking over the thousand Crows and Gros Ventres, as much as to say, "This is my friend." We drove leisurely out towards the river intending to follow its icy course, but the Gros Ventre said to cross the river and strike land-wise direct towards Benton, because, as he gave us to understand, we would be less likely to be ambushed by some possible followers from the tribe. He went a few miles with us, and when he parted our company, I gave him some dozen long plugs of tobacco that I found in a box in the wagon. I never saw him afterwards.

We had before us a cold ride. It was the coldest day of that Northern latitude. We had robes, and I sat in the wagon box wrapped up in them. The drivers were also robe clad. There was snow on the ground, and the day was waning. We had to keep far enough away from the river to head off the ravines that continually ran laterally toward the great river from the High Plateau divide. Night came on, and the three great buttes far away on our right loomed up in the clear atmosphere. The North Star guided us, but the snow deceived us. We were trying to gain Eagle Creek, descend it, and rest at a cabin where the creek empties into the river; the intensity of the cold threatened to overpower us ere we could reach that haven. Its effects were telling on the drivers; it penetrated the hides that covered us, for we had eaten little, and nothing warm, during our imprisonment. The snow hid from view the unevenness of ground ahead of us, and our animals plunged down into a V-shaped ravine before we were aware of the mistake in our course. As the animals leaped up the opposite bank of the ravine, I jumped out in time to let into my place the following team of horses, whose hoofs tore in splinters the tail board of my wagon, and there we came to a sudden stop. We extricated the beasts from the wagons, tied them to the wheels, and huddled all three under robes in the lead wagon—there we constantly rubbed ourselves, for we were benumbed, and the drivers were frozen in parts, fingers and toes—keeping one another awake till the morning in as good natured a way as we could. We were up early and out. I went to the head of the ravine to see our bearings and found that the next ravine was Eagle Creek. We had made the mistake of bearing a few rods too near the direction of the river. We managed somehow to work our caravan out and rounded the head of and then down Eagle Creek to the cabin.

Singularly, we had taken along no provisions when we left McKnight's, the excitement of leaving had blinded every other consideration, but in a box in one of the wagons we found some coffee, the skins of bacon, and some crumbs of cracker, out of which a banquet was prepared that surpassed, and surpasses the memory of, all later festivities. "A passage perilous maketh a port pleasant." We now took a spin on the river but soon wearied of its windings and roundings and left it for the more direct trail of the plateau. Here we encountered the famous big herd of buffaloes stampeding southeasterly, of which Colonel R.I. Dodge speaks in his masterly book on the Indian.[81] The big herd of 1871, which he guessed to number four million—a mere guess certain it is. We drove amidst it the entire day, an opening as we advanced, closing in our rear; at no time during this passage of hours but a hundred guns could have laid low as many of these beasts, and but a few rods at most from the muzzle heading they traveled. The beats of hoofs dinned the air like subdued thunder, the strong jamming the weary, the hale trampling the weak; the calves were hurled hither and thither as if it was a tournament of battledore and shuttlecock. At that season, the excess of hair, with great numbers of them had bunched about the horns, so veiled the eye as to entirely obscure sight. Our immunity, however, was assured, as these brutes with lowered head and nose to the ground easily scented our presence and veered aside as we came on.

From here to Benton we fared well, reaching at night a wood yard on the river where provisions were plentiful and there was a bunk to sleep in. Stopping at the fort below Benton, we reported to the commanding officer of the conditions at McKnight's, and a troop was sent there to find things quieted down. The storm had passed, and a quiet prevailed in the Crow community, born of the fear of Uncle Sam's troops.

I have heard that the following winter, the predatory Sioux dispersed this camp and that McKnight was a victim of his wrath. [McKnight died in 1903, a successful businessman.] At this time, the great continental belt of railway was reaching an arm toward the chief town of the territory, and steamboat traffic was abating in volume.

Editor's Note

Courtenay lost his home months later when Indians destroyed his wood yard and the remnants of Camp Cooke in July 1871. With the headline "Piegans on the War Path," the July 29, 1871 edition of the Deer Lodge paper, the New North-West, *reported on Courtenay's fate and the climate of fear that summer:*

> *Fort Benton, July 18th.*
>
> *EDITOR'S GAZETTE—Mr. Courtney* [sic] *has just arrived with the express from Cow Island. The* Silver Lake *is unloading at that place, put the bulk of her freight, which consisted of annuities for Colonel Black, off at Muscleshell* [sic]. *She had no freight, but had forty-two passengers for Benton. Mr. Courtney* [sic], *while down after the express, was robbed by a war party of Piegans—they taking everything they could carry, and demolished everything they left. They smashed up wagons, looking glasses, furniture, and cut the beds open and scattered the feathers over the floor. They left a candle lit on the floor, and tore down the stockade to make a raft to cross the river. The Indians have cleaned out Camp Cook* [sic] *of every horse. They also cleaned out the Eagle Creek woodyard, and tried to take the horses from the Sheriff, who had been down arresting parties for stealing a skiff. They are known personally by the men on the river as Piegans. Mr. Cenix was shot last night at Eagle Creek. Every place of the river between here and Cow Island has been destroyed by these devils. The main camp of Piegans are now over the British line, and these warriors have come down by Sandy Creek, and are forty or fifty strong, and well mounted. They are expected here almost any time. A good lookout is kept up for their especial benefit. They declare they do not care for anything now; they are where they are not afraid of anything. Everything looks like there will be trouble this winter with the red devils. The Sioux are running the Crows. Last week the Crows killed fifteen Sioux on the road to the Judith. The Gros Ventres have moved up to the Marias. The Crows, Nez Perces* [sic], *and Gros Ventres say the Sioux will own their country after this winter, and consequently are anxious to make peace with the Blackfeet and neighboring tribes for their own safety. The Crows will move with the Nez Perces towards the head of Belt Creek in a day or two, previous to going to their agencies. Yours, &c.,*
> *CORRESPONDENT.*

C.M. Lee recorded in his diary that Courtenay was wounded by gunshot in the winter of 1870–71 by an Indian "who shot him through the thigh with an old trade gun...loaded with a ball wrapped in an old rag." Courtenay moved in the late 1870s to the new town of Miles City on the Yellowstone and opened a real estate office. He married, had four daughters, and prospered there until his death in 1901.

DAWSON COUNTY

On June 1, 1871, I received from Governor B.F. Potts [Benjamin Franklin Potts, territorial governor of Montana] a special commission to proceed and organize the County of Dawson that lay, in part, adjoining the County of Choteau. An election was to be held in August (the time general elections were held in the territories) for delegate to Congress. Members of the legislature also were to be elected. The upper house was called the "Council," and to my surprise, I received notice that the nominating convention at Virginia City had placed me as a candidate therefore for the counties of Meagher, Choteau, and Gallatin. I declined, however, and L. Ratwitt (afterward secretary of state) was substituted in my place on the ticket. It was quite important that to ensure [the accuracy of] the vote of Dawson County, the details of organization should be precise and technically carried out. A great effort was put forth to elect a Republican delegate to Congress, and my erstwhile friend and mining partner, W.H. Clagett, was the candidate in opposition to the Democratic incumbent, James M. Cavanaugh. My duties as county assessor being completed, the job of organizing the biggest county then in the whole world began. The appointment of the usual county officials was not a difficult task, but to thoroughly instruct them in duties pertaining to their respective offices, thus suddenly thrust upon them, was more painstaking, for upon their correct performance of those duties depended much for success. Books and blanks were prepared and a courthouse established in a log cabin surrounded by a stockade where the archives were to have their home and the officials were to

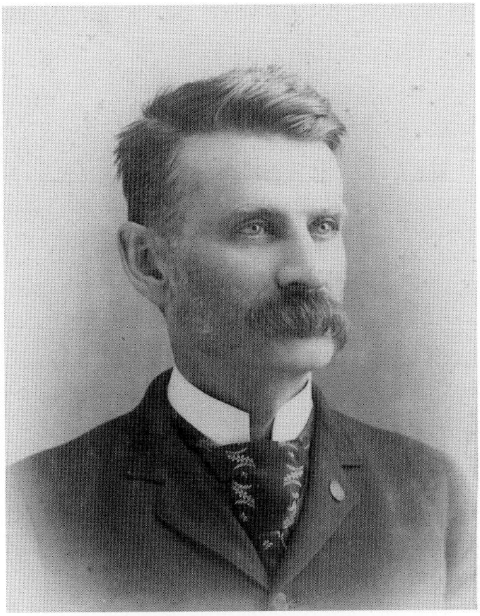

James Howard Lowell, 1897. *Courtesy of Kathy McKenna Downing.*

do their work. Election precincts were defined and election judges and clerk appointed, and to fill all these posts of duty, we feared for a while that an Emigrant Bureau would become necessary. The census for the year before (1870) gives Dawson County a population of 177 whites. The vote cast in August 1871 under this organization was between 300 and 400. The official census of 1880, nine years after, gives 180, an increase in ten years of 3. The vote of Dawson elected Clagett the first representative of the Republicans in Congress. An attempt was made to annul the vote of Dawson, not because of defects in the machinery, for it was found to be impregnable, but because of over-voting, and I have no doubt the attack would have justly succeeded, for there was no such a vote possible of bona fide electors. The governmental structure thus created has continued, though the enormous area of that county (larger than some of the states) has since then been greatly diminished by the change of county lines.

RETURN STATESIDE WITH THE ASHLEY FAMILY

It was the irony of fate that against the wishes of friends in the territory, and in the face of an attractive future—a flood, as it were, in the tide going my way—that the resolution to return to the States had rooted too deep to be changed. Accordingly, the preparations were made to take the last boat down the river. It was the sternwheeler *Miner*, which was expected to reach Benton on its up trip early in August. It was delayed by the falling of water, and was compelled to discharge its freight at Cow Island, two hundred miles below Benton on that account. Meanwhile, a party of us was active in building a mackinaw to carry us to the *Miner*.[82] In this party was the family of Governor James Ashley (who had been succeeded by Governor Potts before-mentioned), consisting of his wife, three young sons, and a still younger daughter. An elderly lady had also come from Helena with the Ashleys for the same trip. Also, a daughter of an old voyageur, Major Culbertson, who was a half-breed, was of the party. She was going to complete her education in the States. An Indian agent and a man with a record were included. I have forgotten their names. I think this made up the party on the mackinaw trip. James M. Ashley was then widely known and called "Impeachment Ashley." He it was who presented to the Impeachment Court the indictment against President [Andrew] Johnson.

He had made an admirable and very acceptable governor of Montana and, socially, was most genial and approachable. Mrs. [Emma Jane Smith] Ashley was an accomplished Lady, and I cherish a very happy remembrance of our talks. On the trip down, we were barred from travels at night, and our progress to the steamboat was slow because of the low water and sluggish

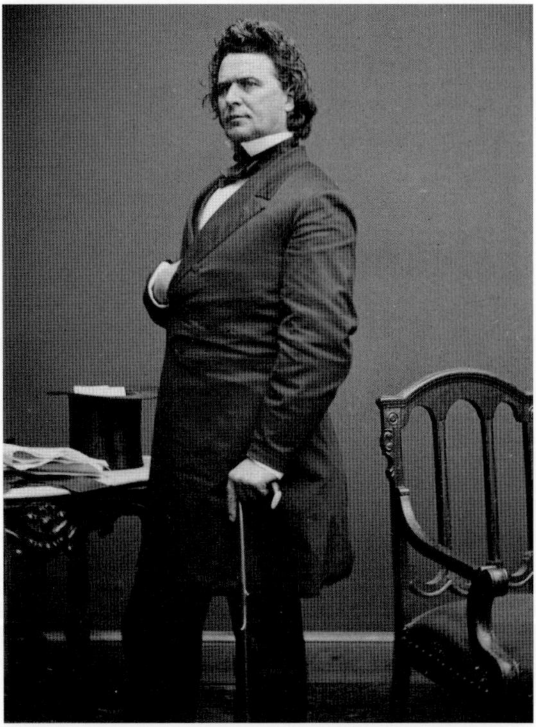

Abolitionist James M. Ashley was a member of the Radical Republicans who pushed for passage of the Thirteenth Amendment, which ended slavery. Ashley served as Montana territorial governor in 1869–70. He married Emma Jane Smith in 1851. They had four children. In the Stephen Spielberg film *Lincoln*, actor David Costabile played his character. *Library of Congress.*

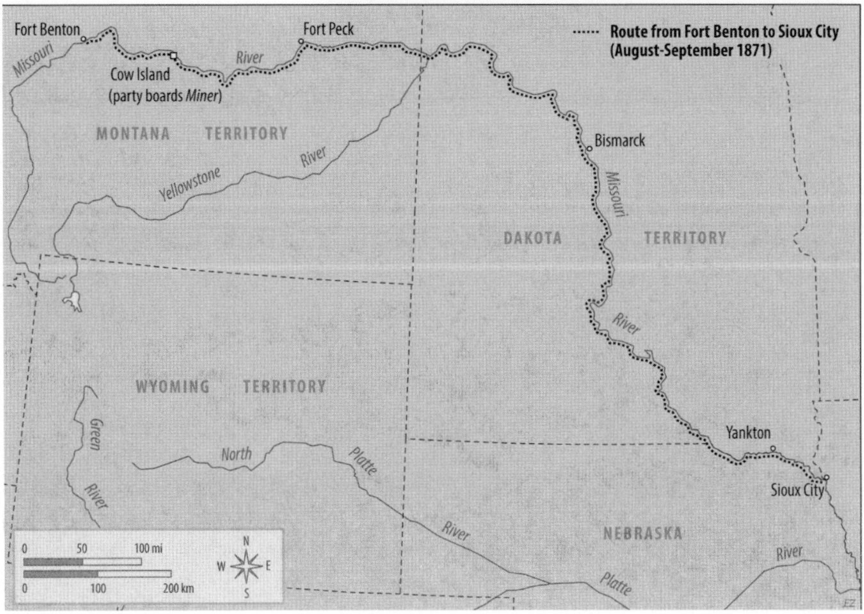

Map by Ezra Zeitler.

current, even with our two oarsmen. Robes were spread for the females of the party at night, and some of us would spread out ashore. The Indian agent and other man were at times "while under the influence," a little rough and boisterous, but we got along pretty well, being some eight or nine days en route. At last, an early start brought us to the *Miner* just before daylight. Our coming was anticipated by those on board the *Miner*, and with some concern for our safety, and immediately we were aboard, we were steaming up for the down trip.

We found on board a party of excursionists, and among them was a correspondent of the *N.Y. Herald*, a daughter of Ex-Governor Faulk of Nebraska, the wife of its congressman, and other most companionable people. The boat was not large, and the accommodations, while limited, were wholesome and as tidy as could be expected in a merchant craft. In a letter received from one of the Ashley boys, now grown to manhood, of date September 1899 and speaking of the trip down, he says: "I recall the Mackinaw ride—reaching the *Miner* in the night—the trip down—the bears, deer, etc. on the banks, the great herds of buffalo that in crossing often stopped the progress of the Steamer and the Indian war dance at Fort Peck. The Indian alarms and the frightened wood choppers, etc."[83]

It was a great sight to witness the struggles of the buffalo as our boat burst upon them in rounding a point of the river. They would be filing along the edge of the water to which they had descended for drinks and be caught where the bank's steepness prevented a land retreat, hence, they would plunge into the river, and practically carpet its surface with their hairy backs. Of course, the excursionists indulged the vicious propensity to kill these lordly beasts only to see them disappear. On one occasion, we succeeded in roping one of the victims, and by the aid of our engine, hoisted it over the bows, and this served to amplify our table with buffalo steak. I have said somewhere that this sinuous river was characterized every two miles with "points," and many of these points, or turns were abrupt, so that a steamer of even the limited length and capacity as ours could not keep the current in rounding these points. The way this was done was to point straight to and strike the bank sharply, and during the recoil, the pilot at the wheel turned the bows to the current and proceeded, steam on. Constant soundings were taken, for the current was very shifty, and ever and anon came the monotonous record of the lineman, "Mark 8," "Mark Twain," etc. Our time record down to Sioux City was eighteen days, several days was consumed in "sparring off" sand bars. At one time, we were three days fast in one of these bars, during which the derrick and engine were constantly at work sparring off—these spars were placed at the bows, one on each side meeting at their tops where wheel and tackle were rigged, and the lifting of the bow by the small engine, and reversing of the stern paddles comprised the operation of "sparring off." As the distance to the States lessened, the speed increased, and longer hours given to the cruise, which covered a distance from Benton to Sioux City of two thousand miles.[84] Meanwhile, on board was a very merry party, and the time did not drag heavily. In the cabin were all sorts of devices to pleasantly occupy the time. When moored at night, a blaze was started on shore by piling up pine knots, which lighted the fore-deck, and [we danced] to the tune of the cook fiddler, in which we all, more or less, took part—especially the young Ashleys, who showed the Unlearned how. At Yankton, we parted with our Nebraska friends, and there we got the consent of the captain to tie up the boat for two hours, during which time the Nebraskans gave us a carriage trip through the town and to the residence of one of them on a fine elevation overlooking the town. At Sioux City, I parted company with my fellow Voyagers and took a train for the East.

It was the latter part of August 1871, and the season's best attire was on exhibition. It is impossible to describe the sensations produced by a change so radical—from a region of evergreen and pine forests relieved only by quakenasp to that of elms, maples, orchards of fruit trees, tame grasses, corn fields, and grain fields, and to witness the products of these—after more than six years beyond these frontiers. As I write, the panorama rises before me as it did when looking out the window of the car; was then seen the groves of trees, and hedged fields, and fruitful farms, churches, schools, swift highways—all the conveniences and arts of the world's highest civilization and the security and peace of a builded and established order. Shut out, as by the slamming of a door, was the billowing prairie sea—the deep gashed ranges of mountain—the illusive mirages—the lordly buffalo—the nimble antelope—the smileless,

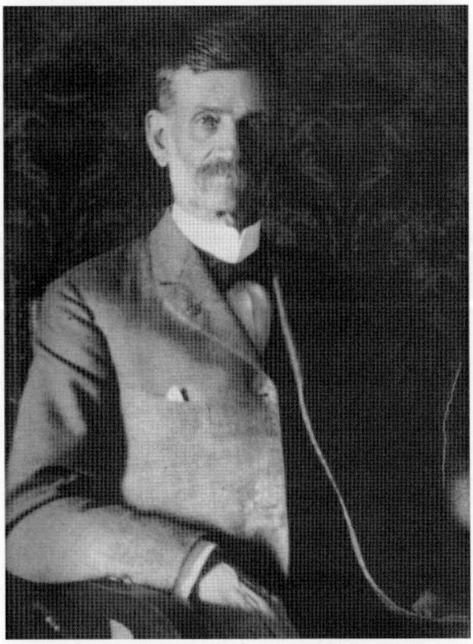

Judge James Howard Lowell, 1917.
Courtesy of David Winston.

sinister, and uncertain red man—the tiresome trail and that expansive feeling when gazing upon illimitable distances—the theater wherein Sherman calls the Indian warfare succeeding the Civil War, the "Buttes of Civilization" throughout the "trans-Missouri region."

The romantic age of the frontier has disappeared. The dim, winding trail of the red man has broadened into a highway of civilization, and the aborigine finds himself within the confines of an unchosen reservation, save when his status has become merged into citizenship. The buffalo—the chase—the warpath—the ghost dance—the sun dance—the endless meanderings, now belong to history's memories. No more is heard the simple chansons with which this child of nature woke the echoes of forest and hill, but instead, his faculties are engaged with soap and whiskey and draw poker and Sunday School, the outward semblance of civilized life.

Epilogue

LOWELL RETURNS TO THE STATES

After six years of wandering after the war, Lowell made good on his promise to collect Katherine Mary Roberts. He quit town in September 1871 and bid a "long and unregretful farewell" to Benton. Hell or low water, he was determined to get stateside.

The family of Senator James Ashley traveled with him. Thirty years later, Ashley's son described a gay party on board the *Miner* as it progressed down the Missouri River from Cow Island to Sioux City:

> *As we were about to set out on this novel and dangerous journey, my Brother, James, came to my Mother and said, "Mother, there is going to be more whiskey than men aboard this boat, I am afraid."*... [Not] *an oath was spoken by all these rough men during the entire trip (at least in the hearing of my Mother), and in every way, the greatest consideration and truest politeness were displayed by the men on board the boat.*[85]

So much for the Wild West.

Upon Lowell's return to Harrisburg, we can assume Kate Mary's father, who had a successful legal practice, coached the young man in preparation for his bar examinations. Lowell's correspondence does not reveal whether he returned to Boston before his marriage to Kate Mary Roberts (now thirty-two) in Harrisburg on January 30, 1873. The couple left on a honeymoon trip to permanently settle in Holton, Kansas, where they wasted no time in starting a family. Holton was the Jackson County seat, in the northeastern part of the

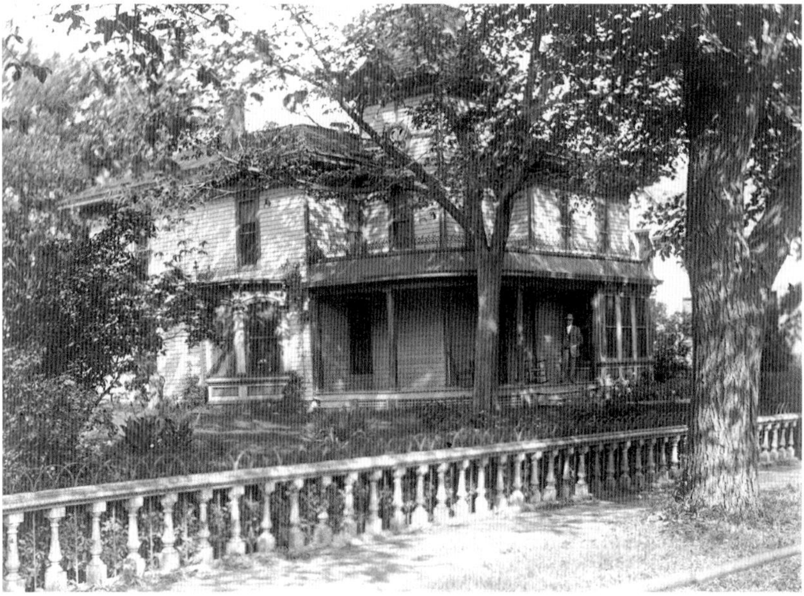

Above: Lowell home at 515 Iowa Avenue, Holton, Kansas. The house was torn down in the 1970s to build a church parking lot. *Courtesy of Tim Sewell.*

Right: James Howard Lowell, late 1880s. *Courtesy of Tim Sewell.*

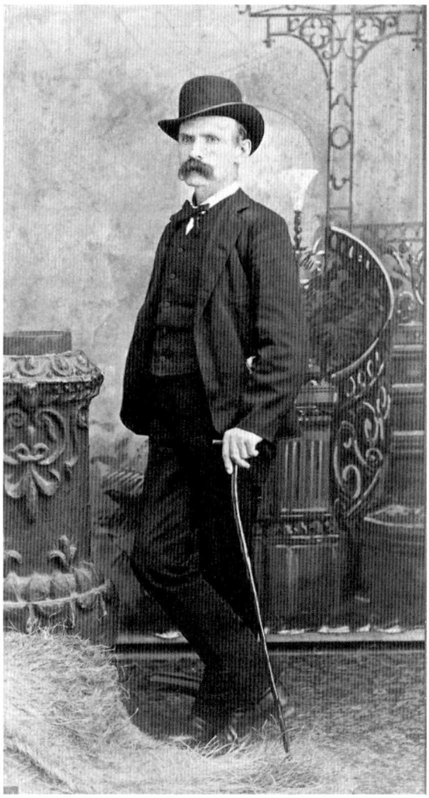

state, a burgeoning and progressive town that was still considered a frontier place. Free State men from Wisconsin who abhorred the establishment of slavery in the West settled the area in the 1850s.[86] Twenty years later, the town offered young families migrating from the Eastern Seaboard good schools, farmland, some mining, and manufacturing.[87]

Lowell built a law practice in Kansas and served as a Jackson County attorney. He ran and was elected mayor twice, in 1885 and 1886, and served as a judge and a presidential elector for the State of Kansas in 1896. When an assassin killed President James A. Garfield in 1881, Holton town fathers invited Judge Lowell to eulogize the late president at local services.[88] As the family grew, the couple moved into a large Victorian clapboard in Holton near the courthouse and raised four children. Lowell never returned to Montana. He died in Holton on February 19, 1925, at age eighty-two. (For the Lowells' obituaries, more about Lowell's descendants, family history, and the provenance of the journal, see the appendix.)

Part II

CORRESPONDENCE

INTRODUCTION TO THE CORRESPONDENCE

To modern readers, it might seem remarkable that in the memoir, Lowell never directly referred to his Civil War experiences, family circumstances, his relationship with Kate Mary Roberts, or even a desire to see his family. Lowell wrote down his experiences for posterity. Men of the period would have considered the sharing of their private lives in a public document unseemly—or worse yet, unmanly. There is even a tradition in the Lowell family of burning personal correspondence after death.[89] Despite Lowell's reticence regarding his love life and interior life in general, his optimistic personality and good humor seep from between the lines and lend the narrative heart. Section II offers a more personal perspective. It includes selected letters written to his sweetheart, Civil War reminiscences, and recollections that he shared with a fellow pioneer near the end of his life. Lowell also corresponded with two of the Ashley children with whom he journeyed back east.

LETTERS TO KATE MARY ROBERTS

After being shot and wounded in the infamous Miller cornfield where so many died at Antietam, Lowell recovered at a temporary hospital in Harrisburg, Pennsylvania. Sparks flew with a lively volunteer nurse, Kate Mary Roberts (1841–1938), whom he married eleven years later. Roberts was one of the enthusiastic young locals who fussed over the recovering Massachusetts Thirteenth boys and sang in a women's quartet for their entertainment. Her father, Colonel John Roberts, was a lawyer whose Quaker antecedents immigrated westward with William Penn. Roberts was a veteran of the War of 1812.[90]

A letter written home by another Massachusetts Thirteenth soldier, John Buttrick Noyes, disabuses one of the notion that recovery in a Civil War–era hospital was all gloom and suffering:

> *Nothing can exceed the Kindness and attention, which the ladies of Harrisburg bestow upon us. All the morning we have been exhibiting ourselves to their gaze…nobly. Oceans of goodies have been brought us, and we are living on the fat of the land.…One or two quite pretty young ladies are particularly devoted to our party for the reason of course that we entertain them in turn.*[91]

> *"Are you acquainted with any of those Mass soldiers?" said a lady to our nurse, "they have such excellent conversational powers."*[92]

Clearly, the Boston boys were removed from bodily peril in that hospital. Lowell's leg wound was sufficient, however, to prevent him from returning to active service. His contributions to the regimental circulars in later years and the letters written to Kate during his travels are filled with reminiscences of their happy hours riding and courting in Harrisburg, "the times when the speed would relieve you of your head dress, hat and all, while your witchcraft of hair would have its recreation as well."[93]

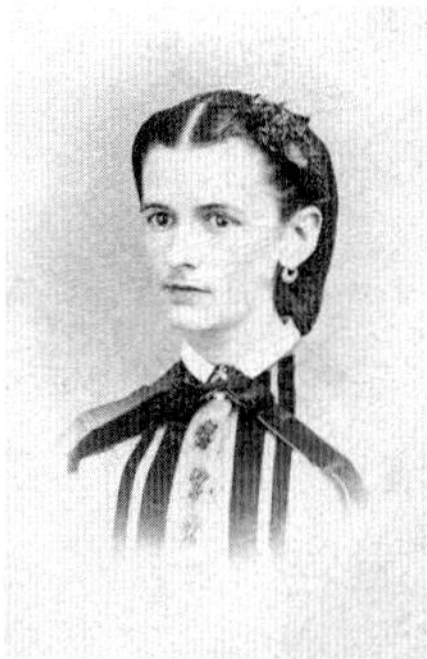

Right: Kate Mary Roberts. *Courtesy of Tim Sewell.*

Below: Portrait of the Roberts family of Harrisburg taken during the Civil War. *Seated left:* Kate Mary Roberts. *Courtesy of Tim Sewell.*

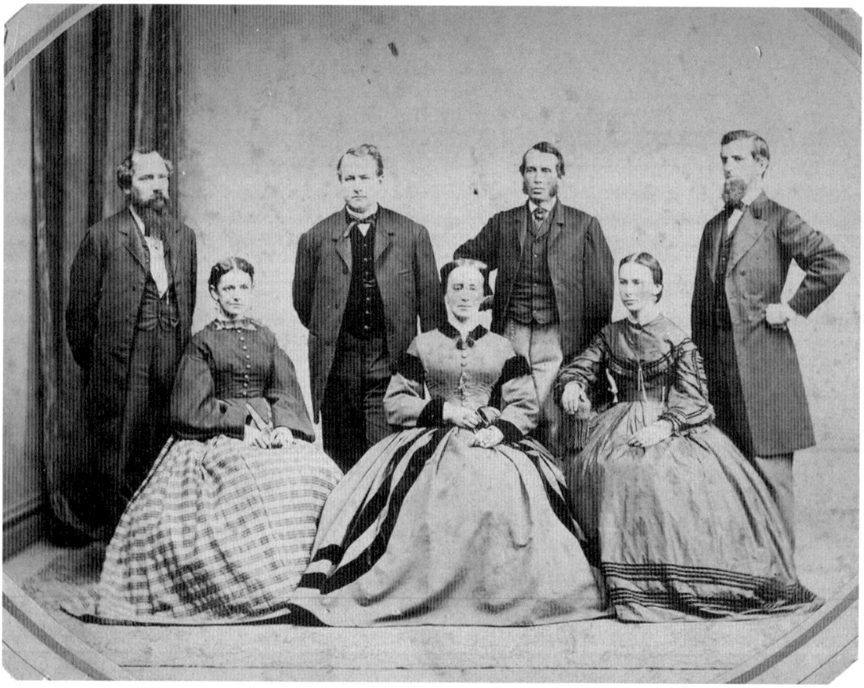

Kate Mary Roberts and Lowell shared a talent for drawing and an appreciation of art. Later, their second son would become an artist and illustrator. Much of Lowell's affectionate correspondence chides her for not writing often enough or apologizes for his lack of epistolary material. While the memoir was written for posterity, the letters are confessional. They give a taste of the disillusionment he felt with mining.

She must have questioned why he chose to seclude himself. He responded, "I am myself at loss to sufficiently account for it and have often regretted that I didn't stop someplace less removed from civilization."[94] He asked her: "So it was supposed that I had faded into a permanent eclipse in the stomach of an aborigine?"[95] The personal letters offer the perspective of a homesick young veteran trying to make his way in the world. He complains, he opines, and he flirts.

Full transcripts of his ten letters reside at www.lowellmemoir.com.

POSTMARKED: MARCH 28, 1866, DENVER

Lowell left his clerking job at the Planter's House hotel in Denver to seek employment with Territorial Governor Charles W. Durkee in Salt Lake City. With the optimism of youth, he and one companion departed early in the season to cross the windswept and desolate Laramie Plains.

Planter's House

Denver, Colorado
March 26, 1866

My Dear Friend.

This is the eve of my departure west for Great Salt Lake City. Imagine me astride a pony gamboling over hill and dale across woodless mountains, destitute of verdure, and rolling barren plains. My companion, a young fellow from Philadelphia, will also gambol over hill and dale, across woodless mountains, destitute of verdure, etc. We have laid in a goodly stock of flour, soda, cream of tartar, salt, pepper, oyster (tinned) bacon, & sardines, six U.S. blankets from which we'll take glimpses of the moon. And with a firmness, which might also be terror and courage, proceed on our winding way. The distance is six hundred miles, which we expect to accomplish in twenty-five or thirty days, if no ill befalls us. Please write me a long letter. I wrote you some days since, asking you to direct to Denver and I now write to inform you of the change henceforth in my address, with greetings to all, I remain,

Yours,
Lowell

Postmarked: December 18, 1868

Thwarted in his bid for employment in Utah, Lowell tries his hand at placer mining farther north, accompanied by thousands of other young hopefuls.

Helena, Montana

Near Diamond City, MT
December 14, 1868

Kate...

Some time since I wrote to our friend McCauley to learn the chances and changes in human affairs at Harrisburg, and though my fears of what might have happened were dispelled in the gratifying reply, the letter itself was essentially meager. I was surprised to hear that you were not (as I had been told you were about to be) married; on the contrary, you were enlivening Harrisburg as usual with your maidenly presence, and residing with your brother. I wonder if this incongruity of statements cannot be traced to an ignorance on your part of the danger involved by those who will come within the pale of your eyes; be that as it may, Kate, there is no longer that obstacle to my writing you, albeit a disability may exist preventative of a reply [another suitor]. But I must get through this preamble and "speak my piece." I received your last letter (I presume), forwarded from S.L. City, in Helena. It was handed me as I was sitting on a huge boulder engaged in mental interrogations as how to inflate, in the quickest possible time, my pocket book, which had just sacrificed its all in a pork chop at a neighboring shop. Pregnant with visions of the wealth I was destined to unearth from the auriferous hills around, I procured the necessary tools and started solus for Deer Lodge, fifty miles distant, said to be fabulously rich. I reached the valley of that name just in time to join a large "stampede" to some new place about thirty miles away. On the way thither I endeavored to get from this and that person of the stampeders some clue to the genuineness of the report of this new El Dorado in wild; somebody had whispered he had a "soft thing," and for all they knew this soft thing might consist of having reduced the question of whether the moon was made of green cheese to a certainty and was regaling himself thrice a day with "rarebits" of which the moon made the chief ingredient. Still the stampede augmented and when we reached our Destination, numbered a thousand at least. Officers were at once elected, President, Recorder, and Surveyor. And recording commenced each claimant coming in order after the manner of seniority as in Post Offices, but being in so methodical a mood as that I fled the ranks and invoking Dame Fortune, set my pegs in a tributary ravine and went to work, and after ten months time spent, my swans turned out to be geese, but having a little courage and a few pounds of flour left, I seized a frying pan, mounted my pony and hastened away from a scene so cruel, a soil so nonfruitful. Thus, Kate, you have the story of mining in a nutshell. Such is the fortune of "Tender footed Pilgrims." Exceptions are rare even among the craftiest pioneers. Returning to Helena, I encountered an apparition in the jovial figure of (O ye Gods) Morrow P. Lowry, an old comrade of mine whom you will remember. The wonder was mutual; the meeting comical considering the individuals and place. Lowry at the time was exhorting his fellow citizens to vote by all means the Democratic ticket, for it was Election, for which I took him to task, after he had taken me to drink. Who could say nay to an invitation under such circumstances? Who blame? Candour is a part of my nature and I have no more confessions to make.

Since then, (fall of '67) I have been in this camp oft and on, as also Lowry. L. often speaks of the ladies I used so shamefully who took part in a Sanitary Fair at Chambersburg, and this leads me to wonder if you don't now and then think of the gyrations we used to enact in the saddle when free of Ha. [Harrisburg] on those dear old roads and drives of ours, and the times when the speed would relieve you of your head dress, hat and all, while your witchcraft of hair would have its recreation as well. My pen is going astray, Kate, but you can well make the allowance. What has become of Miss Barnett, your old chum? Of Mary, and Ella? Of Sissy, Forbes' inamorata? of Forbes himself? (Lord forgive me for negligence in writing.) Fiske? Warner? Waltrous? and many others? Is it true that Hannah is really to be mated? Where is her fidelity? And Lucy (Bless her) how and where is she? What else shall I write about? Shall I tell you the proficiency I have attained in the culinary arts? Of hot "Pones?" Plum Duffs, Doughnuts & & without end that I throw off with a facility that would make your little heart quicken in admiration? Ah me, what a critic I shall be when I once more dwell in the atmosphere of civilization. But fare well for the present. I shall take this to Helena starting tomorrow.

Yours,
Lowell
Diamond City
Montana
(Thompsons Gulch)

Postmarked: March 28, 1869

Disillusioned with mining, Lowell reads law and contemplates returning to the East. He further tests the waters with Kate and shares with her his enthusiasm for art. He responds to her sister's suggestion that he write something for Harper's Magazine, *and relates meeting the famous artist and illustrator A.E. Matthews.*

Fort Benton

Near Diamond City, Montana
February 10, 1869

Kate:

Last night's mail brought me your gracious letter. Thanks for it. I am glad mine led you into nothing worse than a facial eccentricity. Paintings and hysterics of a lady on a crowded street are interesting, yet unutterably piteous spectacles. Be it an admonition to you as it is a relief to me that your letter is, as well, the herself of the writer's unruffled serenity as a chronicle of Harrisburg annals. I will pass over there last and take up some of your enquiries. And first, "Don't you think?" I do: such inordinate presumption in so small a man as McCauley would extort the sympathies of a stoic. I feel myself unable to add anything to your criticism, which I have endeavored to rescue from decay by the immortalizing power of the pencil, as exhibited on last page, but I marvel at such wanton engulfment of an inoffensive fellow creature, not to encourage apostasy in so valiant a youth, he would find an alternative in the counsel of the sagacious Captain Cuttle to that similarly circumstanced oracle Mr. Bunsbey and a rigid yet exquisitely secure asylum in Montana. It's too bad about Lucy F. Her misfortune will be regretted by all who can appreciate a truly excellent lady. My thanks to her sister for her kind intention with respect to the wedding cards. I am vain enough to hope that one passage in your letter was rendered to inspire in me a different ambition than is usually inhaled in these mountains. It is true that men of the vilest nature find their element here. It is also true that the minority who lay claim to respectability have a moral preponderance, ever augmenting as the avenues to enterprise are opened by increasing facilities of communication with the States. It is optional here, as elsewhere, for one to become vile or virtuous, pious or profane, as his tendencies incline, and what for good or evil; climate, habit and association have wrought, *ad hominem*. There is always one consolation for me that my health has wonderfully improved since I left the company of roistering gentlemen. Without that, I could be of little use to myself or friends and there is nothing here that would have enticed me to so "forlorn" a country, and, too, it is but natural that a novice should have been drawn into the vortex from which men ought to issue wiser, if not better men. I refer to gold seeking. On one occasion, I was on my way east, when I met Lowry, and turned back. I am now looking forward to the time when the boats will be navigating the Missouri. So much on a theme in which you can scarcely be more than incidentally interested, but which has been necessary to answer your enquiries. Before I go on, I will say that it was McCauley who wrote me that rumor was rife that you were to be married to Mr. Kelly. Thanks to your sister for her suggestion to write articles with sketches to *Harper's*. A Mr. Maguire is, or has been, engaged on a like undertaking, but whether he completes it or not seems now to depend on his recovery from an unhappy case of *Mania à Potu* [delirium tremens]. The illustrations were to have been furnished by a Mr. Matthews,[96] a gentleman with whom I spent a week or more in the mountains of Colorado, and an excellent artist. He has also been taking sketches from different localities with a view of having them lithographed and published. His works in Colorado are now in print. It comforts my family much to hear that my essay in the "serenely silent art" is being so honored by your sister. I don't remember much about it, but I do recollect that it did not suit me and that I put extraordinary pains on it, which I have since discovered does more injury than good. Do you not find that the case? [He overworked a drawing, or an essay on art.]

Like an unpracticed swimmer plunging still,
with too much labour, drowns, for want of skill.

When you next go to Philadelphia slip into the Academy of Art and take notes from [Benjamin] West's "Death on a White Horse," a work which embodies the mystery of magic strokes. You will be repaid for your trouble and materially assisted in your crayon heads.

So it was supposed that I had palled into a permanent eclipse in the stomach of an aborigine. O horrible, pray give me a more graceful exit than that. Speaking of Indians in this connection, I will mention an incident that happened this morning. A party of Flatheads passed through here last night and camped a mile away. One of them took from my yard an axe, without which I could scarcely be happy. I rode to their camp and caught them all at prayers, a manner of devotion taught them by some Jesuit priests and performed in a manner somewhat unique. I suspect the observance was enforced more by their zealous chief than embraced by his more worldly followers. Be that as it may, I entered the chief's lodge and made known my business, whereupon he strode through the lodges shouting fiercely, and in less than a minute, a down looking rascal appeared with the axe, but quickly put space between him and his terribly incensed chief. I spent a few minutes "talking" with my Nemesis and started to return when, lo! My nag was unsaddled and feeding with the herd, and nothing would do but to sit down to a Buffalo steak, etc. I staid with these jolly chaps an hour or two and called for the horse, which was saddled and made ready the due time by an industrious squaw. It is worth notice that this [illegible] between them and the white the original treaty has remained inviolable and the one, solitary instance, they have adopted many of the customs of the pioneers, cultivated the soil, and herd large bands of horses and cattle, and every fall pass through here on their way to the buffalo range on the Yellowstone and Muscleshell, [*sic:* Lowell employs the same spelling as Meriwether Lewis of the Musselshell River.] the hunting grounds of the Crows whose title, however, they dispute on every such occasion, thereby keeping alive the old warlike customs such as war dances and other superstitious follies, which else would have probably been laid aside along with their many other barbarities. They are returning earlier than usual to save what few horses their foes have failed to steal. These last are likewise foes to the whites whom they have been annoying all winter and so have broken into their occupation of hunting trapping, etc. in these grounds, so profuse in game.

What admirable good sense dame Myers shows in her solicitude for Lill's welfare. Still there is something heartless in that young lady's conclusions to let the chap with three children slide, although [the choice] may be expected in one of her universally allowed perfections. If Lill says truly, the three children had a narrow escape. Leroy Parsons is just the person to give the ploughmen to....[H]e has traveled a good deal and known how to prevaricate. I wonder if Forbes has settled permanently in the land of "the anthropophagic" and men whose heads do grow beneath their shoulders, whereof such things to hear doth Ella seriously incline? [He refers to James LaSalle Forbes, a friend and Massachusetts Thirteenth vet who married another volunteer nurse, Ella Small, and took over his family's indigo plantation in India.] I meant Lilly when I spoke of his inamorata, but I am glad to hear of the Philadelphia one, whom I now recollect as the paragon of vocalists whose charms inspired much literary effort of the sentimental kind in opera-distracted Forbes. Do you know anything of Captain John [illegible, Klement] that used to board at Mrs. Dolls? There were some governmental affairs with which he is, or was connected and with which I am privy to, the solution to which I would, out of curiosity, like to know. If they have been made public you may have heard something about it. The story is too long for this sort of intercourse, even if you should be interested in it. Please remember me to Ella and Mary, Lucy and Hannah.

Yours, Lowell

Having been away since writing the above. I have returned to find it where I left it, although I gave the rascally carrier to put it in the mail. I am very sorry it happened.
March 21st

Postmarked: Diamond City, August 7

Diamond City, M.T.
August 5, 1869

Kate:
I am exceeding glad your advice was so prompt—so near it is to the eve of my departure to the States—a few weeks at the farthest and I shall wave a long and unregretful farewell to these old hills. By what route to go—whether by the Missouri River or by rail—I need some inspiration to decide. Canst thou not propound a solution? I think thou canst. Late advices say that there are many steamboats stranded high and dry on the Missouri, and that that mode of navigation has met with a sudden and violent termination. So, all that remains in that direction would be to charter a boat that will carry five or six persons to be propelled with oars or by means of a sail, according to circumstances. The advantage of this route is its novelty, which is a great argument in favor where one is desirous of making the best of this, the

probable last trip of the kind for a long time—but it is 3100 miles from head of navigation to St. Louis, a long distance surely and will occupy about forty or fifty days. It will take, by the other route, about thirteen days to Chicago, or five days by coach and eight by rail. Here again, a coach ride of five days is fraught with the most poignant suffering and I know a man who has traveled thus whose resentment has not cooled at a distance of five years. Naturally, one, under the circumstances, sighs for an "Avatar" or "Hyperion" to avoid the crooked ways of the Missouri and the debilitating effects of a coach ride.

Business being very dull, I took a tramp of nine days with fishing rods and rifle. We made a party of four and reached this classic village night before last, having had good luck and a jolly time. Glad there were no ladies along for we saw Indian sign and therefore kept pretty watchful, and probably the Indians, if any were about, kept pretty watchful also—for the tribes at this time of year are broken up into small parties, unless on the war path, and when white men are about they can beat us in vigilance. I shot two splendid fat elk and was in at the death of a bruin. It seems that my comrade, whom I had left but a few minutes, came face to face with the gentleman and at once gave him a shot, which took effect in his foot, and fell (they drop always when injured even in the least), but before the assailant could load, the bear came bouncing and bellowing straight at him, upon which said assailant "clomb" a pine and shouted for me, and I cautiously approached the scene. I had little to fear, however, as my rifle carries sixteen loads, and the first shot was enough and penetrated the throat, the most vital "bear shot" that can be made. The lock of my companion's rifle was wrenched out and the stock was pretty well scratched to pieces, he having left it at the foot of the tree which he had climbed and which the bear evidently thought a pretty plaything. We cast our lines in Deep Creek and in consequence, we can tell the largest fish story extant. The creek was literally thronged with the finest, though not the largest, trout ever caught any place. There is really no fun fishing in such a place. For one is continually sad to think his friends and the world besides are not there to applaud and admire. Moral—there is no class of people who enjoy themselves better than a well appointed hunting and fishing party! I said my leave of the mountains would be unregretful—it is so. I have been long enough, though perhaps not more than long enough in this kind of school and my failure is attributable to the perfidy of one in a high public position, Charles Durkee, the Governor of Utah. [Durkee promised Lowell a position in Salt Lake City and failed to make good on his promise.]

Pray, present your cousin my appreciation of her correct taste. If she will join me, we will interdict all from listening, who get "so tired of hearing you talk," and then will have you all to ourselves. As to your letter, in reflecting yourself on the pages you write, you cannot fail to do good, if making your correspondent think the world and all of you is doing good, which proposition may well occupy a little consideration when you get time. Will write you from Leavenworth, at which point, I will probably stay for a while.

In haste for the mail,
Yours,
Lowell

EXCHANGE WITH YELLOWSTONE EXPLORER CHARLES W. COOK

Less than a year before his death, James Howard Lowell exchanged letters with Charles W. Cook of the 1869 Cook-Folsom-Peterson exploration of the Yellowstone region. In the 1860s, Cook and his friends David E. Folsom and William Peterson heard tales of the wonders of the Yellowstone River valley that had filtered though the mining camps from the accounts of explorer and guide Jim Bridger. As park historian and ranger Aubrey Haines (1914–2000) put it: "The valley of the upper Yellowstone was, in their minds, a place of volcanic fires, steaming mounds, and suffocating gases; lifeless and weird..."[97] When other expeditions fell through, Cook and his companions set off to see for themselves. Further explorations led to the region's dedication as a national park in 1872. Yellowstone is believed to be the first such designation in world history.

In 1922, the National Park Service recognized Cook's role in the exploration of Yellowstone at the park's fiftieth anniversary celebration. In February 1924, President Calvin Coolidge wrote Cook a congratulatory letter to commend his service. Perhaps these anniversary activities prodded Lowell to reach out to Cook, who settled in White Sulphur Springs, Montana, near Lowell's old mining camp at Thompson's Gulch.

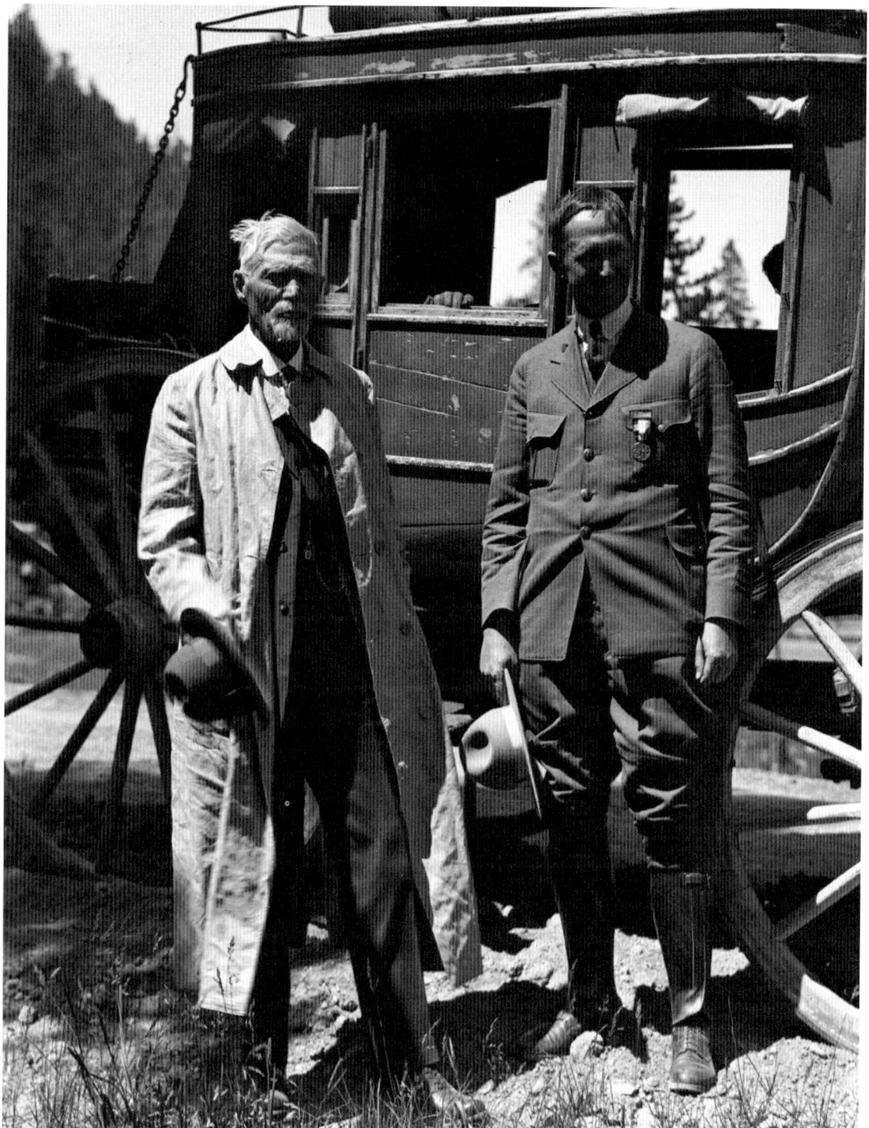

Cook and Yellowstone Park Superintendent Horace Albright on the fiftieth anniversary of the park in 1922. The publicity surrounding the anniversary might have prompted Lowell to initiate correspondence with Cook. *Reproduced courtesy of the National Parks Service, Yellowstone National Park, YELL 37151_2.*

Law office of
James H. Lowell
March 23, 1924
Capt. C.W. Cook,
White Sulphur Springs, Montana

My dear Comrade:

Your two letters and printed matter [have] given me great delight and amazement as well. If I am able to carry out my purpose of a paper on placer mining, your remarkable story of that El Dorado at Diamond with the part you played will color up the dry details. I don't know, one's spirit may be O.K. but other ingredients must combine to achieve the goal, chief among which is the physical. I have read of your trailing the virgin wonders of the Yellowstone with great interest. You may justly be proud. I would love to have been along. At once upon my discharge from war service, I obeyed the call to go out where things awaited opening up. My native Boston had no hold longer on me. When I located here I wrote with some detail the seven years spent west, five in Montana. My first break in mining was with a stampede from Deer Lodge some 8 or ten miles out. I there met one you may recall, Wm. H. Clagett, of the law firm of Dixon and Clagett, later Rep. in Congress. We opened up in a side tributary together. He moved his wife and child there housed in a tent; we got the color on & near bedrock five feet down, it proved a fizzle. I never saw him after, but my law partner from here made his acquaintance in Congress. Do you recall W.A.C. (Whack) Ryan, a reporter on a Helena paper? He afterwards joined an Insurgent outfit in Mexico. Was a General, captured and shot on the way to his fate he hummed an operatic air. About three or four miles down the Deer Lodge Valley was a cabin I occupied a short time after, my mining tilt. One night a party drove up and stopped Whack and another man and two ladies came in to warm up. It seems that they had been to Deer Lodge where Whack and one of the ladies were to be married. She learned that Whack had borrowed a shirt for the ceremony and called the affair off and now they were en route for Helena. Before I forget it, Is your Gov. Dixon any relation to Clagett's partner? It was about this time I came up against a character named Coggswell, an old California miner. Soured through adversity, his clean ups had not realized. We were together three seasons in Thompsons Gulch, starting Sept. 1867. There were two brothers only in the Gulch besides. We appropriated an abandoned set of sluice boxes and opened up a new prospect-bed rock, eleven feet and panned four feet that held color. An average of 14 cents. (I am consulting my minutes written 50 years ago.) If uniform that promised $50.00 per day to the wild game all around. Antelope, Deer, Moose, Elk, Bear. A beautiful landscape stretched away from the ranges, the third season our tail race came up to bed rock and we bought lumber and put in a bed rock flume. Now sure, we had a bonanza. Our riffles were from a Fir tree in blocks two inches thick, cross sawed. Two things prevented, rocks and a tenacious clay that would not wash. Our dump disclosed the latter, yet saved gold that assayed 22 to the ounce. One day after ground sluicing a few days, Coggswell, on getting up in the morning said, "Jim, I'll never strike another pick in this gulch. If you want to hitch up your horse and go with me to Helena." Coggswell was a Spiritualist and was constantly moved to sudden and strange freaks. A very unsocial man of some 45 years. I believe he thought more of me than any other living person. A masterful miney, strong and untiring. I was tall and slightly built but capable of hard work and as untiring as he. I parted from him in Helena, he first signing a transfer of his interest in the mine.

In Helena was a law firm "Shober and Lowry," ever hear of them? A brother of Lowry was a student with them. I had known him in the east when a war pay master clerk in Harrisburg, Pa. when I was being treated in a hospital for a wound received at Antietam. Lowry and I got onto a young strong fellow and we three returned to the mine. We took out some gold and finally I sold the outfit to two pilgrims. Lowry and I went to Fort Benton where I remained until the summer of 1871. I had been for years a student of the science of law and had a good beginning in the practice at Benton. There I became intimate with your late Senator Tom C. Power and through him traded with the Crows and Gros Ventres below Camp Cook. I invested $1000.00 in trading stuff of T.C.P. who also traded at Camp Cook. I can only touch these topics, which may not interest you. A long deferred purpose of marrying a girl I met in hospital at Harrisburg, demanded fulfillment. I left the glorious Montana with great reluctance, to my great astonishment, Mrs. Lowell upbraided me for not returning after locating here. These are mere outlines of a few things of my five years there. I might add that I came there with a flour laden train touching Virginia City en route. Alder Gulch near by I think was being worked as you know the gulch was famously rich and held rock, but a few felt. I presume you do now know the particulars of this mine. I should like to know more of it. The abundant prospect I learned was made the reason for short measure individual claims. Since writing above of the Thompson mine I find I should have pointed out that our bed rock riffles may have caused [left blank] shaped as they were. These fir blocks were round and fitted out two foot wide flume thus naturally, a strong current would very likely carry to the dump over these flat surfaces some gold adhering to the clay that abounded there we had up stream a natural reservoir fed too by a three mile ditch from another gulch. The year I came down river to the states I was assessor of Choteau County. The treasurer was a gambler and depleted the treasury and I left with Mr. Power the collection of my salary, which was delayed two years.

In closing again I wish to say how much your letter and printed matter has interested me. I have given you the additional trouble of wading through this disconnected narrative. One of our age to function a pen, needs restored eye sight, obedient finger joints, amended nerves, absence of profanity, to do a job to rank with the classics.

Wishing you restored vigor
I remain your friend
JAMES H. LOWELL

It may interest you to know that I was one of three to organize Dawson County under a commission from Gov. B.F. Potts; a copy I have. That the votes that were thus obtained enabled the election of Wm. H. Clagett, as Congressman.

Charles W. Cook Replies to Lowell, Less than Three Years before Cook's Death at Age Eighty-Eight

White Sulphur Springs, Montana, June 30, 1924
Mr. James Lowell
Holton, Kans.

Dear Sir:

Your letter was received last evening and I will make an attempt to answer it but will ask you excuse penmanship as I am slowly recovering from a long and severe illness and this is my first attempt to handle a pen and it seems unwilling to move in any direction, but when I get through it if I think you can't make it out I will consign it to the waste basket.

You were in Diamond in 67, the bar was worked out in 66, it was rich. Probably $1,000,000 was taken off of it. I look back now on my early experiences in Diamond with much satisfaction. Hope it will not burden you, I will give you a short chapter, which has never been written. In the spring of 66 I went to work for the Boulder Ditch Co., which supplied water to work the Bar. I had charge of the Ditch to see that it carried all the water possible without the danger of breaking. On coming home one evening I found everything in an uproar, the town against the outlaws. The outlaws had started in to jump claims and one of the leaders had been killed and the members of the Ditch Co. [were] under the protection of the sheriff to keep them from the drunken howling mob of outlaws. The sheriff called on the citizens to help him. 75 men well armed watched all night. In the morning they were taken to Helena under guard to protect them. Had their trial, turned loose. But to leave the territory as the outlaw element was too strong in Diamond. But before leaving Diamond the president of the company called me up and turned all the business over to me. In a few minutes I was made manager of one of the largest placer mining concerns in the territory, I was in a fix. I was but a boy never handled large money or many workmen, I had no boss no one to report to no one to advise or help me. I work [*sic*] twenty men a day and the same at night. Had to clean sluice boxes morning and evening, the most I took out in 24 hours was $16,000 and also had to regulate the water supply and collect the money each week, which usually amounted about $10,000. The dust all had to be cleaned and cared for. I not only handled the company's gold but for another big company. As a matter of history one man [Charles Friedrichs] cleaned up more than one bushel at one time but that was his summer's work. And to show you how we did business in those days, he asked me to clean and sack his dust. He could not guess within 20,000 what he had. My only instructions were to put $5,000 in a sack and I did not see him until the job was completed. I handled gold as a farmer does wheat. This all came into my hands unweighed and uncounted. At the time I did not see anything unusual or peculiar in my position. I thought nothing about it, but looking back on it at this time I can realize the situation and responsibility. I presume no other young man was placed in like circumstance. There is no credit due any one for being honest, that is what we were entitled to expect from any good citizen. When you were in Diamond in 67 I was working company ground in the gulch they had 600 feet, it was very rich. After the claims were all drifted out they were bought up by a company who put in a bed rock floom [flume] and sluiced the whole gulch out. Nothing is left of Diamond, no one lives there, the bare rocks are the tombstones of a dead city. In 69 myself with two companions explored what is now the Yellowstone National Park for which government gives no credit. (I will sent you some Park Bulletins in which is copied our notes.)

You did not state in your letter to whom you sold your gulch mine to. I located about ten miles south at the foot of the hills in 71, the Smith brothers were the principal parties there at that time. They made some money, went into the sheep business and became wealthy both are now dead. Thompson is now a cattle ranch. The country is all fenced. The old road over the range was changed to a good grade, no mining is done at Thompson except on a [illegible] which has not up to the present time proved successful. Birch Creek from hill to valley is owned by Dick Ringling (circus fame). White Sulphur Springs is a well built country village, two solid Banks, two hotels three groceries and six or seven hundred people. We have Electric lights and the best water in the world, while the sulphur springs has wonderful medicinal qualities.

I have been several days writing this as I cannot write much at one time, but I wanted to test my strength. If you cannot read this you will not have lost much. We are having beautiful weather, have had three cold days no snow until about the 10th and this is about gone in the valley but there is much in the hills. If there is anything I have left out which you would wish to know about this section of country just let me know and I will try to help you out.

Yours respectfully,
C.W. Cook

CHARLES SUMNER ASHLEY *1899* LETTER TO LOWELL

The abolitionist and former U.S. senator from Ohio James Mitchell Ashley served as territorial governor of Montana for fifteen months, from 1868 to 1870, during the period Lowell lived in Helena and Benton. The Republican congressman introduced the bill that evolved into the Thirteenth Amendment, which formally abolished slavery in 1865. In 1871, Lowell returned stateside on the steamboat Miner *with Ashley's wife and the couple's four children, including his eight-year-old son, Charles Sumner Ashley. Judge Lowell wrote to C.S. Ashley in 1899 to solicit his childhood reminiscences of the trip. Lowell used a quote from Ashley's reply at the end of the memoir, proving that Lowell completed the journal at the turn of the century, nearly thirty years after he commenced the work.*

C.S. Ashley,
Attorney and Counselor,
The Nasby,
Toledo, Ohio.
August 2nd, 1899.

Dear Sir:

Yours of July 30th is just received. I do not suppose that I have any recollection of the trip down the Missouri, in 1871, differing materially from those of the other passengers on the *Miner*.

The most vivid recollection I have of it is the vast herds of buffalo that swam the River ahead of our steamer, and which we wantonly and uselessly slaughtered by shooting from the decks. I suppose no such herds are now in existence as we saw at that time. It is a pity that these magnificent animals have been exterminated so rapidly.

One recollection we all have, however, which we have frequently expressed, and shall always express, in speaking of the trip. This is our most grateful recollection of the extreme courtesy of which my Mother was the object during all the long voyage in the Mackinaw with men who would usually be spoken of as "rough pioneers." As we were about to set out on this novel and dangerous journey, my Brother, James, came to my Mother and said, "Mother, there is going to be more whiskey than men about this boat, I am afraid." My Mother felt extremely timid about it, but there seemed nothing else to do than go ahead and so we went. You will recollect that they set off the middle section of the boat by placing trunks crosswise of the Mackinaw, with the choicest part of the boat, to my Mother and the aged lady of whom you mentioned; together, I presume with my little sister and myself. Several times each day, the boat was drawn up to the River bank and we were invited to relax ourselves by going and taking a walk; not an oath was spoken by all these rough men during the entire trip (at least in the hearing of my Mother), and in every way, the greatest consideration and truest politeness were displayed by the men on board the boat. Thus, a trip, which was begun with much timidity, has always furnished the matter for the most pleasing and agreeable remembrance.

I sent your former letter, and shall send your last one to my Mother, who is now at East Hampton, Long Island, New York, with my Sister. Possibly, my Mother may feel like writing you some of her own recollections of the matter. At least, I am sure she will be much pleased to read your letter and to have recalled to her memory the events of a very stirring summer of travel.

My Mother's address is "Mrs. James M. Ashley, East Hampton, Long Island, N.Y." There were with her on the trip in question her four children, James, Henry, Charles and Mary.

I do not know precisely what your intentions are, but if you are to get out some publication relating to this trip I should much like to have the opportunity of purchasing it.

Yours very truly,
C.S. Ashley

THE CIVIL WAR CORRESPONDENCE

The nineteenth-century migration west was fueled by the hunger for gold and the yearnings of young American men seeking adventure and healing after the war. Lowell calls these fellows "Argonauts of the plains." The upheavals of the conflict had ruptured the routines of family life, education, and work. The returning soldiers found the economy transformed, particularly in the South, where a young man might return home to find his family dispersed and his home destroyed. The rituals and traditional occupations of young adulthood were unfamiliar to them after camp life—perhaps even trivial. Headlines boasting of rich farmland, gold, and silver ignited their ambition. So it was with Jim Lowell. Despite his being shot in the upper thigh at Antietam, his war service had otherwise hardened him for the journey. He wasn't just an artistic city boy with literary ambitions anymore. He knew how to shoot.

It is impossible to know whether Lowell would have set off for parts unknown if he hadn't experienced the disruptions of war. His enlistment in 1861 effectively wrenched him from Boston and a future career in lithography. Several of Lowell's regimental comrades from the Northeast made their way west after the war, including the important early photographer of Native Americans Will Soule, with whom Lowell maintained a lifelong correspondence.[98]

LOWELL'S REGIMENT

The memory of the Massachusetts Thirteenth Regiment is burnished by regimental historians from the past and in the present day through the work of its modern descendants. In 1893, Charles E. Davis Jr. drew upon the diaries and recollections of fellow soldiers to compile the highly readable regimental history *Three Years in the Army: The Story of the Thirteenth Massachusetts Volunteers*.[99] In our era, we owe the title of regimental historian to Bradley Forbush, a great-great-grandson of the Massachusetts Thirteenth soldier William Henry Forbush, of Company K. Starting in the 1990s, Brad Forbush began collecting a complete set of the Massachusetts Thirteenth circulars. The circulars were pamphlets sent out to the men as invitations to their annual reunion in Boston. They served as a conduit for the men's war recollections and status updates. Lowell was a frequent contributor, and excerpts of his letters are included in this section, along with a letter he wrote in 1904 to his second son, James Henry Lowell, recalling his service. Also included is a letter Lowell wrote to his brother just after Antietam.

Lowell's life trajectory shifted on April 14, 1861, when Fort Sumter surrendered. Five days later, the people of Boston were celebrating the anniversary of the Battle of Lexington when news arrived that Southern Rebels had attacked the Sixth Regiment in Baltimore.

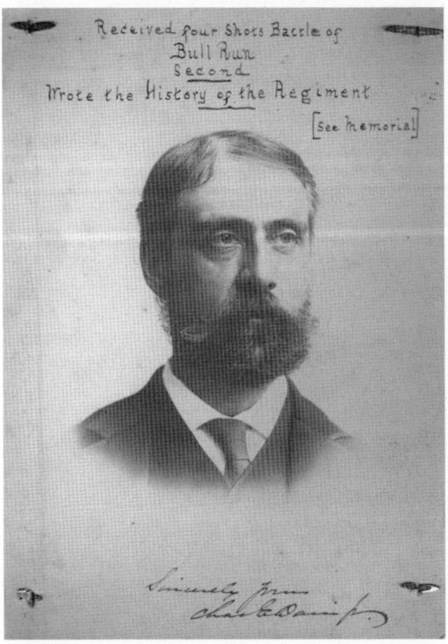

Lowell's comrade-in-arms Charles E. Davis Jr. from Company B wrote the Massachusetts Thirteenth regimental history. *Photograph from Lowell's personal photo album, courtesy of Tim Sewell.*

Charles Davis's regimental history offers this account of the turmoil:

> *Only one subject possessed the public mind—to protect the government from the clutches of traitorous hands....Many of the young men who left lucrative positions were guaranteed them on their return by their employers. The generous impulses of all were awakened by the danger that threatened the country.*[100]

In this climate, the nineteen-year-old Lowell enlisted in the Massachusetts Thirteenth Regiment, Company A, in July 1861. Surely, his grandfather and great-grandfather's Revolutionary War service figured prominently in the stories he heard as a child.

Apparently, the newly recruited Company A boys thought they were hot stuff. "They are a damned impertinent lot," wrote brigade commander General John J. Abercrombie, "fit only for the guardhouse."[101] Many of the young men, who were required to pay a fee of $12.50 for uniforms and equipment, were handpicked from Boston's best-known families.

Under Colonel Samuel Haven Leonard, they developed into the grudgingly complimented and somewhat infamous regiment known for its competitiveness, spit and polish, and back talk. In anticipation of a high-level review in 1861, the Boston boys, as the saying goes, *put on the dog*:

> *We were notified in advance that this was to be an unusual occasion, so the boys shined their buttons, brushed their coats, blacked their boots, and last but not least, adorned themselves with paper collars purchased from the sutler. This prinking which the boys indulged in occasionally, just to remind them of days gone by, and which gave the regiment the sobriquet of "Band-box guard," reached the ears of Colonel Coulter, of the Eleventh Pennsylvania, who was bound to have a little fun at the regiment's expense. Now it happened that "Dick" Coulter was the owner of a brindle bulldog called "Sally," who was famous throughout the brigade for her intelligence, and had a habit of sticking close to the colonel's heels with her neck labeled "13," and a white glove fastened on each paw. During the whole of the ceremony, "Sally" trotted about in plain sight, a most ludicrous object, affording a deal of amusement to all who witnessed it.*[102]

Early in the war, the men made an effort "to adorn and beautify" their camp at Darnestown, Maryland, by placing evergreen trees in front of the tents and by erecting arches made of boughs to mark each company

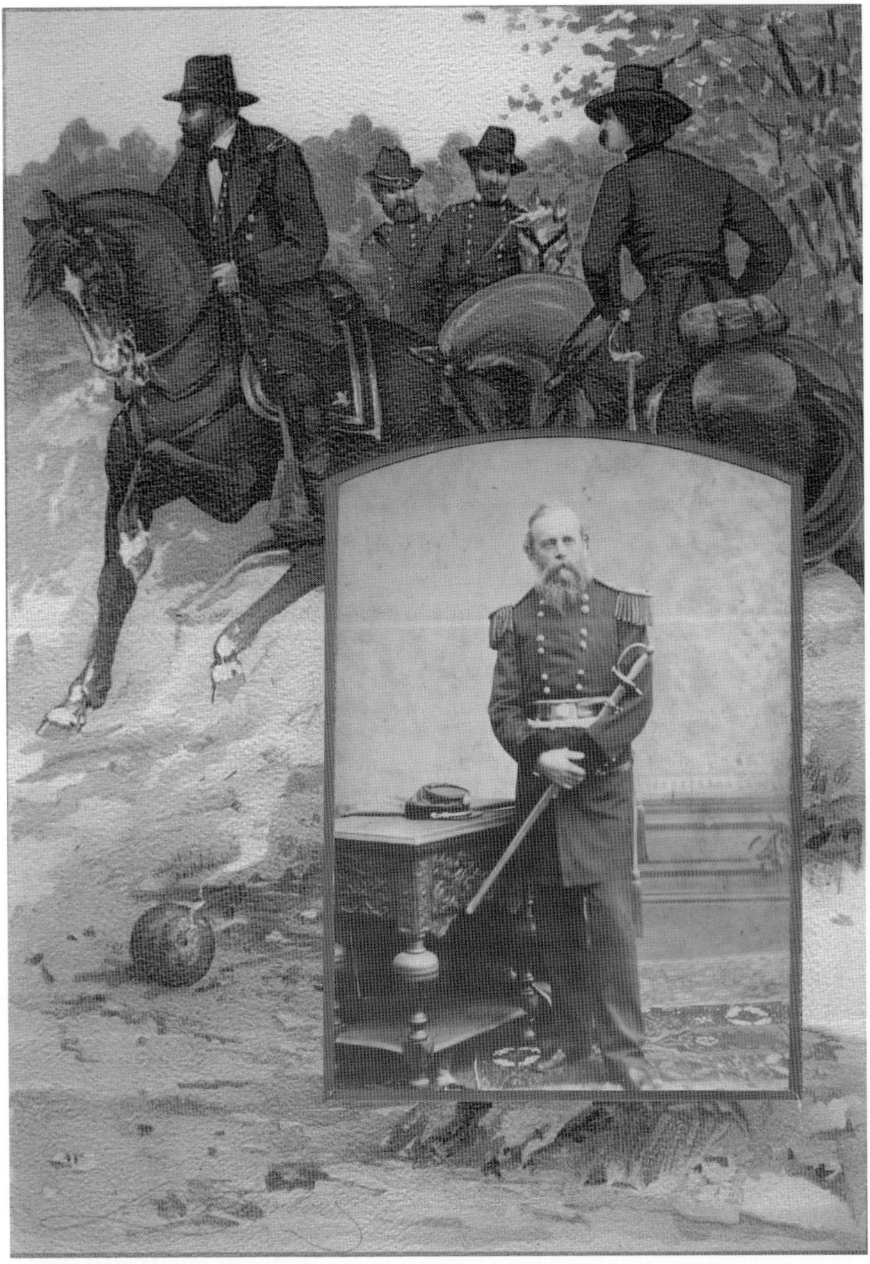

Brigade commander of the Massachusetts Thirteenth Regiment Colonel Samuel Haven Leonard. *Photograph from Lowell's personal photo album, courtesy of Tim Sewell.*

street.[103] The rows of marching soldiers bedecked in polished brass buttons and ornament were intended to cast a *glow* upon reviewing officers, but their efforts at cleanliness were not just for show. The Thirteenth boasted a record of merit in the low percentage of deaths from disease, due in part, to the men's addiction to soap and water: "It's as difficult to overcome as drinking or the use of opium," Davis wrote.[104] Those Boston niceties must have seemed quaint a year later on the battlefield at Bull Run (Second Manassas):

> *One's teeth would chatter, chatter the whole night long, making sleep impossible. Shaking with the cold, enduring the agony of pain from undressed wounds and the pangs of hunger, it seemed as though the nights would never end. A good many men pegged out under this combination who might have lived, possibly, had they been removed to the hospitals early in the week. By the fourth day, the stench on the field, from decaying bodies, was almost unbearable….On Thursday afternoon, an old man, not far from sixty years of age, with a bag on his shoulders, was seen prowling about the field, apparently, for the purposes of gain, as he was seen frequently to bend his body as if engaged in searching the dead. Presently it was discovered that no such motive prompted his action, inasmuch as his bag was filled with apples and biscuits which he was distributing to men on the field, giving one to each, according to choice, that as many as possible might have even a mouthful. To each and every one visited, he proffered a kind and encouraging word, and it is possible that many a fellow's courage was kept alive by his patriotic undertaking.*[105]

A year later, another patriotic civilian, a newspaperman, saved Lowell's life by dragging him off the battlefield at Antietam.[106]

Contrary to military records, Lowell records first being wounded at the Second Battle of Bull Run (Second Manassas), and the index of the regimental history written by Charles E. Davis Jr. cites Lowell as having been wounded in that battle. Nevertheless, the wounds he suffered must have been minor. Military records reveal only one incident, a gunshot wound to the left leg suffered at Antietam. By the time the Massachusetts Thirteenth made its way to the battlefield north of Sharpsburg to meet General Robert E. Lee's forces near Antietam Creek on September 17, 1862, the troops no longer resembled a glittering bandbox brigade:

> *Instead of bright uniforms, with gilt buttons and shoulder knots,* [a new recruit] *found us with ragged trousers, ill-fitting blouses, and torn and*

> *faded caps—the result of long marches over dusty roads and bivouacking in ploughed fields, that made us look more like a regiment of tramps than soldiers.*[107]

At this point, the Boston men more closely resembled their Confederate adversaries, who had marched for weeks subsisting on little but green corn and unripe fruit. Thousands of the Southern men were unshod as they passed north of the Mason-Dixon line to meet the enemy on its own turf.[108]

The men of the Massachusetts Thirteenth headed into the Battle of Antietam as part of Brigadier General George Lucas Hartsuff's brigade (Hooker's First Corps, Rickett's Second Division, Hartsuff's Third Brigade consisting of the Sixteenth Maine, Twelfth Massachusetts, Thirteenth Massachusetts, Eighty-Third New York, and Eleventh Pennsylvania). Hartsuff took a hit as they moved out, so the command passed down to Colonel Richard Colter, Eleventh Pennsylvania. The men emerged from the woods at 6:25 a.m. and approached the infamous David R. Miller cornfield under heavy shelling and fire from Hays's and Lawton's Louisiana and Georgia brigades. As historian James McPherson noted in his book on Antietam: "Many cornfields were the scene of fighting during the Civil War, but this one was ever after known as *the* Cornfield."[109] The firefight flattened the crops and shredded men's firearms to pieces in their hands; 45 percent of the Massachusetts Thirteenth were either killed or wounded holding the front line.[110] Lowell suffered a gunshot wound to his upper left leg. He recounted the experience in a letter written to his son years later and noted that a *New York Sun* correspondent risked his life to drag him to safety. As an elderly man, he still regretted not getting the man's name to thank him.[111]

In *Miller Cornfield at Antietam*, historian Phillip Thomas Tucker wrote: "And at no single place on the battlefield's twelve square miles during a dozen hours of combat was the contest more lethal than in the Miller Cornfield. To determine the destinies of the two republics, no combat during the war's four years compared to the sheer intensity of the brutal struggle that raged throughout the cornfield."[112]

In all, 301 of the Thirteenth went into the battle; 165 came out in one piece when their cartridge boxes were empty.[113] The Massachusetts Twelfth Regiment, fighting just west of the Thirteenth, suffered the highest percentage of casualties in a battle that produced the highest number of American casualties of any single battle in U.S. history.[114]

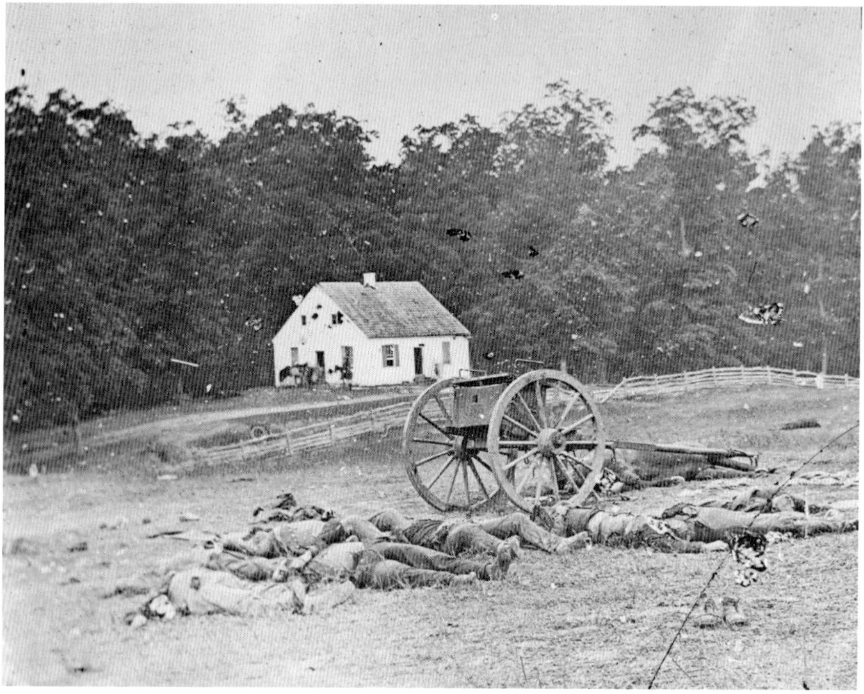

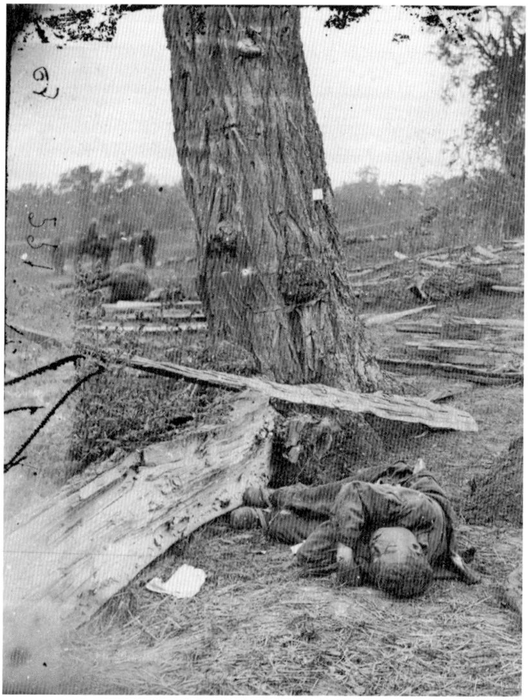

Above: Antietam, Maryland. Bodies in front of the Dunker Church. *Photograph by Alexander Gardner, 1862, Library of Congress, LC-B811-562.*

Left: Antietam, Maryland. Confederate unburied, where they fell. *Photograph by Alexander Gardner, 1862, Library of Congress, LC-B811-551.*

The outcome at Antietam proved that McClellan's unsuccessful Army of the Potomac could stand their ground and fight, particularly when they were defending northern territory. The morning after, Massachusetts Thirteenth major Jacob Parker Gould tipped his hat to his men in a letter written to Colonel Leonard:

> *It was the severest battle I ever expected to witness. The Manassas was a skirmish compared with it....Hartsuff's Brigade is complimented, how much praise must be awarded to the 13th who stood so long so bravely. I am proud of them.*[115]

In many respects, the Union victory at Antietam was a turning point. It gave Abraham Lincoln the confidence to issue his Emancipation Proclamation and discouraged the European powers from entering the war in support of the Confederacy. Yet the Union soldiers groused at McClellan's unwillingness to pursue Lee's army over the Potomac and finish them off.[116]

Lowell's leg wound kept him off the field of battle for the remainder of the war. He worked as a clerk in the medical director's office, then in mustering and disbursement, and, finally, at the provost marshal general's office in Harrisburg until he mustered out in August 1864. During this period, Lowell met and befriended Morrow P. Lowry,[117] a character who would make a surprising reappearance in Lowell's life in Montana. Lowell also contracted a mild case of smallpox while he was working in the medical director's office in Harrisburg. The immunity he developed enabled him to doctor Piegans and whites while he lived in Benton.

In the Civil War correspondence, one can't help but note how Lowell's perspective changes over time from his writings as a young, wounded soldier, when he characterizes the enemy as enjoying overwhelming numbers, to the late-life recollections, where he betrays 20/20 hindsight: "There was always a 'Lion in the Way' with McClellan..."[118]

As a veteran, Lowell joined the fraternal organization known as the Grand Army of the Republic and maintained two keepsake photo albums of his comrades and Union officers. The proud confidence he shared with the Massachusetts Thirteenth boys served him well as he navigated throughout the untamed West.

Post-Antietam Letter to Brother

Lowell wrote in the margin: "This letter was written by James H. Lowell shortly after Antietam (Sept. 17, 1862)."

Hospital Harrisburg Oct 8th 62

Dear Brother

Yours of the 22nd was received on the 30th I think having first gone to the Regt. I sent a line to you giving the particulars of the battle my wound is getting along favorably and am able to get around with a crutch quite well. If you wish to do anything for me you can send the 5 dollars which I need to invest in a lap and necessarys. I have my Descriptive List but cannot get my pay until the last of the month the amount you will please add to that which I owe you now and await the payment which will come some time

I intend to visit Boston in about a month and I hope when the Government goes to work with a single eye to crushing the Rebellion as Rebellions always have been crushed, then I will join them. I will not hazard my life again under the present system of warfare. I have been in 7 battles and now no nearer the end of the war than when I crossed into Virginia nor so near with the taxation now being imposed on the South and the Drafting of every man will make these strong enough for our Million. They are a sanguine and desperate people notwithstanding the Newspaper talk of the North. I believe as Gen. Banks says that there is too much confidence placed on the strength of our army. Fools and Non Military men imagine that McClellan is going to bag and capture 150,000 men with 100,000 men and take Richmond with an inferior force with such Generals as Lee & Jackson to contend against. Such men can easily draw the wool over the president's eyes while if he would listen to a General like Banks, the war would soon end.

Please forward the money as quick as possible and tell father to write.

Yours truly

James

enclose a stamp and paper

LETTER TO FATHER

After suffering a gunshot wound to his left leg at the Battle of Antietam in September 17, 1862, Lowell recovered in Harrisburg, Pennsylvania, and served in the medical director's office. He wrote to his father and begged for a letter and a photograph.

Medical Director's office
Harrisburg Jan 18th 1863

Dear Father

Thinking that perhaps you would like to hear from your son, I take this time to inform you that I am well and getting on finely in my Business. My duties have been rather arduous for the last month but now they are very much easier. I am among friends and do enjoy myself here. I think that Harrisburg is the place for me. If I were out of the Army, I would easily get a good situation here. I am acquainted in many good families here and pass the time very pleasantly. I heard from Lydia [Lowell's sister, who was two years older] a short time ago. She was not very well. How do you get along with your work? It is so long since you wrote to me I shall expect a lot of news when you do write and I wish you send me your Photograph. Tell George [his brother, four years elder] to send me his. I forgot to speak of it in my last letter to him. Give my regards to all inquiring friends. Goodbye.

James

LETTER TO SON

The sixty-two-year-old Lowell recounted his Civil War service to his son James Henry Lowell.

Law Office of
James H. Lowell
Holton, Kansas, July 17, 1904

Dear Jim:
When Sumter was attacked early in 1861, Old General Winfield Scott was in command of the U.S. troops. Shortly after, Col. McClellan [George B. McClellan, Commander of the Army of the Potomac] had a small scrap in W. Va. and the affair was reported a success, this gave McClellan notoriety and the old man Scott laid down in his favor. But before this, a great hue and cry of "On to Richmond" with the 75,000 of Lincoln's first call brought out Gen. [Irvin] McDowell, who yielded to the demand and the 1st Bull Run was the result. This was considered a tremendous battle at the time, but if you look sharp, it was a small affair compared to the Second of the name. McClellan went to work organizing and the year was spent at it up to March 1862. The Potomac was patrolled to Hancock and the winter spent in shifting and drilling.

Our regiment went South July 14, 1861,[119] and camped within a stone's throw of the battlefield of Antietam, at Sharpsburg, but the companies of our regiment were hither and thither up and down the river. We were called "The Advance Guard of the Upper Potomac." My Company, "A," and "B" Company were sent to Hancock where we staid the better part of the winter '61–'62 supporting a battery there. Our duty was to prevent the destruction of a dam, which turned water into the canal leading to Washington.[120] McClellan's plan was to transfer a large army to the Peninsular, there to battle for Richmond leaving an Army under McDowell, and one in the Shenandoah under Banks to protect Washington. Simultaneous with the movement to the Peninsular, the McDowell crowd, 40,000, and Banks crossed over the river at various points. My brigade under an old Granny named [Major General Robert] Patterson (who was shortly retired) was attached nominally to Banks, and we crossed separately from other troops and marched at night entering Martinsburg about midnight. Nigh day, we pushed toward Winchester, the rebels falling back.[121] Winchester was fortified and as we approached the early dawn in battle line and looked at the line of earthworks ahead, you may possibly think that:

Each horseman drew his battle blade
And furious every charger neighed
To join the dreadful revelry [122]

The cold facts, however, were somewhat different. My regiment had in advance deployed as skirmishers, its Company "A" (of which I was one) each other regiment was likewise covered by an extension of skirmishers, thus:

. . . .

Co. A

―――――――――――――――

Reg't

So you observe we skirmishers were favored with a much closer view than the regiment, and the port holes [cannon] stared at us as we neared them most fearsomely. Old Man Patterson said something about charging; it must have been <u>not</u> charge, for we <u>did</u> charge with our usual disobedience of his orders. Our Wisconsin fellows got there first and planted the Stars and Stripes on the abandoned parapet. We learned that Jackson had retired a couple of hours earlier. Aside from a few skirmishes and forays, this was our first baptism in warfare. I was glad they had left, and although pretty well worked up, I would say: "Better mistaken suspicions than one close encounter." We staid under Banks a while and were kept going up and down, out and in of the Valley of Shenandoah, scrapping a little here and there, and worked Hard. A noble soldier, Gen. [George Lucas] Hartsuff, came to command our brigade, and we joined McDowell at Falmouth (on the Rappahannock). This was in May. We took an immediate dislike to McDowell, a reasonless, foolish dislike.

We do not like you Doctor Fell
The reason why we cannot tell
But this we know, and that full well
We do not like you Doctor Fell.

But long before the close of war, we knew him to be a brave, wrongly accused, and wrongly discredited officer. Looking back,

I believe he would have been the peer of the best of our Generals had he been given a fair chance.

Lincoln visited and reviewed us here.[123] It was a great pageant, 45,000 strong. He rode a small horse, his legs reaching way down and his beaver [hat] of that period reaching way up. McClellan was storming the rebels on the Peninsular. No one understood why we were not moving his way. The war was waging out West and an officer named John Pope was reported capturing an Island—No 10—and bagging 10,000 rebs. A clamor went up to get him the Virginia job. This new genius came to us—relieving McDowell in July 1862 and issued a general order that was read to us at dress parade. It was a program of immediate slaughter, where at, we gave our guns a special clean up. He joined us on the Rappahannock and led us 14 miles south to Rapidan, the same night we arrived, a stealthy retrograde began which ended in the fortifications at Washington, or Arlington Heights. This interval was a holy terror in warfare. Pope tried to check the enemy at the Rappahannock. He sent my brigade over to the south side with a battery to hold off Jackson's advance, the army proper being on the north bank. For 2 days and until morning of the 3rd, we lay there only partially protected while the batteries roared and the shells hurtled around, and occasionally dropped among us. I know of no one who likes that kind of fighting. You can neither dodge nor hit back. Then followed a race toward Manassas, or Bull Run. Our way lay toward Thoroughfare Gap and to occupy the heights above. We got part way into the gap and encountered Longstreet's sharp shooters and presently his division. They cleaned us out handsomely, and we suffered quite a loss, especially the Wisconsin regiment. Our brigade was alone and comprised the 12th Mass., (Col. [Fletcher] Webster, son of Daniel), the 13th Mass., the 9th N.Y., [83rd NY] the 13th Wis., 4th Pa. (Col Coulter.)[124] The weather was torrid, and exhaustions were numerous for we were going a fast pace. Off we went toward Bull Run and there a half day was spent in aligning troops. We were several times shifted and finally just after noon, marched toward McDowell and staff on a high ground. When the ball opened, this we all concede was the worst place the troops got into. In less than 10 minutes from the beginning, McDowell in person led our brigade to Bald Hill. He was the incarnation of War himself, and we went in yelling like demons. Bald Hill had already been swept clear of every live soldier sent there, how long we remained that survived, I don't know but our remnant broke and escaped.[125] I helped take off a gun of Matthew's battery, a famous battery, virtually knocked to pieces, every horse and most of the men killed or hurt.[126] McClellan had got back from the Peninsular and was relieved from command. His troops or part were sent toward us as we sullenly walked back to Arlington Forts. Here, our rags were replaced by fresh clothing and our feet, newly shod. Lee now schemed to break over the Mason Dixon Line, promptly, he crossed the river into Maryland. McClellan was reinstated and we had a night's march through Georgetown and Washington across Long Bridge and the morning found us on Maryland soil hiking to Frederick, thence, to South Mountain. Hooker now commanded our division, Hartsuff, still our Brigadier. Hooker was ever present full of vim and keen for a scrap. He was a fine specimen, conceited, brave and enterprising. His night work, where we saw him every little bit, getting us over that mountain, is very vivid to me. Our regiment was there in the center and he would go afoot through our ranks way up stealthily in advance with only an orderly, then return and give his orders. By these stages, we reached the summit about 2 o'clock in the morning fighting every inch with General [A.P.] Hill confederate. Two days later, the 17th September come on Antietam, and here closed my field service as a soldier, unless you count the auxiliary service in the Gettysburg campaign as volunteer in the trenches across the river at Harrisburg, July 1863. My escutcheon reads, Harpers Ferry—Pritchard Mills—Berkley Springs—Winchester (the real Battle of)—Newton—Middleburg—Cedar Mountain—Rappahannock Station—Thoroughfare Gap—Manassas 2nd—Chantilly—South Mountain—Antietam, more or less seven—gunning in them all.

The story is too much for a letter. It will give you the idea you want in fixing my whereabouts in the reading of the Potomac Army. You are pretty near right about Lee and Jackson, but don't think for a moment that there was excess of valor in the rank and file of their armies over ours. You are right about Burnside. The supremacy of Halleck, the office General at Washington curtailed the initiative of every subordinate in the field. Splendid material existed, but men like Reynolds, men of genius, would have nothing to do with it, and refused leadership when offered. I have a letter written by me to my father October 13, 1862, in hospital, complaining of the conduct of the war in terms you have expressed as your deductions from reading. It was the universal topic among soldiers and seriously affected the morale of our army. There was always a "Lion in the Way" with McClellan. Pope was a fraud, and Burnside, an incompetent. Hooker failed, not in his plan, but his tactics. We were outwitted constantly until Grant, who had carte blanche and unlimited means, doggedly wore out the enemy. My regiment was composed of the best material in point of natural ability and intelligence—more of such men in it—than any regiment I ever saw. And McDowell, Banks, and even Pope have substantially attested it. You will notice that the work we had to do between March and September 1862 shows a big record.

Parker represents, as you say, the restoration of old-time, sane democracy. Of the Cleveland stamp. It will take time to purge it of its vitiated element, its tomfoolery, its Bryanism, with its demagoguery. The Republican Party has absorbed every good that belonged to it, at the time it left me. Parker seems strong in the East and South and he will lead a strong fight. In my view, he was wisely chosen. In the west Roosevelt will lead but he will have difficulty in carrying N.Y., if the signs are correctly read. The Republican Party needs a Hanna to arouse it to the impending danger. We are not fighting the Populism that masqueraded in '96 and 1900, but a sane and awakened democracy. Look out for the fur to fly. George was here two days last week. He is touring, and in Leav'th [Leavenworth] today (Sunday). His team is ahead.[127] I saw two games at Topeka and enjoyed it. Geo. pitched one of them. All well.

James
Pa

I might as well finish my enlistment period of 3 years by saying, when I got able, I left the hospital as detailed Clerk in the Medical Directors Office, then Chief Clerk Mustering and Disbursing Officer, then Chief Clerk in Provost Marshal General's office, at Harrisburg. I was ordered to report (I have the order) to Boston to be mustered out August 1, 1864. I was tendered as a civilian, a chief clerkship at Harrisburg at $100 per month and accepted until the war closed in 1865. My salary was raised to $150.

MASSACHUSETTS THIRTEENTH CIRCULARS

James Howard Lowell contributed letters to eleven regimental circulars. The following selections are of particular interest. In Circular 23, Lowell recounted an incident where the Company A men were displaying their bayonet skills and their youthful vanity. The contemptuous reaction of a local matron revealed her identity as a Southern spy. Circular 27 offers an incident from the journal where he met a fellow Boston man in Montana. Lowell wrote his last contribution four years before his death. In Circular 34, he related how a newspaperman saved his life by dragging him off the battlefield at Antietam.

Full transcripts reside at www.lowellmemoir.com.

Circular 23

HOLTON, KAN., Dec. 9, 1909.
CHARLES E. DAVIS, JR., Boston, Mass.
DEAR COMRADES ALL:
[...criticizes the practices of quoting bylaws and permitting advertisements in the Circulars, which he calls the sale of "our accumulated rubbish."]

I wonder how many survivors of Company A remember the following incident; I have seen nothing of it in any of the circulars. The impression it left on my mind at the time has never molted a feather and I am tempted to relate it in my awkward way. In the winter of 1861, three or four companies of the regiment were sent to Hancock as part of the "Advance Guard." Company A was quartered in a brand new brick 3-story house; the pony mess (to which the writer belonged) camped in the low-ceiled attic. Now, as Company A figured in the role of skirmishers of the regiment, a part of our training was the bayonet drill. One day a series of bayonet drills took place in the attic, an arena wholly unsuited for that character of warfare, and the result was that the ceiling looked like one vast cane bottom for a chair, and the lamentations of the Irishman who owned the property when he discovered the casualties brought Sergeant [David] Whiston to the scene. Orderly Sergeant Whiston was a pretty good detective, but he was clean off-scent in this instance. The bayonet warfare of Company "A" did not end here. On one of those delightfully fine days of a Maryland winter, Bob Henderson (of cherished memory), then a sergeant, was ordered to bring out the company for bayonet drill. For the occasion we were groomed to the top notch—buttons glistening in the sunshine we were proudly marched up street halting in front of a mansion whose balcony above contained two Union officers with a female between. One was a surgeon with rank as major. With bayonets fixed we got to business, going through the manual with bugle calls. The whole thing was so sudden and unexpected that the vain pedantry of the performance did not at once get to our inner consciousness, as it did later on. Our distinguished audience on the balcony condescended to clap us politely, and the show was going merrily on when the bugle noted us to lie down, and down we went, immaculate plumage, polished buttons, and all in Maryland dirt. At once a voice—of a woman—from the balcony "see Lincoln's niggers." Instantly Sergeant Henderson took a hand, and we were marched to our quarters, where a discussion took place without the formality of a chairman and secretary and in which the names of the holy Trinity served to give emphasis. We were not long in deciding what to do, and with Sergeant Henderson for a leader we retraced our steps to the mansion and going to the door the sergeant slammed the knocker; the door presently opened with the major in front, who demanded the sergeant's business. "I wish to speak to the person who insulted these Federal soldiers," said the sergeant. Quoth the major: "You can't cross this threshold except over my dead body." Behind the major stood the "person," who said, "Major, I will speak to the sergeant." Then followed a retraction of the offensive words and an apology, and thus disarmed, we returned to our quarters. The incident was closed as to the "person," not so as to the major. Our return was enlivened by repeated "three groans for the dead body," that could be heard by the rebel pickets on the Virginia shore. At the foot of the stairway or entrance to our quarters was constantly kept a guard or sentinel. This guard, as part of his duty, was unofficially charged to announce the appearance of the major whenever seen in the vicinity. On one or two occasions this happened, and in each instance we formed a line in double column on the curb, and gave the major our complimentary salute, "Three groans for the dead body." It was currently reported that the major at his own request was relieved from further service at Hancock. But before the major's departure, the woman took hasty leave. Her mission as a spy became by this incident too plainly evident to admit of doubt. She was not a resident, a palpable courtesan, and her flight none too soon for her own good.

With best wishes to all,
JAMES H. LOWELL.

CIRCULAR 27

HOLTON, KANS., Dec. 1, 1913.
MY DEAR CHARLES, JR.:

The selections in Circular 26 were fine, and the good, dietary sketches are something to think over after reading. Warner's sketch of the blue and gray at the late reunion at Gettysburg called to mind, by contrast, a little incident that occurred in '69 in the mining region of Montana. A matter of business took me to see the president of a gold placer mining enterprise. They were digging a water ditch on a big scale, and apparently, the diggers were all unreconstructed rebels. It was nightfall when I reached the ditch line, and man and beast were about all in. I drew rein at a cabin of one of the diggers. A big fellow came out, and a heated colloquy took place. He said he was a Georgian, and had a hand in licking Yankees, and would like to do it again. No damned Yankee from Mass. could sleep under his roof, and the sooner a Mass. soldier got off his ditch contract the better for him. I had my foot in the stirrup to remount, when he took hold of the rein to detain me. "Hold on," he said, "no true Southerner forgets to be hospitable." He picketed the horse out where it could feed on the nutritious bunch grass, and we entered the cabin. My protests were in vain, and he was a big man besides, and would have his way. A neater kept cabin was hard to find. There were books and papers; the furniture hand made from the surrounding timber. Canned meats and fruits were on the shelves. The dirt floor looked clean and swept. On the deal table I saw a volume of Hume's *History of England*. I got into a fit of thinking. He busied himself getting supper—mixed a batter, and was soon flipping slap-jacks in a frying-pan; then he broke the tense silence. "What town did you say you hailed from in Mass.?" "Look here," said I, "Quit your damn shamming, and what town in Mass. did you come from?" "Boston!"

His name was Hopkins; he had served through the war in a regiment of Mass., I have forgotten the number. He asked me to stay with him a day or two and help stand off annoying neighbors who would come in pairs to taunt and vent their spleen and hatred of Yankee's, thinking to freeze him out of his ditch contract. It worried him, but he was amply able to keep up his end. I run up against many in Montana, first and last, of the horde of ex-rebels that had poured into that Territory at the close of the war, who were amiable and content to bury the hatchet; some fine fellows, among whom was the president of the ditch company, whom I first met in 1866 in Salt Lake City.

Wishing a happy reunion on the 13th,

Cordially,

Lowell.

P.S.

Some very clever lines were written some years ago, I may have them somewhere, on the futility of swearing. The argument was that smoking and chewing tobacco, and the satisfaction they gave to some particular sense, found a contrast to swearing, that satisfied no sense whatever.

An officer of the U.S. Army—a General—was delivered of a dictum carrying a better argument, and in harmony with the outburst of G. Washington, to wit:

"Profanity, sir, is the unnecessary use of profane language."

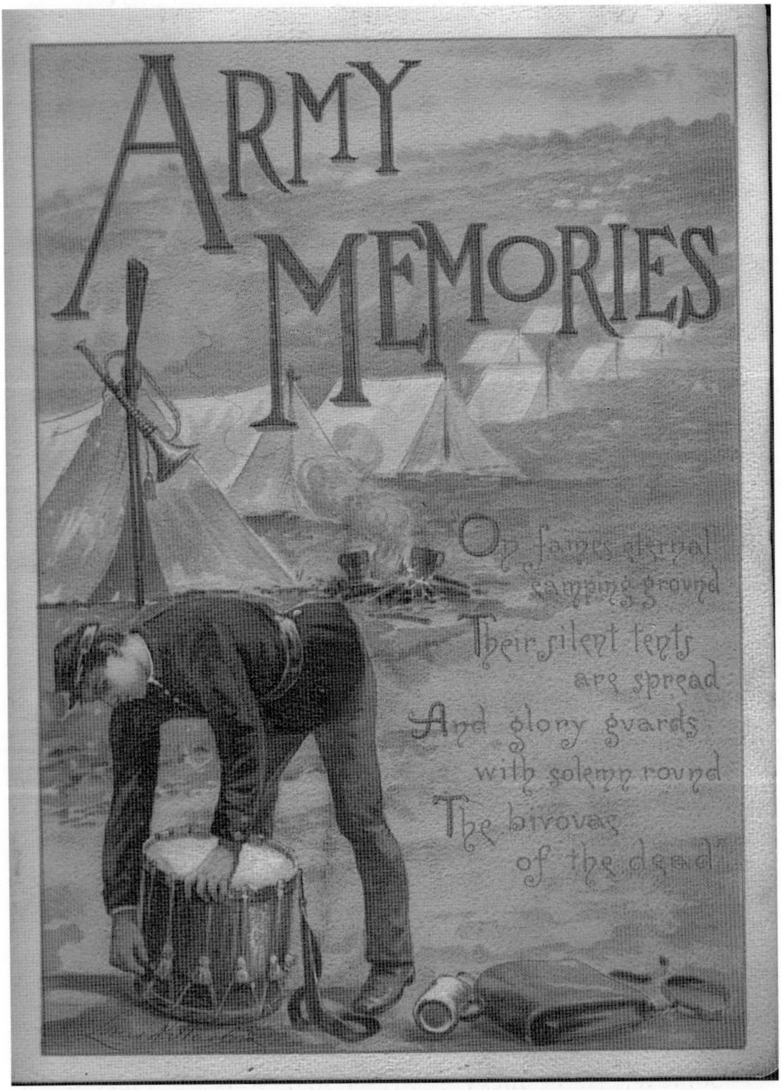

Page from Lowell's army keepsake photo album. *Courtesy of Tim Sewell.*

Circular 33

HOLTON, KANSAS, Sept. 11th, 1919.
MY DEAR COMRADE SWAN AND COMRADES ALL:

I have just read the nine short letters of the nine aged and esteemed veterans in Circular 32 with a thrill of comradeship, which I must acknowledge here. Our ages are separated but by a few years at most and doubtless we generally share more or less the inconveniences hinted at in the letters. [Lowell was seventy-seven.] But, glory be, old age is not necessarily an unhappy period. It will come with good cheer to those who can say: "I have fought the good fight; I have finished my course; I have kept the faith; and when the summons comes for my departure, I am prepared to go—not like the galley slave scourged to his dungeon, but like one who draws the drapery of his couch about him and lies down to pleasant dreams." [2 Timothy 4:7] The going out of such a life is like the going down of the sun into the mellow haze of an Autumnal evening. Our attention is constantly called to the inevitable, that a strictly old man's league that admits of no recruits, puts it squarely up to us to make all the hay possible while the sun shines. Therefore, may you have a cheery time on the seventeenth, a day so full of memories of youth, of vigor, of sacrifice, of valor. The natal period of our glorious comradeship, and we who are camping out will remember you and the day.

Yours,
LOWELL, Co. A.

Circular 34

HOLTON, KANSAS, Sept. 10, 1920.
MY DEAR SWAN AND COMRADES:

I wish I could be with you the 17th. Have read and enjoyed the Circular and I find in it, in Comrade Walker's Article, a text for reminiscences of hospital life, and events that followed in its train.

Antietam has always been a theme of deep interest—a sort of starting point in my life. A few days ago I fished out a Government map of the battlefield given me by Charley Davis (of devoted memory) of good size and the location of hay stacks as they were, and gave it to the Secretary of the Kansas State Historical Society, who welcomed it with great enthusiasm.

I had two assistants from the firing line to the haystacks on the farm of Samuel Luffenberger. [*sic* Poffenberger] One was a Penn. bucktail, who, when we got past the rear guard, bolted. There came along, under fire, a fellow about my age in civilian rig, who stuck to the job. [...of supporting Lowell off the battlefield and escorting him to the triage area among the hay stacks on the farm.] He took down my name, regiment, etc., saying, "I am a correspondent of the *New York Sun*." How stupid of me not to take his name and address that I might remember to commend his bravery later! The space at this stack hospital was crowded and we remained there till evening, during that time first aid only was given. And there was disclosed the machine like habit of the drilled soldier—more interested in the fortunes of the firing line they had just left than the injury he received there. "How are things going?" was the topic discussed, while the surgeon was making his rounds. The tragedy of the firing line was the tragedy of the wounded, and *its* fortunes, *their* fortunes. That night we were taken to Hagerstown, and our second hospital was "The little White Church," thence the next day through the Cumberland Valley to Harrisburg, where a hospital on Chestnut Street—the Sunday School room of the German Reformed Church, was opened for some of us—a frame dining room in the rear. It was a new thing there and our treatment was lavish for quite a while, and always of the friendliest. Eight boys of the 13th were there, possibly I may miss others—John B. Noyes, Robt. Armstrong, Eugene A. Fiske, James L. Forbes, L.L. Dorr, James Dammers, William S. Soule,[128] Alfred Brigham. The service was good. A rule was early laid down that all emotions except those of cheerfulness should be stifled; and I recall no infraction of this law. My cot was next to Dammers. A quartette of singers often delighted us. Dammers' lung was pierced with a bullet, but no one was his superior in keeping out the blues, being a ventriloquist, he startled the quartette on one occasion by an interruption from the opposite side of the ward of a cock crowing. This resulted in a riot of laughing. Dorr, Dammers and self survive. An intimacy—life long—with Forbes, Soule and Fiske has been my good fortune. Forbes inherited a large landed estate in India through an uncle. Fiske lived in Santa Fe many years and served a term as Attorney General of New Mexico. You know of Soule. But I must not encroach on your time and patience. It will interest you to compare Walker's Article and this scrawl with the following authentic account of a hospital at Waterloo. By Surgeon C. Bell.

This is the second Sunday after the battle and many wounds are not dressed. It is impossible to convey to you the picture of human misery continuously before my eyes. At 6 o'clock a.m. I took the knife in my hand and continued incessantly at work til 7 in the evening, and so the second day, and again on the third. All the decencies of performing surgical operation were soon neglected. While I amputated one man's thigh, there lay at one time thirteen, all beseeching to be taken next—one full of entreaty, one calling on me to remember my promise to take him, another execrating. It was a strange thing to feel my clothes stiff with blood and my arms powerless with the exertion of using the knife.

At the time he speaks of the principle of anesthetics had not been discovered.

I intended to include in my hospital experience, and state that being detailed as a clerk in the Medical Director's office, I caught a case of small pox from a convalescent who had business here, and in consequence put in a couple of months—alone, except a man nurse—in the pest house at Camp Curtin, just outside the city. Cordial greeting to all.

Yours,
LOWELL, of A.

APPENDIX

Lowell's Descendants and the Provenance of the Journal

James Howard Lowell and Kate Mary had two sons and three daughters.

George Alexander, born in 1874, pitched minor league baseball for the Joplin Miners.

James *Henry* Lowell—our hero's second son, my great-grandfather, who was often mistakenly identified as James Howard Lowell Jr.—was born in 1876. He inherited the art bug from his parents and set his sights on New York City, where he met his wife, Anna Clotilda Brocaw, of St. Louis, at the Art Students League. He was a painter and illustrator who did political cartoons, advertisements, and book illustrations. The couple had two girls. They left their first home near the New York Botanical Garden in the Bronx to settle in White Plains, New York.

Lowell's third child, Ellen, was born in 1879. She taught music in Holton and never married. Another baby daughter, Blanche, failed to survive her first year. Their youngest child, Kate Roberta, was born in 1885 when Kate Mary was in her forties. Kate Roberta married a widower named Brutus Sewell and raised a son by his first marriage and two children of her own.

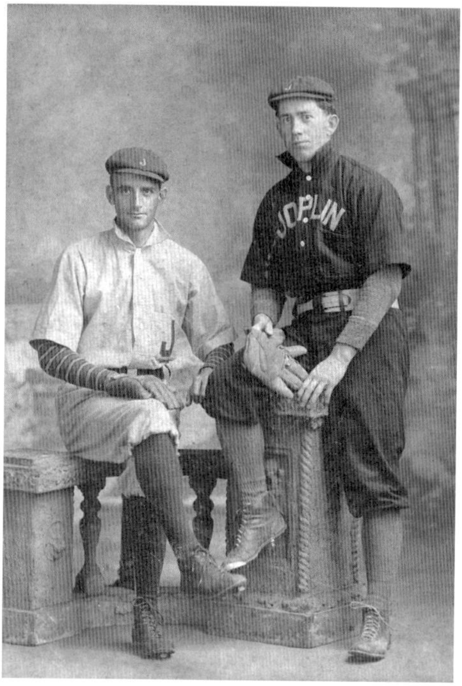

Left: Lowell's eldest son, George Alexander Lowell (*left*), and an unidentified teammate, 1903 Joplin Miners. *Courtesy of David Winston.*

Below: Second-eldest son James Henry Lowell (*standing*) took this picture of his family around 1895 using a timer. *Seated from left to right*: daughter Kate Roberta Lowell, Kate Mary Roberts Lowell, daughter Ellen Lowell and James Howard Lowell. *Courtesy of Tim Sewell.*

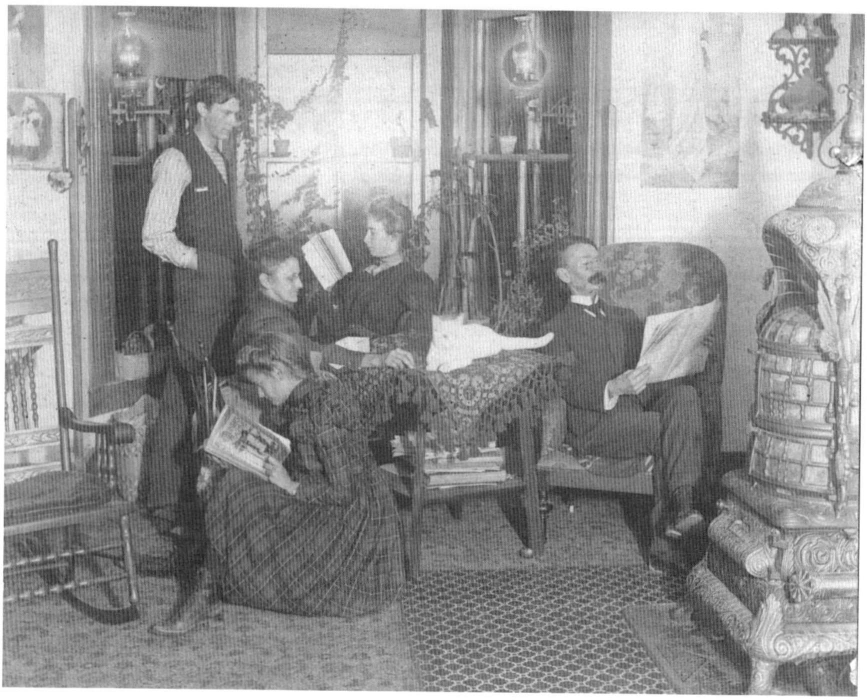

In later years, Lowell pursued his interest in family history and took care to maintain the graves of the Putney forbearers. He researched the Lowell family coat of arms and wrote the third chapter about the family's transatlantic history for Delmar Lowell's 1899 genealogy.[129] Despite his early wanderings, Lowell seldom ventured from Holton but sent his regrets along with his dues to the annual reunion of the Massachusetts Thirteenth veterans in Boston. He never returned to Montana. In later years, the "Judge," as he was familiarly known, sheltered his elder brother, George Malcolm Lowell, who had been down on his luck and had fallen into debt while prospecting in New Mexico.

Lowell stayed in active communication with his Company A friends until his death on February 19, 1925, at age eighty-two. From his obituary, one can sense the regard Judge Lowell inspired in Holton: "To him his profession was a sacred duty of his life. He recognized and appreciated the importance of the trust imposed upon the lawyer, the demand for the highest integrity

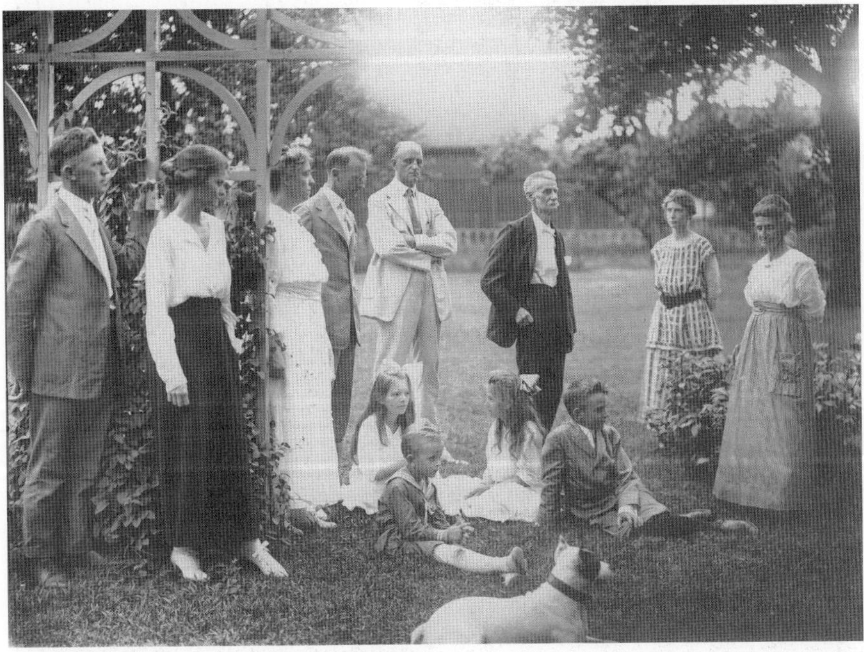

Lowell family portrait taken around 1920. *Standing left to right*: Brutus Edgar Sewell Sr., Kate Roberta (Lowell) Sewell, Clotilda (Brocaw) Lowell, James Henry Lowell, George Alexander Lowell, James Howard Lowell, Ellen Roberts Lowell and Katherine Mary (Roberts) Lowell; *seated*: Marion Roberts Lowell (Nanny), Jesse Howard Sewell, Anna Clotilda Lowell and James P. Lowell. *Courtesy of Tim Sewell.*

and the necessity for constant study."[130] Upon hearing of his death, Lowell's regimental buddy Walter Swan offered this succinct encomium: "He was indeed a noble and plucky fellow."[131]

Kate Mary continued living at 515 Iowa Avenue until her death on January 18, 1938, at age ninety-six. She was Holton's oldest citizen.[132] After the Lowells' unmarried daughter, Ellen, died in the mid-1970s, a local church bought and demolished the house to make room for a parking lot. The journal passed to Lowell's second son, James Henry Lowell, who had moved from the Bronx to White Plains, New York. Upon his death in 1966, the notebook remained with his unmarried younger daughter, Anna Clotilda Lowell, who acted as custodian of the family history and relics from the pre-Revolutionary period. Clo died relatively young, in 1972, and left the journal to her only sister, Marion Roberts Lowell Rendell. Grandmother Marion, whom we called "Nanny," died in 1989 and passed it to her only child, Marion Lowell Rendell Seaton, my mother. The notebook remained in her drawer in Glen Rock, New Jersey, until her death in 2012.

ANCESTRY

Although much is made of the Boston Lowells and their Brahmin status, this particular Lowell does not appear to have sprung from a twig of the family tree that possessed great means. He was a contemporary and distant cousin of the famous branch of the Lowell family that produced the poets James Russell Lowell and Amy Lowell, the astronomer Percival Lowell, and the famed Harvard president Abbott Lawrence Lowell. The family emigrated from Bristol, England, in 1639, within the Great Migration that lasted from 1620 to roughly 1640. Genealogists have traced the Lowell family even further back to link it with Edward I, also known as Edward Longshanks, King of England, who ruled from 1272 to 1307.[133]

James Howard Lowell's branch was more modest. It stemmed from Putney, Vermont, to where his ancestors had migrated from Newburyport, Massachusetts. On the Connecticut River in Putney, Lowell's great-grandfather Moses (b. 1726 in Newbury, Massachusetts) and Moses's son Jacob built a well-to-do farm. The following passage is taken from James Howard Lowell's handwritten genealogy:

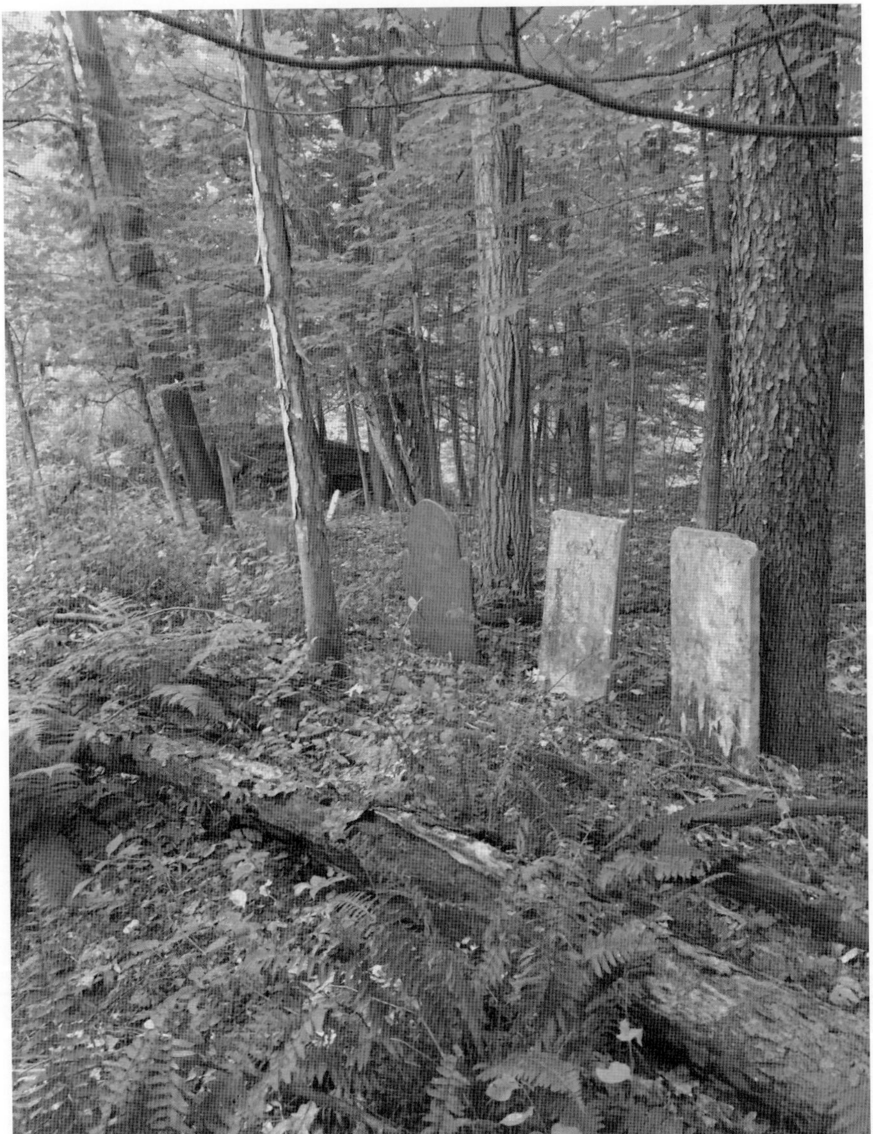

Lowell Cemetery, Putney, Vermont. *Author photo*.

> *About 12 miles up the Connecticut River from the City of Brattleboro, is a hamlet named Putney, in Vermont. Some two miles farther up the river and skirting its bank is the Lowell homestead. In February 1787, Moses Lowell, g. gr. of James H. Lowell, bought and moved to this spot and built thereon a house that is still standing and occupying the land. It's described as Lots 24 & 25, each containing 50 acres, Town of Putney. The title was put in the name of Moses' son, Jacob. Here were born the 13 children of Jacob and Sally* [Keyes] *Lowell. Like most of the farms about there the land rises into a hill as it recedes from the river. The location is very attractive. The house is of fair size and of substantial build, as also are the barn and outbuildings—the river road runs through the farm, leaving between it and the river a scope of farming land, and it is on this portion—near the river and on its bank—that the family burial plot is. Several years ago, about 1896, James H. Lowell had this plot put into shape, a substantial fence and gate put there, the growth of sumac and brush removed, and the place made sightly, and yearly cleaned up. There are 14 of the family buried there.…At the Stone of Moses is the government marker of a Revolutionary Soldier.*[134]

Moses and son Jacob both fought in the Revolution. Pieces from Moses and Sarah Bradbury Lowell's pewter wedding service and their glass saltcellars remain in our family to this day. Jacob's ninth child was Lowell's father, born in 1826 and named—in the spirit of the age—George Washington Bradbury Lowell. G.W.B. Lowell left Putney as a young man to earn a living in Boston as a cabinetmaker and contractor. He married Lydia Marie Grant of Kennebunkport, Maine, in 1832 and had five children.

Our author, James Howard Lowell, was the youngest of the five, born on June 12, 1842. Lowell's mother died when he was three years old, and the father remarried when he was six. Unlike many of the Boston Lowells, this young man did not attend Harvard, but from his writing style and literary references, one can glean that he received a serviceable education in Boston, which he described in a short autobiography as "Graduate High School—Lithographic Student."

The family was artistic. His elder brother John Zanidorus Lowell owned a design and engraving firm before the Civil War. Lowell himself was an apprentice lithographer when the war broke out. Perhaps the elder brother made this engraving of his younger brother on page 32—we do not know for sure.

OBITUARIES

James Howard Lowell and Katherine Mary (Roberts) Lowell

Holton Signal, February, 26, 1925[135]

JUDGE LOWELL DIES THURSDAY

James Howard Lowell was born at Boston, Mass., June 12, 1842. He died at Holton, Kansas, February 19, 1925, aged 82 years, 8 months and 5 days. He was the youngest son of George Washington Bradbury Lowell and Lydia Maria (Grant) Lowell. He was direct in line of descent from Percival Lowell who came from Bristol, England, and settled in Newbury, Mass, in 1639.

His early life was spent in Boston, Mass., where he graduated from the high school, and was a lithographic student when the civil war began. At the age of 18 [*sic*] he enlisted in Co. A 13th Mass. Vol. Infantry, serving three years. At the battle of Antietam he was wounded, and while convalescing was chief clerk in the mustering and disbursing office and Provost Marshall's office. He was discharged at Harrisburg, Pa. Early in the spring of 1865 he came west and at Atchison, Kansas joined an overland train to Denver, and from there, by way of Salt Lake City went to the territory of Montana. Here he engaged in mining, trading with the Indians, and later engaged in the practice of law at Benton, Montana. In 1869 he was clerk of the 2nd Judicial District of that territory, county assessor of Choteau county and commissioner under appointment of Governor B.F. Potts to organize the county of Dawson. In 1871 he returned to the states and located at Holton, Kansas, where he has since resided and been engaged in the practice of law.

In January 30, 1873, he was united in marriage to Kate M. Roberts, daughter of Colonel John Roberts, at Harrisburg, Pa. To this union five children were born. George A. now of Muskogee, Okla., James H., now of New York City, Ellen R. of Holton. Blanche, who died when about one year old, and Kate R. Sewell of Lancaster, Kansas.

During his residence in Holton, he has occupied many positions of trust, having been police-judge and mayor of his home city, county attorney of Jackson County, and presidential elector for the state of Kansas in 1896. He was a member of Holton Lodge A.F. & A.M.,[136] of which he was master for four years from 1886 to 1890. He was an honored member of Will Wendell Post, G.A.R.[137]

This briefly epitomizes the life history of a man who had lived beyond four score years, almost fifty-four of which had been spent in this community. But how little it tells of the real work and worth of the man. Born in that city which has been recognized as the seat of education and culture, his early life was spent under the influence of such men as Emerson, Holmes, Longfellow, Whittier and his relative, James Russell Lowell from whom he imbibed a love of the beautiful in literature and art, yet had the pioneer spirit of his ancestors and was liberal minded enough to mingle with and become part of the great west. He was a force in the moulding [*sic*] of the intellectual and social character of the state of his adoption.

He loved his home and his country. He appreciated that the building of one was the best way to preserve the other. He understood the political principles upon which this government was founded and believed in them to the extent that he risked his life and gave his blood for the preservation of the union. In his many addresses to his comrades and his fellow citizens, and in his writings he upheld the highest ideals of American citizenship, the influence of which will live long after the speaker and writer has been forgotten.

To him his profession was a sacred duty of his life. He recognized and appreciated the importance of the trust imposed upon the lawyer, the demand for the highest integrity and the necessity for constant study. He had a judicial mind, well trained and never lost his interest in the subject of law, even after his failing health in the last few years of his life compelled him to give up active practice.

Judge Lowell, as he was familiarly called, retained the respect and esteem of his fellow townsmen throughout his long residence among them. They knew him for what he was a moral, upright man, equally interested with them in the improvement and advancement of the city, county and state. He was especially interested in the schools, he was a staunch friend of Campbell University as long as it continued, realizing that in education lay the surest safeguard of the rights and liberties of the public. His passing away leaves his family and friends in sorrow, alleviated by the blessed memory that his life was long and full of service. Service to his country in the time of its peril; giving the young years of his life to the development of new territory; upholding the standard of his profession; ever on the side of morality and justice and ever extending the helping hand to friend and neighbor.

"Soldier, rest thy warfare over, Sleep the sleep that knows not breaking; Dream of battlefields no more. Morn of toil nor night of waking."

Funeral services in charge of Rev. Munneke, assisted by Rev. Penick, were held from the home Saturday afternoon. The music consisted of a quartet composed of Mrs. P. A. Adam, Mrs. Hurd, B. E. Canfield and Bert Kennedy, accompanied on the piano by Doris Roebke. There were many floral tributes, showing the high esteem in which Judge Lowell was held.

Judge Lowell's old army comrade Major Webster,[138] of St. Louis, came out to attend the funeral and the part he took added much to the impressiveness of the occasion.

Jackson County Signal, Jan. 20, 1938

HOLTON'S OLDEST RESIDENT DIES

Mrs. Katherine Lowell Dies at Her Home at 515 Iowa Avenue on Monday Evening

Holton's oldest citizen, Mrs. Kate M. Lowell, 96 years old died at her home in Holton, at 515 Iowa avenue, Monday evening. Funeral services will be held at the home this afternoon at 2:30 o'clock, conducted by Rev. Fred M. Newlin of the Presbyterian Church.

Mrs. Lowell was born at Harrisburg, Pennsylvania, May 20, 1841. She was united in marriage to James H. Lowell in Harrisburg, Pennsylvania, January 30, 1873. Mr. and Mrs. Lowell came immediately to Holton on their wedding trip and continued to make their home here.

To this union four children were born, Miss Ellen R. Lowell, of Holton, James H. Lowell, of White Plains, New York, and Kate and George deceased. She also leaves to survive her nine grandchildren and four great-grand children.

Mrs. Lowell has continued to live in the same home in Holton for sixty-three years. In her younger life she took an active part in the cultural activities of the community. In her home town in Harrisburg as a girl she was an artist and musician of distinction.

Mrs. Lowell first met her husband when she sang with a young ladies' quartet in a hospital in Harrisburg to which Judge Lowell, then of Boston, who was brought having been wounded in the battle of Antietam in the Civil War. When he recovered a romance followed and they were married in Harrisburg.

LETTER FROM WALTER SWAN TO SAMUEL DERRICK WEBSTER

Upon Lowell's death, Walter Swan of the Massachusetts Thirteenth Regiment (Company A) wrote to Samuel Derrick Webster (Company D). Sam Webster was a color bearer who spoke at Lowell's funeral.

Postmarked Dorchester, Mass., Feb 24, 1925

Grand Army of the Republic, Department of Massachusetts, Benjamin Stone Jr., Post No, 68
Benj. Stone, Jr. Post, No. 68, G. A. R.
Grand Army Hall, 91 Park Street

Dear Sam,

Your postal of the 20th, notifying me of our dear Comrade Lowell's death on the 19th inst. just received. Needless to say, it gave one quite a shock for I was going to write him a letter today and send him a letter that I received from Brooke of Co. A. whom he mentioned in his letter of Jan 21st which I am returning to you with this. It was probably his last letter, and how cheerful he seemed to be with all his ailments. How we shall miss his interesting letters. He was indeed a noble and plucky fellow. In his death you and I certainly have sustained a severe loss, you particularly as you were privileged to see him occasionally. Shall look for a letter from you with particulars of his death. Trusting that you are well.

Fraternally
Swan

NOTES

Introduction

1. AVMJ, Massachusetts Thirteenth Circular 34, 216–18.
2. Ibid.
3. JHL letter to KM, December 26, 1869, www.lowellmemoir.com.
4. Grant, *Personal Memoirs*, chapter 15.
5. For more on Charles W. Cook (1839–1927) and the 1869 Cook-Folsom-Peterson expedition, see National Park Service, Yellowstone National Park: Its Exploration and Establishment, Biographical Appendix. www.nps.gov/parkhistory/online_books/haines1/iee4.htm.
6. Cook, Folsom, Peterson, and Haines, eds. *Valley of the Upper Yellowstone*.
7. AVMJ, JHL letter to C.W. Cook, March 23, 1924, 187–89.
8. Ibid.
9. AVMJ, C.W. Cook letter to JHL, June 30, 1924, 190–92.
10. Overholser, *Fort Benton*.
11. Frazier, *Great Plains*, 163–65. "Some historians maintain that Fort Benton was the wildest town in the West. Unfortunately, unlike Dodge City, it had no newspapers during its early days, so nobody really knows."
12. Overholser, *Fort Benton*, 261–62; JHL letter to KM, November 10, 1869, lowellmemoir.com.
13. The U.S. Army built Camp Cooke in 1866 to protect steamboat traffic en route to Benton but abandoned the fort in March 1870. The fort was located on the south bank just upstream from the mouth of the Judith River. Lowell's trade took place in the winter of 1870–71, a period when

only the civilian post sutler, Joseph H. McKnight, and his employees remained at the structure they named Fort Claggett [*sic*] after William Horace Clagett.

14. Graybill, *Red and the White*, 127.
15. Ibid, 147. The higher casualty number is cited by Graybill from a firsthand account given by Joseph Kipp. Kipp worked as a scout for Baker in 1870 and led the army to the Piegan camp.
16. Ibid, 125.
17. Wheelan, *Terrible Swift Sword*, 253.
18. Wylie, *Blood on the Marias*.
19. Overholser, *Fort Benton*, 261.
20. Canfield, ed., *Diary of a Forty-Niner*, entry from May 26, 1850. The diary of Alfred T. Jackson, a miner who migrated to California from Norfolk, Connecticut, in the 1850s, is a classic of frontier lore.

Dull Day Jottings 1872

21. JHL borrows from James Russell Lowell's 1865 Harvard *Commemoration Ode*, line 10, "That is the best blood that hath in't most iron to edge resolve with."
22. Isely and Richards, *Four Centuries in Kansas*, "The first train was drawn by 1,200 mules and carried 150,000 pounds of freight." Two distinct Butterfield stage lines ferried supplies west in the 1860s. John Butterfield founded the first in 1858. It carried mail through Missouri along a southern route to California. David A. Butterfield (no relation to John) launched a second route in 1865, the one Lowell joined. This second, northern trail ran west through Kansas to Denver, Colorado, roughly paralleling modern U.S. 40 and, ultimately, to Salt Lake City. This Smoky Hill route had the advantage of adequate water supply, but it bisected Indian hunting grounds. The Butterfield Overland Despatch closed in 1870 shortly after the first transcontinental railway line was complete.
23. Former Wisconsin senator Charles W. Durkee was Utah's sixth territorial governor.

The Plains Across: Kansas to Colorado, 1865

24. The *Atchison Free Press* announced in a September 25, 1865 headline, "First Coach Through to Denver." Lowell disputes this date, but a stagecoach did arrive in September. His wagon train arrived in November.
25. Isely and Richards, *Four Centuries in Kansas*, 62–66. The Kingdom of Quivira refers to a region in modern Kansas explored by Francisco Vazquez de Coronado of Spain in 1541. The story handed down portrays an Indian slave taken captive by the Spanish who describes a region rich in gold somewhere to the north. This province became known as Quivira. If Coronado had found gold in Kansas, little doubt the territories of the Louisiana Purchase would have remained Spanish. He describes the land itself as "being very fat and black and being well watered by the rivulets and springs and rivers." The slave who lured the Spanish explorer north was likely a native Wichita Indian who wanted to escape captivity.
26. In his period memoir, freighter and native Frenchman Alexander Toponce calls these extra beasts on a wagon train, the *cavayard*, a drove of horses or mules. Toponce, *Reminiscences*.
27. For more on that initial stagecoach experience see Davis, "Stage Ride to Colorado," 137–50.
28. Castle McLaughlin, curator of North American ethnography, Peabody Museum of Archaeology and Ethnology, Harvard University, attributes the "white man's voice" to the English-speaking skills of Charles Bent, a mixed-race member of the Cheyenne and Lakota Dog Soldiers who were active on the plains in 1865. "Charley" was three years younger than Lowell. His father was the trader William Bent; his mother, Yellow Woman, was Cheyenne. After Charles, his half-brother George, and his mother survived the Sand Creek Massacre of 1864, Charles joined the Dog Soldiers in attacking the invading U.S. Army and settlers. In 1867, he died in battle at age twenty-two. His elder brother George first fought against the U.S. Army as a Confederate soldier. He established himself later as an interpreter, negotiator, and Cheyenne historian.
29. Historian Charles R. Wetzel cites October 2, 1865, as the date Indians first attacked the BOD coach at Monument Station. Wetzel, "Monument Station, Gove County," 251, http://www.kshs.org/publicat/khq/1960/1960autumn_wetzel.pdf.
30. Ibid.

Denver: Clerking at the Planter's House Hotel

31. Speaker of the House Schuyler Colfax; President pro tempore of the U.S. Senate Lafayette S. Foster; U.S. Senator James Rood Doolittle of Wisconsin, who reported on Indian affairs and published *The Condition of the Tribes*, known as the Doolittle Survey of 1865.
32. Abraham Lincoln appointed William Gilpin the first territorial governor of Colorado. Gilpin's vision of a West connected by railroads with Denver as its hub lured many to the territory.

Salt Lake City Bound, 1866

33. Jim Bridger was a trapper and guide thought to be the first white man to encounter the Great Salt Lake in 1824. Bridger explored the Upper Yellowstone River Valley. In 1843, he established Fort Bridger, which opened the overland route by Bridger's Pass to the Great Salt Lake.

The Mormon City: Lowell Meets Brigham Young

34. Prophet Brigham Young (1801–1877) took over leadership of the Church of Latter-day Saints three years after the murder of founder Joseph Smith in 1844. Young organized the Mormon exodus from Missouri and then established Salt Lake City in what was then a part of Mexico in 1847. President Millard Fillmore appointed him Utah Territory's first governor and superintendent of American Indian affairs in 1851. Young was the longest-running LDS president and served as church leader for twenty-nine years.
35. Heber C. Kimball and George A. Smith were foremost counselors to Brigham Young. Kimball (1801–1868) and Smith (1817–1875) were two of the original "Quorum of the Twelve Apostles" of the Mormon Church. George A. Smith was a first cousin of Latter-day Saints founder Joseph Smith.

North to Montana: Wintering in Deer Lodge, W.A.C. Ryan

36. In 1870, a miner from British Columbia, Jesse "Cariboo Jack" Fairchilds, discovered gold on Mount Pisgah (renamed Caribou Mountain) in

southeastern Idaho. He acquired his moniker in the Cariboo Mining District of British Columbia. Over the protest of locals, the U.S. Forest Service created Caribou National Forest and changed the spelling from Carriboo (or Cariboo, or Caraboo) to *Caribou.* At the time, residents pointed out that herds of caribou had never lived in the area, but the service went ahead with the change. Lowell's spelling varied.

Diggings with William Horace Clagett

37. Dixon, "Sketches of the Life," 249–57; Vollmer, *Illustrated History*, 1066–67.
38. Robison, *Confederates*, 23. James Michael Cavanaugh was elected delegate from the Territory of Montana and later served as a U.S. representative from Minnesota.

Helena: A Chance Encounter with Morrow P. Lowry

39. This passage hints that Lowell wrote this section between 1889 and 1893, the years attorney Joseph Kemp Toole served as Montana's first governor.
40. Thomas Jefferson (Jeff, or T.J.) Lowry partnered with John H. Shober in Helena to form Shober & Lowry in 1867. Shober joined the Sully Expedition and landed in Helena, Montana, in September 1864. Jeff's brother, Morrow P. Lowry, who was also a lawyer, followed him to Montana after the war. See John H. Shober Papers, 1832–1952, Collection MC69, Box 1/ Folder 2, Montana Historical Society Research Center, Archives, Helena, Montana. Regarding John H. Shober, "He mined in Nelson and Holmes Gulches, while beginning his law practice in Helena. In 1865 he ran for district attorney and defeated Cornelius Hedges. He won that office again in 1867. That year Shober also formed a law partnership with Thomas J. Lowry." (The Jeff Lowry to which JHL refers.)

Thompson's Gulch: The Antelope Hunt

41. Thompson's Gulch is named for Jack Thompson, an Englishman who was one of the early discoverers of Confederate Gulch in 1864. For more on Thompson's Gulch and the Montana gold camps, see Fynn, *Goldpans, Guns & Grit*, 94–96. Flynn also quotes JHL's letters to KM, 150, 154, 156.

42. Hampton, *Life and Death*, 40, 178. The diary of C.M. Lee mentions two stragglers arriving in his camp on the Musselshell River in 1868 from Thompson [*sic*] Gulch.
43. William Cullen Bryant's 1832 poem "The Prairies," 7–10.
44. Lowell quoting his cousin James Russell Lowell's 1867 *Biglow Papers, Second Series*, ch. 4, "Fitz Adam's Story," 267–68.

A New Deal

45. JHL's letter to explorer C.W. Cook described Coggswell, AVMJ, 187–88: "A very unsocial man of some 45 years. I believe he thought more of me than any other living person. A masterful miney, strong and untiring. I was tall and slightly built but capable of hard work and as untiring as he."
46. Lowell refers to the Dickens character Edmund Sparkler, well meaning, but thick, from *Little Dorrit*.
47. See AVMJ, regimental Circular 27, 213–15, for another recital of this incident.
48. The practice of wolfers using poisoned buffalo carcasses as bait made enemies among the native tribes. The baits lured and killed off domesticated dogs, work animals that were essential for pulling travois and for sounding early warning of approaching intruders. Some tribes ate dog; others found dog-eating repugnant. Hampton, *Life and Death*, 18–19. A wolfer could expect a bait to kill forty to sixty wolves and then sold them for $2.50 each.

Tomahawk Jurisprudence and Vigilante Justice

49. Dillon, *Montana Vigilantes*, 231–73, offers history of the nascent legal system in Montana during this period.
50. Overholser, *Fort Benton*, 385–86, describes the same incident at Morgan's well. He identifies the victim as the son of the Blackfeet headman Mountain Chief and the culprits as bull whackers who were punishing the chief for the alleged murder of frontiersman Joseph Spearson. More on the "place of skulls" in Lepley, *Birthplace of Montana*, 54.
51. Overholser, *Fort Benton*, 386, recounts the execution and refers to Pipeneaux Wypert by his nickname, "Bowlegs," only. Quoting the recollections of W.S. Stocking (the head of the family with whom Lowell

boarded), Overholser identified the father of the papoose as Baptiste Racine. The incident occurred in April 1871. Lowell also spells the name Pipineaux.

52. The date of this poem's initial publication was 1888. Lowell must have written this section after that date.
53. *Helena Weekly Herald*, "Fort Benton Letter," February 15, 1872, 4.
54. Overholser, *Fort Benton*, 254.
55. AVMJ, JHL letter to KM, December 14, 1868, 176–78.
56. Fold3.com, https://www.fold3.com/image/35465698, Navy Widows' Certificate, Pension #8836, Widow's Certificate, 19, 74–75. The U.S. Navy rejected an 1895 initial pension application by Lowry's wife, Libbie D. Lowry, when the pension office ruled her husband's fatal pneumonia was not connected to his naval service: "There is abundant credible testimony, however, that there was no noticeable or known disease of the lungs for many years after discharge, or until after the deceased had returned to his old home in Pennsylvania from Montana, where he had been for several years after discharge, and where he had become strongly addicted to drinking intoxicated liquors, which habit he indulged in so excessively until near the time of his death some attributed his death and his lung and stomach troubles to that cause alone, or principally."

Benton 1869–71, the Kanackers

57. Lowell likely refers to the Mètis people, now recognized as a mixed race, aboriginal culture of Canada. He employed an archaic term for "Canuck." The term "Kanackers" (Lowell varies the spelling) possibly derives from the Iroquois word *kanuchsa*, the resident of a *kanata* or community.
58. Schultz, *With the Indians*, 18. "The choicest part of [the buffalo] was the so-called 'hump,' or in frontier language, the 'boss ribs.' These dorsal ribs rose gradually from the centre of the back to a length of twenty inches and more just above the point of the shoulders, and were deeply covered with rich tenderloin."

Stern-Wheeled Boats

59. The *Chippewa* and *Key West* were the first steamboats to arrive at Benton, the head of navigation, in July 1860.

60. Lepley, *Packets to Paradise*, 40-42; Hampton, *Life and Death*, 12. The number of steamboats docking at Benton reached a high of thirty-nine in 1867. By 1874, only six boats reached Benton. There was an upsurge again in the 1880s.

The Baker Massacre

61. The Baker Massacre took place on January 23, 1870, on the Marias River, not the Teton. The two rivers converge and empty into the Missouri just downriver from Benton, which could explain why Lowell misidentifies the river. On New Year's Day 1870, the superintendent of Indian affairs for Montana Territory, Lieutenant Colonel Alfred H. Sully, met with several Blackfeet chiefs on the *Teton* River north of Fort Shaw to warn them to subdue their young warriors and return stolen horses. The massacre, however, occurred on the Marias, and is often referred to as the Marias Massacre. (For more on Sully's role, see Graybill, *Red and the White*, 107.)
62. AVMJ, Circular 34, JHL wrote, "[B]eing detailed as a clerk in the Medical Director's office, I caught a case of small pox from a convalescent," 218.
63. JHL wrote "A.E. Campbell," but U.S. Army records list the assistant surgeon as Archibald B. Campbell. U.S. Adjutant General's Office, *Official Army Register for 1870*, 21, https://www.fold3.com/image/312121793?rec=303553014. Huckabee, "Camp Cooke," 19. Huckabee cited a report written in 1868 by Post Surgeon N.[*sic*]B. Campbell that said the army intended Camp Cooke to be a transitory post.
64. In contemporary source documents, one often comes across the pejorative term "good Indian," implying "dead Indian." In this passage, Lowell likely alluded to an infamous quote attributed to General Phillip Sheridan: "The only good Indian is a dead Indian." In fact, Sheridan denied the quote, but he is reported as having said, "The only good Indians I ever saw were dead." (Wheelan, *Terrible Swift Sword*, 253.) Here, Lowell is likely referring to Brevet Major General William S. Harney, a cavalry officer and famous Indian fighter.
65. *New North-West* (Deer Lodge, MT), August 27, 1869, Image 2, Chronicling America, Library of Congress, http://chroniclingamerica.loc.gov/lccn/sn84038125/1869-08-27/ed-1/seq-2.pdf.
66. Wylie, *Blood on the Marias*, 197.

67. Ibid., 182. Wylie quotes the Horace Clarke Affidavit, Heavy Runner Records, 1914–1921, MF 53, Montana Historical Society; Martha Edgerton Plassmann Papers, MC 78, MHS.
68. Graybill, *Red and the White*, 127. Quoting cavalry officer, Lieutenant Gus Doane.
69. Ibid., 236–43.
70. Dodge, *Hunting Grounds*, loc. 625.

Indian Trading and Adventure: Senator Thomas C. Power, Courtenay's Wood Yard

71. Huckabee, "Camp Cooke," 60–67. Lifelong friends T.C. Power and J.H. McKnight came west together in the 1860s and supported each other's businesses throughout their lives. McKnight's brush with Lowell occurred when McKnight worked as a clerk at Camp Cooke on the Judith River before McKnight formed his own trading business at Fort Shaw with backing from Power. J.H. McKnight and Company Records, 1865–1914, MC56, Montana Historical Society, Research Center Archives, archiveswest.orbiscascade.org. The army abandoned Camp Cooke less than four years after it was built at the mouth of the Judith River, in part, because it was too remote and overrun with rats.
72. Hampton, *Life and Death*, 182. The 1870 U.S. Census records a New Yorker named Robert Gordon twice: first in Benton at age twenty-one, then working downriver at a wood yard at age twenty-two.
73. Ibid., 178, Hampton gives a short bio of William "Bill" Courtney [*sic*]: "Born in London in 1823, Courtney received a fair education before emigrating to the United States in 1858. After seven years of "operating a business" in New York City, he purchased a stock of goods and moved, first to the Yellowstone valley, and then to the Judith Basin where he exchanged his goods for furs and robes obtained by the Indians of the area. In 1870, the census taker found him located in Fort Benton operating as a wood dealer." Advertisements bought by Courtenay in the Miles City, Montana paper spell his name "Courtenay." "William Courtenay Dead," *Anaconda Standard*, November 3, 1901, 16, newspapers.com; "William Courtenay: Another of Montana's Pristine Settlers," October 31, 1901, 3. For more on Courtenay and Camp Cooke, see Huckabee, "Camp Cooke." Courtenay is also described in Monahan and Biggs, *Montana's Wild and Scenic*, 116, 120–23.
74. A.k.a. Deadman Rapids, or Drowned Man's Rapids.

Gordon's Stronghold

75. Hampton, *Life and Death*, 135. The partner's name was likely George Horn.
76. Montana Memory Project collection of digitized National Archives microfilm publications. Letters Received by the Office of Indian Affairs 1824–1881, Roll 490, Montana Superintendency 1864–1880, http://mtmemory.org/cdm/ref/collection/p15018coll41/id/16471.

A Feast and a Trade: Revenge, Murder, and Siege at Camp Cooke

77. Hampton, *Life and Death*, 121. Musselshell gunsmith C.M. Lee's diary entry from January 7, 1871, mentioned word of a trade at Camp Cooke with Crow and Gros Ventre.
78. For more on the Charles H. Barstow collection of ledger drawings: http://www.msubillings.edu/library/SpecialCollections/BarstowHistory.htm. The collection itself: http://arc.lib.montana.edu/indian-great-plains/search.php?type=ledger+drawing.
79. Hampton, *Life and Death*, 53–55. The C.M. Lee diary described an incident in May 1869 in which settlers at Musselshell thwarted an Indian assault (possibly Assiniboine), then boiled and displayed the skulls of their victims on the levee (May 14, 1869 entry) to ward off future attacks. During the same incident, Lee also described John Johnson, the infamous "Liver Eating Johnson," tasting the liver of a victim.
80. Ibid., 126, 135. The February 6, 1871 C.M. Lee diary entry recounted a slightly different version of these events. Lee recorded that Lone Tree was wounded in both arms and that it was his brother who was killed. He noted that the incident took place at Little Rocky and that the disagreement was not over a young girl but had to do with a whiskey deal gone bad with traders Tom Hardwick and Charley Morrison. He said that Hardwick shot the Crows with his Henry rifle. The April 3–4, 1871 entries mentioned that Bob Gordon and his partner, George Horn, had gone missing. (Horn is likely the partner whose name Lowell could not recall.) Lee's diary recorded that the Crows were still agitating for revenge three months later and were blaming Johnny Cochran and a man named Dean for killing their chief. He also mentioned that the Assiniboine had killed two or three wolfers on the Marias River.
81. Dodge, *Hunting*; Dodge, *Our Wild Indians*. Dodge was General William Tecumseh Sherman's aide-de-camp.

Return Stateside with the Ashley Family

82. "River Route," *New North-West,* July 29, 1871, noted that the *Miner* was at Cow Island and would "receive passengers at very low rates from Benton. If you want to go to America at low rates, now is the time."
83. AVMJ, August 2, 1899, C.S. Ashley letter to JHL, 193–95.
84. "How to Come," *New North-West*, April 8, 1870, listed the distance as 2,000 miles. Even allowing for the eventual straightening and channeling of the river, measures of river distances on the Missouri in the 1860s were generous. In 2015, the National Parks Service office of the Missouri National Recreation River in Yankton, South Dakota, gave the distance as 1,320 river miles.

Epilogue

85. Ibid.
86. Cordley, *Pioneer Days*, 270.
87. Blackmar, *Kansas*, 865; Tuttle, *New Centennial History*, 618–19.
88. "In Memory of Garfield," *Holton Recorder*, September 29, 1881.

Introduction to the Correspondence

89. Sankovitch, *Lowells of Massachusetts*, 1–3.

Letters to Kate Mary Roberts

90. Lowell, *Historic Genealogy*, 197.
91. John Buttrick Noyes Civil War Letters (MS Am 2332), Houghton Library, Harvard University, September 22, 1862 letter from Noyes (1838–1908) to his sister Martha from the temporary hospital at Girl's School house, corner of Cherry and Raspberry Alleys, in Harrisburg.
92. Ibid., Noyes, September 30, 1862 letter to his father, George Rapall Noyes. They were both Harvard graduates; the father was a divinity professor.
93. AVMJ, JHL letter to KM, December 14, 1868, 176–78.
94. JHL letter to KM, December 26, 1869, www.lowellmemoir.com.

95. JHL letter to KM, February 10, 1869, www.lowellmemoir.com.
96. Alfred Edward Matthews, an artist professionally known as A.E. Matthews (1831–1874), produced a widely distributed series of pencil sketches and lithographs of the American West and Civil War battle scenes.

Exchange with Yellowstone Explorer Charles W. Cook

97. Cook, *Valley of the Yellowstone*, xii.

The Civil War Correspondence

98. Belous and Weinstein, *Will Soule*.
99. Davis, *Three Years*.
100. Ibid., xiii.
101. Ibid., 222.
102. Ibid., 199.
103. Ibid., 12.
104. Ibid., 88.
105. Ibid., 116.
106. AVMJ, Circular 34, 216–18.
107. Davis, *Three Years*, 131.
108. Tucker, *Miller Cornfield*, 34.
109. McPherson, *Antietam*, 117–18.
110. Davis, *Three Years*, 135.
111. AVMJ, JHL letter to son, July 17, 1904, 205–10.
112. Tucker, *Miller Cornfield*, 13.
113. Priest, *Antietam*, 48–49, 91, 333; Bowen, *Massachusetts in the War*, 239–40, cites Thirteenth Massachusetts casualties as 139: 15 dead, 120 wounded, 4 missing.
114. Bowen, *Massachusetts in the War*, 224–25. Twelfth Massachusetts losses: 283: 70 killed, 183 wounded, 30 missing.
115. Letter from Major Jacob Park Gould to Colonel Samuel Haven Leonard, September 18, 1862, http://www.13thmass.org/1862/antietam.html#mozTocId698782.
116. Davis, *Three Years*, 142.
117. Morrow P. Lowry (1844–1888) worked as acting assistant paymaster in the U.S. Navy (18641865) in Pennsylvania for the stern-wheel steamer

USS *Naiad*. Lowry, who was a lawyer, ran into Lowell out west and lured him to Benton. AVMJ, JHL letter to KM, December 14, 1868, 176–78.

118. AVMJ, JHL, July 17, 1904 letter to son, 205–10.

119. The Thirteenth Massachusetts actually left Boston on July 29, 1861, and arrived in Hagerstown, Maryland, on August 1, 1861. In JHL's case, he likely enlisted on July 14.

120. The Chesapeake & Ohio Canal was an important Union transportation route ferrying coal from the West to Washington, D.C.

121. The Thirteenth Massachusetts arrived in Martinsburg at midnight March 1–2, 1862. On March 5, they marched ten miles to Bunker Hill. March 11, the regiment advanced six more miles to Stephenson's Depot, then farther to take Winchester on March 12, 1862.

122. JHL quoted "Hohenlinden" by Thomas Campbell (1777–1844).

123. Lincoln reviewed the company at Falmouth, Virginia, on May 23, 1862. The temperature was ninety degrees. Secretary of War Edwin Stanton, Secretary of State William Henry Seward, and General Irvin McDowell were also present.

124. Likely, the Thirteenth Wisconsin was not present, as he recalled here. Two of the Thirteenth Massachusetts died in this fight.

125. They were surrounded on three sides with artillery blasting at them. Thirty-eight soldiers of the Thirteenth Massachusetts died in less than a half hour. The fight at Bald Hill took place on August 30, 1862, part of the Second Battle of Bull Run, or Second Manassas.

126. Lowell is referring to Captain Ezra Matthews, First Pennsylvania Light Artillery, Company F. Note from descendent and historian Brad Forbush: "Lowell must have helped remove the guns after the regiment retreated from Bald Hill. Matthews' battery was stationed nearby at the Henry house and did not go up Bald Hill with them. Possibly, Lowell saw them in trouble and stopped to help in the confusion of the retreat."

127. Lowell's eldest son, George Alexander Lowell, was a professional baseball player, a southpaw pitcher, with the Joplin Miners and several other teams.

Massachusetts Thirteenth Circulars

128. Belous and Weinstein, *Will Soule*. William S. Soule (1836–1908) became an important photographer of the post–Civil War period. He is known principally for his portraits of the Plains Indians taken at Fort Sill, Indian

Territory (Oklahoma) from 1869 to 1874–75. Soule's work is an important visual record from the era when the tribes were still defiant "in a métier and in costume closer to their own choosing than required of them later by photographers. His subjects were not the Indians of twenty, or even ten, years later, dressed and posed to demonstrate the Indian as the white man wished to see him." In late 1874 or 1875, Soule returned to Boston, where he partnered with W.D. Everett in a photography business.

Appendix

129. Lowell, *Historic Genealogy*, xxxiv–xlix. For JHL's contribution to the history of the Lowell coat of arms, xviii; JHL's genealogical entry, 197.
130. *Holton Recorder*, February 20, 1925.
131. AVMJ, letter from Walter Swan to Samuel Derrick Webster, February 24, 1925, 228. Webster spoke at Lowell's funeral service. He was a color bearer in the Thirteenth Massachusetts.
132. "Holton's Oldest Resident Dies at Age 96," *Jackson County Signal*, January 20, 1938.
133. Steward and Child, *Descendants*, 4.
134. James Howard Lowell's informal genealogy is in possession of Allen Sewell of Long Beach, California.
135. JHL obituary, *Holton Signal*, February 26, 1925. This obit was likely written by Will Beck (1873–1967), son of the founder and publisher of the *Holton Recorder*.
136. Ancient Free and Accepted Masons.
137. Grand Army of the Republic, a fraternal organization of former Union soldiers who served in the Civil War.
138. Thirteenth Massachusetts veteran Samuel Derrick Webster was not a major in the regular Union army. He was active in the GAR and might have held the ceremonial post of major in that organization.

SELECTED BIBLIOGRAPHY

Allen, Frederick. *A Decent Orderly Lynching: The Montana Vigilantes*. Norman: University of Oklahoma Press, 2004.

Anaconda Standard. "William Courtenay Dead." November 3, 1901.

Bailey, Ronald H., ed. *The Bloodiest Day: The Battle of Antietam*. Alexandria, VA: Time-Life Books, 1984.

Beidler, X. *X Beidler Vigilante*. Norman: University of Oklahoma Press, 1965.

Belous, Russell E., and Robert A. Weinstein. *Will Soule, Indian Photographer at Fort Sill, Oklahoma 1869–74*. Los Angeles, CA: Ward Ritchie, 1969.

Birge, Julius C. *The Awakening of the Desert*. Boston: Gorham, 1912.

Blackmar, Frank W. *Kansas: A Cyclopedia of State History, Embracing Events, Institutions, Industries, Counties, Cities, Towns, Prominent Persons, Etc.* Vol. 1. Chicago: Standard Publishing, 1912.

Blake, Henry N. "Henry N. Blake: Proper Bostonian, Purposeful Pioneer." *Montana: The Magazine of Western History* 14, no. 4 (Autumn 1964): 31–56.

Bowen, James L. *Massachusetts in the War, 1861–1865*. Springfield, MA: C.W. Bryan, 1889.

Brands, H. W. *The Man Who Saved the Union, Ulysses Grant in War and Peace*. New York: Doubleday, 2012.

Callaway, Lew. *Montana's Righteous Hangmen: The Vigilantes in Action*. Norman: University of Oklahoma Press, 1982.

Canfield, Chauncey L., ed. *The Diary of a Forty-Niner*. New York: Turtle Point Press, 1992.

Carlson, Paul H. *The Plains Indians*. College Station: Texas A&M University Press, 1998.

Chernow, Ron. *Grant.* New York: Penguin, 2017.

Cook, Charles W., David E. Folsom, William Peterson, and Aubrey L. Haines, eds. *The Valley of the Upper Yellowstone—An Exploration of the Headwaters of the Yellowstone River in the Year 1869*. Norman: University of Oklahoma Press, 1965.

Cordley, Richard. *Pioneer Days in Kansas*. Boston: Pilgrim Press, 1903. Kindle edition.

Cyclopedia of Virginia and the District of Columbia of the Nineteenth Century: Eminent and Representative Men of Virginia and the District of Columbia in the Nineteenth Century. Madison, WI: Brant & Fuller, 1901.

Davis, Charles E. *Three Years in the Army: The Story of the Thirteenth Massachusetts Volunteers from July 16, 1861, to August 1, 1864*. Boston: Estes and Lauriat, 1894.

———. *Three Years in the Army*, n.p.: Forgotten Books, 2012.

Davis, Theodore R. "A Stage Ride to Colorado," *Harper's New Monthly Magazine* 35 (July 1867): 137–50.

Deverell, William F., and Anne F. Hyde, eds. *The West in the History of the Nation, A Reader*. Vol. 1. *To 1877*. Boston/New York: Bedford/St. Martin's, 2000.

Dillon, Mark C. *Montana Vigilantes: 1863–1870, Gold, Guns & Gallows*. Boulder, CO: Utah State University Press, an imprint of University Press of Colorado, 2013.

Dimsdale, Thomas J. *The Vigilantes of Montana*. Guilford, CT: TwoDot, 2003.

Dixon, W.W. "Sketches of the Life and Character of William H. Clagett" in *Contributions to the Historical Society of Montana: Transactions, Officers and Members*. Vol. 4. Edited by the Historical Society of Montana. Helena, MT: Independent Publishers, 1903, 249–57.

Dodge, Richard Irving. *The Hunting Grounds of the Great West; A Description of the Plains, Game, and Indians of the Great North American Desert.* London, Chatto & Windus, 1877. Kindle edition.

———. *Our Wild Indians: Thirty-Three Years' Personal Experience among the Red Men of the Great West*. Hartford, CT: A.D. Worthington and Company, 1883. Kindle edition.

Donovan, Tom. *Hanging Around the Big Sky: The Unofficial Guide to Lynching, Strangling and Legal Hangings of Montana, Book One: Legal Hangings.* Great Falls, MT: Portage Meadows Publishing, 2007.

———. *Hanging Around the Big Sky…Book Two: Extra Legal Hangings.* Great Falls, MT: Portage Meadows Publishing, 2008.

Doyle, Susan Badger. *Bound for Montana, Diaries from the Bozeman Trail*. Helena: Montana Historical Society Press, 2004.

Farr, William E. *Blackfoot Redemption: A Blood Indian's Story of Murder, Confinement, and Imperfect Justice*. Norman University of Oklahoma Press, 2012.

Flynn, Kelly. *Goldpans, Guns & Grit: Diamond City from Territorial Gold Rush to Montana Ghost Town*. Townsend, MT: Hidden Hollow Hideaway Cattle and Guest Ranch, 2006.

Frassanito, William A. *Antietam, The Photographic Legacy of America's Bloodiest Day*. Gettysburg, PA: Thomas, 1978.

Frazier, Ian. *Great Plains*. New York: Picador, 1989.

Goodwin, Doris Kearns. *Team of Rivals: The Political Genius of Abraham Lincoln*. New York: Simon & Schuster, 2006.

Gottfried, Bradley M. *The Maps of Antietam*. New York: Savas Beatie, 2012.

Grant, Ulysses S. *The Personal Memoirs of U.S. Grant*. Vol. 1. *1885*. N.p., Ægypan, n.d..

Graybill, Andrew R. *The Red and the White: A Family Saga of the American West*. New York: Liverwright Publishing Company, 2013.

Greenslet, Ferris. *The Lowells and Their Seven Worlds*. Boston: Houghton Mifflin Company, 1946.

Hampton, H. Duane. *Life and Death at the Mouth of the Musselshell: Montana Territory—1868–1872*. Stevensville, MT: Stoneydale, 2011.

Harber, Nora E. *Our Fort Benton, The Birthplace of Montana*. Fort Benton, MT: River Press, 1930.

Hoig, Stan. *The Battle of the Washita: The Sheridan-Custer Indian Campaign of 1867–1869*. Garden City, NY: Doubleday, 1976.

Holton (KS) Recorder.

Hoover, Mary Ellen, Elin Williams Neiterman, and E. Dianne James. *From Your Loving Son: Civil War Correspondence and Diaries of Private George F. Moore and His Family*. Bloomington, IN: iUniverse, 2011.

Huckabee, Rodger Lee. "Camp Cooke: The First Army Post in Montana—Success and Failure on the Missouri." Master's thesis. Boise State University, 2010. http://scholarworks.boisestate.edu/cgi/viewcontent.cgi?article=1153&context=td.

Isely, Bliss, and W.M. Richards. *Four Centuries in Kansas*. Topeka: State of Kansas, 1944.

J.H. McKnight and Company Records, 1865–1914. "Historical Note." MC56, Montana Historical Society, Research Center Archives. http://archiveswest.orbiscascade.org/ark:/80444/xv19499/op=fstyle.aspx?t=i&q=0&f_names=J.H.+McKnight+and+Company

Koury, Michael. *Military Posts of Montana.* Bellevue, NE: Old Army Press, 1970.

Lepenteur, Charles. *Forty Years a Fur Trader on the Upper Missouri.* 1898. Kindle edition.

Lepley, John G. *Birthplace of Montana: A History of Fort Benton.* 2nd ed. Missoula, MT: Pictorial Histories Publishing Company, 1999.

———. *Blackfoot Fur Trade on the Upper Missouri.* Missoula, MT: Pictorial Histories, 2004.

———. *Packets to Paradise, Steamboating to Fort Benton.* Missoula, MT: Pictorial Histories, 1999.

Library of Congress. *Chronicling America: Historic American Newspapers.* http://chroniclingamerica.loc.gov/lccn/sn84038125/1871-07-29/ed-1/seq-1.

Lowell, Delmar R. *The Historic Genealogy of the Lowells of America.* Vol. 6. *From 1639 to 1899.* Rutland, VT: Tuttle, 1899.

McLaughlin, Castle. *A Lakota War Book from the Little Bighorn: The Pictographic "Autobiography of Half Moon."* Cambridge, MA: Houghton Library of the Harvard Library, Peabody Museum Press, 2013.

McPherson, James M. *Antietam: The Battle that Changed the Course of the Civil War.* New York: Oxford University Press, 2002.

Monahan, Glenn, and Chanler Biggs. *Montana's Wild and Scenic Upper Missouri River: A Guidebook for the Upper Missouri National Wild and Scenic River and the Upper Missouri River Breaks National Monument.* Anaconda, MT: Northern Rocky Mountains Books, 2001.

Montana Historical Society, Michael Stephen Kenned, ed. "Montana Gold: A Pictorial Feature." *Montana: The Magazine of Western History* 14, no. 3. (July 1964): 20–26, 49.

Montana Memory Project, collection of digitized National Archives microfilm publications, microcopy 234, Letters received by the office of Indian Affairs 1824–1881. Roll 490. Montana Superintendency 1864–1880. 1870. http://mtmemory.org/cdm/ref/collection/p15018coll41/id/16471.

Northwest Digital Archives (NWDA), MC 56. Guide to J.H. McKnight and Company Records, 1865–1914. http://nwda.orbiscascade.org/ark:/80444/xv19499.

O'Neil, Paul. *The Rivermen.* New York: Time Inc., 1975.

Overholser, Joel. *Fort Benton: World's Innermost Port.* Helena, MT: Falcon Press Publishing Company, 1987.

Parker, Nathan Howe. *Missouri as It Is in 1867: An Illustrated Historical Gazetteer of Missouri.* Philadelphia: J.B. Lippincott, 1867.

Pope, Charles Henry. *Pioneers of Massachusetts: 1620–1650*. Boston: New England Historic Genealogical Society, 2013.

Priest, John Michael. *Antietam: The Soldiers' Battle*. New York: Oxford University Press, 1989.

Robison, Ken. *Confederates in Montana Territory: In the Shadow of Price's Army*. Charleston, SC: The History Press, 2014.

———. *Yankees & Rebels on the Upper Missouri: Steamboats, Gold and Peace*. Charleston, SC: The History Press, 2016

Sankovitch, Nina. *The Lowells of Massachusetts*. New York: St. Martin's Press, 2017.

Schultz, James Willard. *With the Indians in the Rockies*, 1912. Kindle edition. Hardpress.net, 2014.

Sears, Stephen W. *Landscape Turned Red, The Battle of Antietam*. Boston, Mariner: 1983.

Shrady, George Frederick, Thomas Lathrop Stedman, and W. Wood, eds. "Army and Navy News." *The Medical Record: A Semi-Monthly Journal of Medicine and Surgery*, vol. 5. New York: William Wood & Company, 1871.

Spritzer, Don. *Roadside History of Montana*. Missoula, MT: Mountain Press, 1999.

Steward, Scott C., and Christopher C. Child. *The Descendants of Judge John Lowell of Newburyport, Massachusetts*. Boston: New England Historical Genealogical Society, Newbury Street Press, 2011.

Thompson, Francis M. *A Tenderfoot in Montana*. Helena, MT: Montana Historical Society Press, 2004.

Toponce, Alexander. *Reminiscences of Alexander Toponce*. Ogden, UT: Katie Toponce, 1923.

Tucker, Phillip Thomas. *Miller Cornfield at Antietam: The Civil War's Bloodiest Battle*. Charleston, SC: The History Press, 2017.

Tuttle, Charles R. *A New Centennial History of the State of Kansas: Being a Full and Complete Civil, Political and Military History of the State, From Its Earliest Settlement to the Present Time*. Madison, WI: Inter-State, 1876, 61819.

Twain, Mark. *Roughing It*. New York: Library of America, 2004.

U.S. Adjutant General's Office. *Official Army Register for January, 1870*. Washington, D.C.: January 1, 1870. https://www.fold3.com/image/1/312120758.

U.S. Department of Transportation and State of Montana Department of Highways. "Missouri River Bridge and Approaches Near Winifred, Montana." *Supplement, Environmental Impact Statement*. N.p., 1979. https://books.google.com/books?id=EcQ1AQAAMAAJ&printsec=frontcover&source=gbs_ge_summary_r&cad=0#v=onepage&q&f=false.

Vollmer, John P. *An Illustrated History of North Idaho: Embracing Nez Perces, Idaho, Latah, Kootenai and Shoshone Counties*. St. Paul, MN: Western History Publishing, 1903.

Von Drehle, David. *Rise to Greatness: Abraham Lincoln and America's Most Perilous Year*. New York: Henry Holt, 2012.

Wetzel, Charles R. "Monument Station, Gove County." *Kansas Historical Quarterly* 26, no. 3 (Autumn 1960): 250–54, http://www.kshs.org/publicat/khq/1960/1960autumn_wetzel.pdf.

Wheelan, Joseph. *Terrible Swift Sword: The Life of General Philip H. Sheridan*. Cambridge, MA: Da Capo, 2012.

White, Helen McCann, ed. *Ho for the Gold Fields, Northern Overland Wagon Trains of the 1860s*. St. Paul: Minnesota Historical Society, 1966.

Wischmann, Lesley. *Frontier Diplomats, Alexander Culbertson and Natoyist-Siksina' Among the Blackfeet*, 2000. Norman: University of Oklahoma Press, 2004.

Wischmann, Lesley, and Andrew Erskine Dawson. *This Far-Off Wild Land: The Upper Missouri Letters of Andrew Dawson*. Norman: University of Oklahoma Press, 2013.

Wylie, Paul R. *Blood on the Marias: The Baker Massacre*. Norman: University of Oklahoma Press, 2016.

Yellowstone Journal (Miles City, MT). "William Courtenay: Another of Montana's Pristine Settlers Follows the Way of All Flesh." October 31, 1901.

INDEX

N

O

P

R

S

T

V

W

Y

ABOUT THE EDITOR

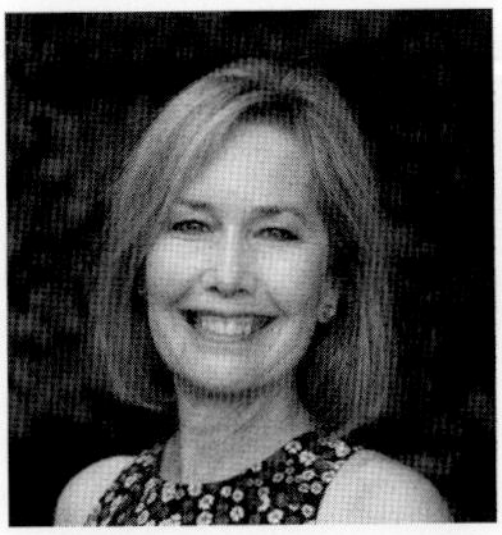

Katharine Seaton Squires's primary career was in the news business, first as an on-air reporter, then as a writer-producer for CBS News, CBS Sports, NBC Sports, and CNBC. She worked on three Olympic Games as a writer and producer. She holds a BA in art and English from Rutgers University, Douglass College, and an MA from the University of Missouri Graduate School in journalism. Squires served in the U.S. Peace Corps as a tuberculosis-control volunteer in the Republic of Korea.

Squires's rescue of Lowell's memoir from her mother's dresser drawer in 2012 set into motion a wide-ranging study of the American Civil War and post–Civil War history. Kate shares a birthday with her great-great-grandmother Kate Mary Lowell.